PENGUIN BOOKS

RAMESSES

Joyce Tyldesley is Honorary Research Fellow at the School of Archaeology, Classics and Oriental Studies at Liverpool University, and a freelance writer and lecturer on Egyptian archaeology. Her previous books include *Daughters of Isis: Women of Ancient Egypt*, *The Mummy: Unwrap the Ancient Secrets of the Mummies' Tombs*, *Hatchepsut: The Female Pharaoh* and *Nefertiti: Egypt's Sun Queen*.

RAMESSES

EGYPT'S GREATEST PHARAOH

JOYCE TYLDESLEY

PENGUIN BOOKS

PENGUIN BOOKS

Published by the Penguin Group
Penguin Books Ltd, 80 Strand, London WC2R 0RL, England
Penguin Putnam Inc., 375 Hudson Street, New York, New York 10014, USA
Penguin Books Australia Ltd, 250 Camberwell Road, Camberwell, Victoria 3124, Australia
Penguin Books Canada Ltd, 10 Alcorn Avenue, Toronto, Ontario, Canada M4V 3B2
Penguin Books India (P) Ltd, 11 Community Centre, Panchsheel Park, New Delhi – 110 017, India
Penguin Books (NZ) Ltd, Cnr Rosedale and Airborne Roads, Albany, Auckland, New Zealand
Penguin Books (South Africa) (Pty) Ltd, 24 Sturdee Avenue, Rosebank 2196, South Africa

Penguin Books Ltd, Registered Offices: 80 Strand, London WC2R 0RL, England

www.penguin.com

First published by Viking 2000
Published in Penguin Books 2001
6

Copyright © J. A. Tyldesley, 2000
All rights reserved

The moral right of the author has been asserted

Set in Monotype Bembo
Printed in England by Clays Ltd, St Ives plc

For my parents Anne McGregor and William Tyldesley

Contents

List of Plates

Photographic Acknowledgements

AKG London: 6, 15
Henning Bock: 12
Erich Lessing: 7, 14
Robert O'Dea: 16
Bildarchiv Preussischer Kulturbesitz, Berlin: 17, 25
British Museum: 1, 2
ET Archive: 20
Giraudon, Paris: 3, 5, 9, 10, 11, 13, 21, 22, 23
Michael Holford: 4
Scala, Florence: 8, 18, 19
Werner Forman Archive/E. Strouhal: 24

List of Figures

Preface

Chapter 1

Chapter 2

Chapter 3

Chapter 4

Chapter 5

Chapter 6

Chapter 7

Chapter 8

List of Maps

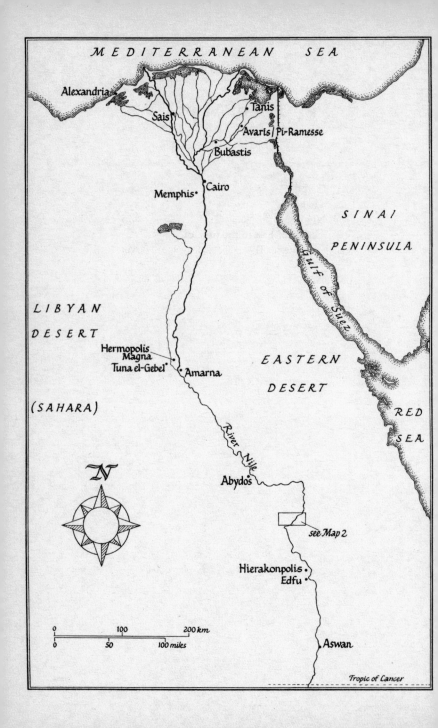

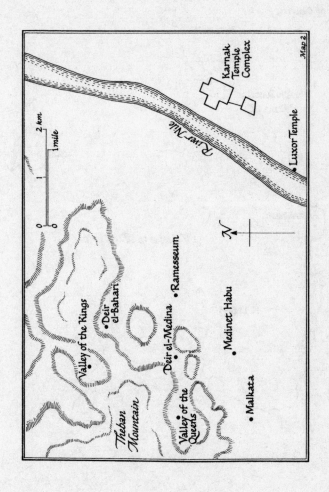

Valley of the Kings

Theban Mountain

Deir el-Bahari

Valley of the Queens

Deir el-Medina

Ramesseum

Medinet Habu

Malkata

Karnak Temple Complex

Luxor Temple

River Nile

N

0   1   2 km

0   1 mile

Map 2

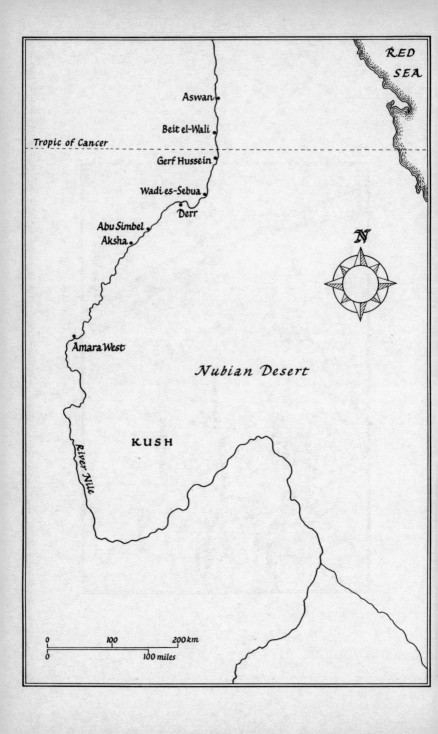

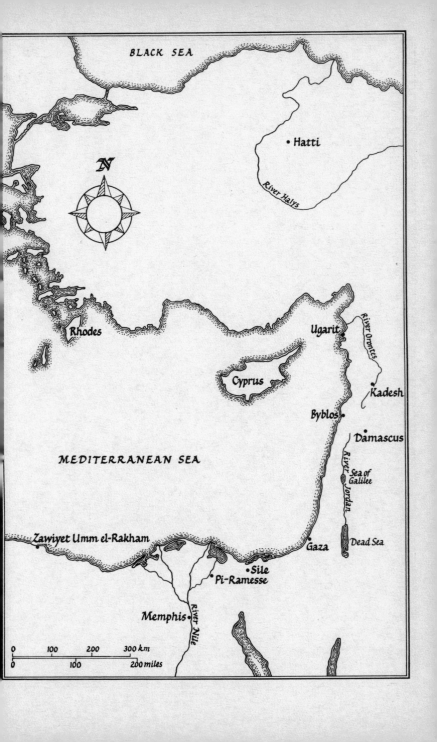

Acknowledgements

Professor Kenneth Kitchen has very generously devoted a great deal of his precious time to reading this text and answering my queries. I am very grateful to him. I would also like to thank Steven Snape for his tireless assistance with references and illustrations. Philippa and Jack tried, and sometimes managed, to be quiet while I worked: thank you.

Preface
New Readers Start Here

Egyptology – the study of Egypt's distant past via a combination of linked disciplines including archaeology, history and the sciences – attracts a disparate band of devotees with varying degrees of knowledge. Many so-called 'amateur' Egyptologists are as well informed as any professional and will already be familiar with the complexities and pitfalls of their chosen subject. Other readers, those new to the delights of ancient Egypt, may feel less confident in their understanding of the background to this book. Egyptology has over the years developed its own terms and conventions, which in extreme cases make more specialist publications inaccessible to the general public. The following notes are therefore offered as a brief introduction for all new readers, and as an *aide-mémoire* to the more experienced.

Egyptologists invariably use dynasties and individual regnal years rather than calendar years to date the events of the past. Under this system Ramesses II may be classified as the third king of the 19th Dynasty, a sub-division of Egypt's New Kingdom. We know that Ramesses reigned for over six decades. His precise calendar dates are by no means certain but on current evidence 1279–13 BC (or less likely 1290–24 BC) seem the most probable; 1304–1238 BC, which may be found in some older references, is now known to be incorrect.[1] By dating the events of Ramesses' reign to individual regnal years we are ensuring the greatest possible accuracy in our history by establishing a small island of chronological stability in a sea of unconfirmed dates. No one can be in any doubt that regnal Year 7 followed regnal Year 6, even though there may be intense academic debate over the precise calendar equivalent of Year 7. Although it may appear somewhat impractical to modern eyes, this regnal year dating system was used successfully throughout the dynastic age, with Egypt's year numbers starting afresh with each new monarch. A summary of Egypt's vast history is provided in Table 1 (p. xxv), allowing Ramesses to be set in his proper historical context.

During the New Kingdom every king of Egypt acquired, at his succession, a series of five names or titles which reflected aspects of his kingship. These names/titles took the form of little sentences and were effectively political statements or statements of allegiance to particular gods. Thus, as he assumed the throne, Ramesses became:

1. *The Horus King*, Strong Bull, Beloved of Right, Truth.
2. *He of the Two Ladies*, Protector of Egypt who curbs the foreign lands.
3. *The Golden Horus*, Rich in Years, Great in Victories.
4. *King of Upper and Lower Egypt*, Usermaatre [Setepenre was added from Year 2 of his solo reign]
5. *Son of Re*, Ramesses II, Beloved of Amen.

The last of these names, known as the nomen, was the king's personal name, the name which had been given to him at birth and which his immediate family would have continued to use after his accession. The preceding name, the throne name or prenomen, was his more formal appellation, used in diplomatic correspondence; thus foreign rulers correctly addressed Ramesses as Usermaatre (User-Maat-Re, literally 'Strong in Truth in Re'). Only the nomen and the prenomen were written within the cartouche, the oval loop which protected and distinguished the names of all Egyptian kings and some of their queens. Ramesses' inscriptions generally bore his nomen and prenomen plus as many additional names/titles as space would permit. The full complement of names and titles would be reserved for the most important of his monuments.

It is difficult to know where to begin writing the history of any one pharaoh as no monarch can be isolated from his country's immediate past. The Ramesside kings, *arrivistes* with a strong urge to justify their hold on the Egyptian throne, constantly looked to the precedents set

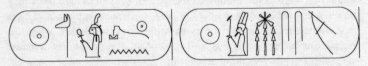

Fig P.1   The cartouches of Usermaatre Setepenre Ramessu Meriamen: Ramesses II, Beloved of Amen

by the successful pharaohs of the preceding dynasty, finding particular inspiration in the military exploits of Tuthmosis III and the internal policies of Amenhotep III. It is therefore necessary to understand something of 18th Dynasty history in order to appreciate the motivations of the 19th Dynasty kings. Many authors delve back to the dawn of the dynastic age in order to provide a full historical background to their study. I have chosen to start the story of Ramesses with the late 18th Dynasty rule of Horemheb, the pharaoh who did much to establish the stability of the 19th Dynasty after the upheavals and political uncertainties of the unconventional Amarna period. This book therefore forms the final volume in a loose trilogy encompassing the history of the New Kingdom, the earlier books being *Hatchepsut: the female pharaoh*, and *Nefertiti: Egypt's sun queen*. Readers requiring more background information are referred to the suggested Further Reading given at the end of the book. The notes that accompany each chapter have been used to suggest more specialized references in English, French and German.

Egyptologists, like detectives, piece together evidence gleaned from a variety of sources in order to reconstruct the events of the past. Unfortunately the ancients were not in the habit of burying carefully constructed time-capsules and so the evidence which has survived the centuries invariably comes complete with its own particular flaws and biases. There is certainly no need to apologize for the quality or quantity of information recovered from Egypt – we know far more about the life and thoughts of the ancient Egyptians than we do of, say, their contemporaries living in the British Isles – but new readers should be aware of some of the challenges posed by the evidence.

The randomly preserved historical record is heavily biased towards formal documents and monumental inscriptions, and so provides us with little or no insight into the mind of the ordinary Egyptian. Problems of translation may further obscure the meaning, if not the words, of any given text. Similarly, it is inevitable that the archaeological record of any country will provide an incomplete and varied assortment of data as everything that has survived has done so by chance. In Egypt this problem is exacerbated by the convention of building towns and cities in the Nile Valley, reserving the desert and cliffs for mortuary architecture. Daily life was conducted within mud-brick buildings, while stone was used to construct temples and tombs. With time the mud-brick houses, palaces and offices have crumbled away while the stone buildings have survived to give a distorted view of a dynastic Egypt obsessed by thoughts of religion and death.

Recently a more insidious form of bias has crept into the Egyptological record; the deliberate selection of information to promote a cause. Traditionally, the Egyptologist gathers his or her facts and then uses them to build a theory. Occasionally this process may be reversed; the theoretical model is developed and then tested against all the available evidence. Now there is a growing tendency for this procedure to be distorted with some 'authorities' first developing a spectacular thesis and then seeking out the evidence to prove it. Deliberately or not, evidence which contradicts the theory is conveniently ignored.

Who can blame the authors? The results of their biased research can prove both popular and lucrative. Who can blame the publishers? They know that a sensational new work of 'history' will always outsell a more rigorously argued thesis. And, above all, who can blame the readers who buy the books? Professionally presented these works of semi–scholarship can prove beguiling. Almost every year our bookshops are blessed with a new bestseller claiming on the most flimsy of evidence to reveal at least one of the mysteries of the ancient world. Those who criticize, no matter how well-armed with facts, are generally dismissed as being over-cautious, fuddy-duddy or lacking in imagination. Needless to say, this book will take a traditional approach to the presentation of facts. The history of Ramesses II is a fascinating story in its own right and needs no artificial enhancement to make it acceptable to the modern reader.

The Egyptians wrote their hieroglyphic texts without vowels, using consonants not found in our modern alphabet. In consequence, although we can read and understand the ancient writings we cannot be certain of the correct pronunciation of any word or name. This explains why different authors refer to the same individual by seemingly different names. Ramesses II, for example, variously appears in print as Ramesses, Ramses, Ramesse and Remeses while Queen Nefertari occasionally occurs as Nofretari. Throughout this book the most simple and widely accepted version of each proper name has been used with Ramesses preferred to the increasingly popular Ramses as the former most accurately represents the original Egyptian name. I follow current convention in using the words king and pharaoh interchangeably.

The Amarna Letters are a group of clay tablets recovered from the short-lived capital of Amarna. Written in cuneiform script, and in the Akkadian language, they represent the Egyptian archives of diplomatic correspondence during the reign of King Akhenaten. The archives include both letters received from foreign rulers and copies of the Egyptian replies.

In 1827 John Gardner Wilkinson, one of the pioneers of Egyptology, developed a system for numbering the tombs of Thebes. So practical was his scheme that today, almost two centuries later, the tombs are conventionally identified by number and prefix; KV (Valley of the Kings), WV (Western Valley), QV (Valley of the Queens) or TT (Theban Tomb). Thus KV7 is the tomb of Ramesses II, QV66 that of his principal and most famous wife, Nefertari. The Deir el-Bahari cache, a collection of royal and high-ranking dynastic mummies, was recovered from the tomb of the Pinodjem family, TT320.

Notes

1 For a discussion with detailed references of the possible chronology of Ramesses and his reign see Hasel, M. G. (1998), *Domination and Resistance: Egyptian military activity in the southern Levant 1300–1185 BC*, Leiden: 151–2. See also Bierbrier, M. L. (1975), *Genealogy and Chronology of the Late New Kingdom*, Warminster.

Egypt's Dynastic History

Years BC

3000	Archaic Period (Dynasties 1–2)	Unification of Egypt
2500	Old Kingdom (Dynasties 3–6)	Djoser step-pyramid at Sakkara / Great Pyramid of Khufu at Giza
2000	First Intermediate Period (Dynasties 7–11)	
	Middle Kingdom (Dynasties 11–13)	Theban kings re-unify Egypt
1500	Second Intermediate Period (Dynasties 14–17)	Hyksos kings in Northern Egypt
	New Kingdom (Dynasties 18–20)	Amarna Period / Ramesses II
1000	Third Intermediate Period (Dynasties 21–25)	Kings at Tanis / Nubian kings
500	Late Period (Dynasties 26–31)	
	Ptolemaic Period	Egypt part of Roman Empire

A.D.O

1

Introducing Ramesses

Some of Egypt's kings and queens have emerged from the obscurity of the tomb in sudden and spectacular fashion. The decoding of hieroglyphics, a tantalizing mystery until 1822, revealed the unexpected existence of the two aberrant New Kingdom pharaohs Hatchepsut and Akhenaten. The 1912 recovery of a magnificent portrait head from the ruined city of Amarna brought the beautiful Queen Nefertiti back to life. Above all, the unparalleled 1922 discovery of a virtually intact royal tomb in the Valley of the Kings allowed the hitherto insignificant boy-king Tutankhamen to triumph over death. Ramesses II, however, has never been in need of such a renaissance. Over the three millennia that have passed since his reign, his name – albeit in a distorted form – has never been forgotten.

Sixty-six relatively peaceful years on the throne had allowed Ramesses ample opportunity for self-promotion. By the time of his death in 1213 BC his monuments and image were to be found in every corner of his realm. The name of Ramesses was known and respected throughout the varied but inter-related kingdoms which made up what archaeologists now term the 'Ancient World' – a wide circle of states encompassing Northern Turkey, Iran, Central Africa, Libya and the Balkans and extending as far west as Italy and even Spain. Within Egypt the highly efficient royal propaganda machine had elevated Ramesses to the status of living legend with divine attributes. In Nubia, Ramesses had already become a fully fledged god. A fortunate combination of circumstances – optimal Nile floods leading to good harvests, international stability and, of course, the extraordinary longevity which caused Ramesses to outlive not only his contemporaries but many of his children and grandchildren – had allowed Egypt to enjoy a continuity of government which was the envy of her neighbours. Whether by good luck or good management, Egypt flourished under Ramesses, and her people were grateful.

Death enhanced rather than diminished the king's reputation and so we find the late Ramesses serving as a role model for most, if not all, subsequent pharaohs. Many of his immediate successors adopted the name of Ramesses, choosing to associate themselves with their hero in an obvious manner even though they were not his direct descendants. Thus the much weakened 20th Dynasty saw a series of identically named rulers stretching from Ramesses III to the unfortunate Ramesses XI whose reign marks the end of the New Kingdom. Only one of these kings, Ramesses III, came anywhere close to emulating the achievements of his namesake.

Later still, the artists of the Third Intermediate Period, a time of disorientating political fragmentation, looked back to the images of the stable 18th and 19th Dynasties, adapting a selection of earlier royal poses in order to emphasize particular political or religious messages. Scenes which had originally been designed to feature Ramesses now reappeared incorporating less charismatic pharaohs. The kings of Tanis (Dynasties 21–22), a city constructed almost entirely from reused Ramesside monuments salvaged from the near-derelict city of Pi-Ramesse, were particularly interested in their illustrious predecessor; King Psusennes even chose to include a valuable antiquity – a genuine Ramesses II ritual brazier – in his own burial equipment. The later Tanite kings, far from being related to Ramesses, were the descendants of defeated Libyans who had been transported to the eastern Delta as prisoners of war either by Ramesses or by his son. The comparison with the glorious reign of Ramesses was a somewhat wistful one; instead of controlling a mighty empire the Tanis kings enjoyed only the most tenuous grasp over the south of Egypt, while Nubia was entirely beyond their control. Nevertheless, many of these kings chose Ramesses' throne name Usermaatre in an attempt to recapture some of the lost brilliance of Egypt's golden age. The kings of the 30th Dynasty, the last native Egyptian dynasty to rule Egypt, continued this interest in Ramesses-abilia; they indulged in the rebuilding of Ramesside monuments which were eventually completed under Ptolemaic rule.

Meanwhile the cult of the divine Ramesses, established during the king's lifetime to promote Ramesses as a living god, continued to flourish. This cult long outlived the Egyptian dynasties so that the pious were still offering to Ramesses at Abydos, Memphis, Tanis and Abu Simbel many centuries after the king's death. The Graeco-Roman priesthood were proud to trace the roots of their religion back to pharaonic times and, making full use of the papyrus archives attached to their great temples, were happy to incorporate elements of the ancient texts into their rituals.[1] The reputation of the great Ramesses still stood high. It therefore seemed natural that the Graeco-Roman priests of the Theban god Khons-the-Planmaker, having decided to boost the profile of their rather insignificant deity, should look to Egypt's most charismatic monarch to accomplish their ends. The priests rewrote their mythology to allow Ramesses a starring role alongside Khons. An engraved stela, erected in their temple, told how King Ramesses had despatched a healing statue of Khons to cure Princess Bentresh, youngest daughter of the king of 'Bakhtan'. The statue was, of course, entirely successful in its mission and Khons eventually returned home in triumph. This tale, although loosely based on a muddle of events occurring during the reigns of Amenhotep III and Ramesses II, had become substantially distorted over the centuries so that its value as a historical narrative is minimal. It does, however, allow us a clear indication of the aura of mystery and glamour which, in 200 BC, still surrounded Ramesses and his court.

Manetho, the 'Father of Egyptian History', included Ramesses Mia-mun or Rapsakes in his Egyptian chronology. The Bible, too, preserved the name of Ramesses and of his capital city Pi-Ramesse.[2] However, with time, the distinction between fact and fiction became blurred so that the real Ramesses gradually evolved into a semi-mythical figure in his own land, just as today the Celtic King Arthur is regarded by many as an ill-defined combination of true king and mystical being, or the historic King Alfred is remembered more for his fictional cake-burning activities than for his actual reign.

The Greek and Roman tourists who visited Egypt's ancient ruins at the end of the pharaonic age were entertained with epic tales of the mighty Ramesses told by the persuasive locals. Herodotus, writing in 450 BC of 'King Rhampsinitus', most probably a combination of Ramesses II and Ramesses III, retells two such unlikely stories.[3] One involves the king visiting the land of the dead to play dice, the other is an amusing story of theft and cunning:

King Rhampsinitus had decided to build a treasury to hold his vast collection of silver. Unfortunately he employed a dishonest builder who incorporated a removable stone in the outer wall of the chamber allowing access to the royal treasure. On his deathbed the builder passed this secret on to his two sons who started to make regular visits to the treasury.

The king was very puzzled. He could see that the room was sealed and yet each time he visited there was less and less silver in the coffers. Eventually he set a trap which caught one of the thieves. He, realizing that he was doomed, implored his brother to cut off his head so that his body would go unrecognized. This was duly done and the second thief made his escape carrying away his brother's head. The king, shocked to find a headless corpse in his sealed treasury, ordered that the body be placed on public display. Anyone weeping for the anonymous thief might be presumed to know his identity. However the plan failed. The surviving thief was able to dupe the guards and make off with his brother's corpse.

A subsequent attempt to trap the thief using a beautiful princess as a decoy also fails, and eventually Rhampsinitus is forced to admit defeat. The thief is surely the cleverest man in Egypt, and as such deserves respect. A free pardon is issued, the thief makes himself known to pharaoh, marries the beautiful princess and, presumably, lives happily ever after.

Herodotus was never the most discriminating of historians and he happily mixes myth with history when he tells us that his King Rhampsinitus was a mighty builder whose statues were still, as he wrote, treated as objects of veneration by the Egyptians:

His monuments were in the western gateway of the temple of Hephaestus [the Memphite temple now known as the Temple of Ptah], and the two statues which stand in front of this gateway, called by the Egyptians Summer and Winter, each being 25 cubits in height. The statue of Summer, which is the northernmost of the two, is worshipped by the natives and has offerings made to it. The statue of Winter, which stands towards the south, is treated in exactly the contrary way.

This assertion is substantially correct. Ramesses II did indeed build at the Temple of Ptah, and he was responsible for a series of colossal statues erected in the Memphis area.

Writing in 60 BC Diodorus Siculus also recorded the work of a monumental Egyptian builder. Diodorus was particularly impressed by the Ramesseum, the mortuary temple of Ramesses II on the west bank at Thebes which he knew as the 'tomb of Ozymandias', and by the seated colossal image of the king which dominated the entrance to the temple. Paraphrasing his fellow historian Hecataeus of Abdera he described this statue in some detail:

Beside the entrance [to the temple] are three statues, each carved from a single block of black stone from Syene. One of these, which is seated, is the largest of any in Egypt, its foot alone measuring over seven cubits . . . it is not merely for its size that this work merits approbation. It is also marvellous because of its artistic quality and excellent because of the nature of its stone, since in a block of so great a size there is not one single crack or blemish to be seen. The inscription on it runs: 'King of Kings I am, Ozymandias. If anyone would know how great I am and where I lie let him surpass my works.'[4]

This same colossus, now fallen and fragmented, may still be visited within the precincts of the Ramesseum. Ozymandias is an obvious corruption of Ramesses' pre-nomen Usermaatre. Diodorus was unaware that his Ozymandias, and 'King Remphis' who appears elsewhere in his narrative, were one and the same. Later Pliny and Tacitus, too, were to write of a 'King Rhamsesis' or 'Rhamses' without any real understanding of who this king might have been. Other classical authors added to the muddle by confusing the monuments and deeds of Ramesses with those of the two great 12th Dynasty Kings Sesostris [Senwosret] I and III under the umbrella name 'Sesothes'. And so, as Egypt's dynastic history sank slowly into oblivion, the names and reputation of Ramesses/Ozymandias/Sesothes lived on, heavily disguised in the classical texts which were to form the backbone of the Western educational system for many centuries.

Almost two millennia later, and over two thousand miles from Thebes, the name of Ozymandias resurfaced in somewhat unexpected fashion. In 1817 Percy Bysshe Shelley published 'Ozymandias', his poetic impression of the once mighty Ramesses:

I met a traveller from an antique land
Who said: Two vast and trunkless legs of stone
Stand in the desert. Near them, on the sand,
Half sunk, a shattered visage lies, whose frown,
And wrinkled lip, and sneer of cold command

Tell that its sculptor well those passions read
Which yet survive, stamped on these lifeless things,
The hand that mocked them, and the heart that fed:
And on the pedestal these words appear: 'My name is Ozymandias, king of
    kings: Look on my works, ye mighty, and despair!'
Nothing besides remains. Round the decay
Of that colossal wreck, boundless and bare
The lone and level sands stretch far away.

'Ozymandias', Shelley's most powerful sonnet, is today one of the best-known poems in the English language. It should go without saying – but unfortunately often does need to be said – that Shelley's poetry cannot be read as a literal description of any particular Ramesside sculpture.[5] Shelley was a poet, not an archaeologist. He never travelled to Egypt and his harsh, beautiful verse was most probably inspired by a series of visits to the British Museum as, in 1817, Shelley was living in London while making plans for his departure to the Continent.[6] 'Ozymandias' undoubtedly owes much to Diodorus Siculus – Shelley was an accomplished classical scholar – and it seems highly likely that Shelley was also influenced by one or more of the guide books to the ruins of Thebes which were becoming highly popular with Britain's educated classes.[7]

The early 19th century was an age of intrepid adventurers. Egypt's sand-covered monuments, largely unrecorded and unexplored, held a fascination for European travellers who, journeying alone along the Nile, returned home to publish exciting accounts of fallen temples, mummified bodies and deserted tombs. Ancient Thebes and the Valley of the Kings had been identified by Claude Sicart as early as 1716, but it was Napoleon's abortive 1798 Egyptian expedition which really fuelled public interest in Egypt's ancient past. As a military campaign Napoleon's mission must be counted a failure but his three-year military occupation of Cairo led to the publication of one of the most remarkable books ever written: the *Description de l'Egypte* (1809–22), an impressive 21-folio encyclopaedia incorporating the work of over a hundred artists and scholars in a full-scale survey of Egypt, her natural resources and ancient ruins. Thus the potential of Egypt as a source of antiquities to rival those of Greece and Rome was fully revealed to the Western world.

Some canny investors had already recognized the value of Egypt's unwanted monuments. With the full cooperation of the Egyptian authorities, teams of professional archaeologists (today we would class them as treasure seekers) were now being hired to collect antiquities – often a dangerous and difficult task requiring considerable engineering expertise – which could be sold for great profit in the West.

In 1817 the British Museum had just taken delivery of the 'Younger Memnon', a portrait head of Ramesses II recovered from the second courtyard of the Ramesseum. This colossal head, a gift from Mohamed Ali to the Prince Regent, was officially recorded as a donation from the British Consul, Henry Salt, and the Swiss explorer, Johann Burckhardt. Salt and Burckhardt had in fact paid for the head to be transferred from Thebes to London by the ex-circus strongman and master of publicity, Giovanni Battista Belzoni. The new arrival drew the crowds, and the Egyptian galleries of the British Museum became a popular haunt of London's upper classes. Belzoni, completely in tune with the fashions of his time, was later to use painted plaster casts taken from the walls of the newly discovered tomb of Seti I to re-create a pharaoh's tomb in the highly suitable setting of the Egyptian Hall, Piccadilly. The highlight of his exhibition proved to be the public unwrapping of a genuine Egyptian mummy.

Soon after the publication of 'Ozymandias' came the deciphering of the hieroglyphic script. Jean François Champollion, following the pioneering work of Thomas Young and William Bankes, was able to fit together the sun sign *Re* and the sign of three fox skins *mise* to make the name *Re-mise* or Ramesses, a coup which was quickly followed by the reading of the name *Thoth* (ibis) -*mise* or Tuthmosis. Now it was possible to read the cartouches of the kings and, after a brief period of intense confusion as linguists and historians struggled to fit the newly restored names into the distorted framework preserved by the classical authors and the Bible, the essential bones of Egyptian history were laid bare. Inevitably this led to more public interest, more exploration and more excavation, and with this increased activity came more Ramesside finds. For the first time the true scale of Ramesses' monumental building works could be appreciated by modern observers. His architecture was seen to dominate the Egyptological landscape and his literature quickly entered the public domain. Ramesses grew famous once again.

Fired with enthusiasm, the newly literate Egyptologists set to work. The Great Abu Simbel Temple, which had been rediscovered by Burck-hardt in 1813 and cleared of sand by Belzoni in 1817, attracted the attention of both epigraphists and archaeologists. The tomb of Ramesses, known since antiquity and plundered very soon after the king's death, was the subject of a detailed inspection by the Prussian Expedition of 1844. Finally, in 1881, came the ultimate Ramesses discovery: the recovery of the king's mummified body as part of the Deir el-Bahari royal cache.

More recently, the extraordinary rescue of the Nubian Ramesside temples from the waters of the Aswan High Dam, the international mission to restore the damaged mummy of the king, and the remarkable conservation project which has preserved the beautiful tomb of Queen Nefertari in the Valley of the Queens, have all ensured that Ramesses and his court are never long out of the public eye.

Outside academia Ramesses has featured in a series of novels and plays and has even hit the bestseller list as the hero of Christian Jacq's quintet of Egyptian novels.[8] Jacq's Ramesses is handsome, courageous and good hearted. In Anne Rice's glittering, gothic tale, *The Mummy*, the king becomes a more complex figure, a lonely man twisted by love.[9] In 1909 Ramesses made his first appearance on the silver screen, starring in the horror-tale *Mummy of the King Ramses*. In December 1923 Cecil B DeMille's silent screen epic *The Ten Commandments* opened; it is rumoured that DeMille, inspired by recent discoveries in Egypt, had to be dissuaded from replacing Ramesses with the more commercially acceptable Tutankhamen. DeMille's more famous 1956 film of the same name starred Charlton Heston as Moses and Yul Brynner as Ramesses. More recently Ramesses appears in the DreamWorks animated interpre-tation of the Exodus, *Prince of Egypt*.

Given his life-long obsession with oppression and tyranny, plus the then widespread misunderstanding of the Ancient Egyptians as a race of ruthless slave-drivers, it was perhaps inevitable that Shelley would inter-pret his Ozymandias as a cold and cruel despot. Little more than sixty years later enough was known about Ramesses to allow Miss Amelia B Edwards to devote an entire chapter of her ground-breaking travel guide *A Thousand Miles up the Nile* to 'the central figure of Egyptian history'.[10] Remarking that the king seems omnipresent in modern Egypt – 'We seem to know the man – to feel his presence – to hear his name in the air. His features are as familiar to us as those of Henry the Eighth or Louis the Fourteenth. His cartouches meet us at every turn' – she summed up his character and his reign:

... it is safe to conclude that he was neither better nor worse than the general run of Oriental despots – that he was ruthless in war, prodigal in peace, rapacious of booty, and unsparing in the exercise of almost boundless power. Such pride and such despotism were, however, in strict accordance with immemorial precedent, and with the temper of the age in which he lived.

Miss Edwards belonged to an archaeological generation that was not afraid to use strong or emotive terms when evoking the characters and the motives of the long dead, although as she wisely remarked 'every attempt to evolve his personal character . . . is in fact a mere exercise of fancy'. She was certainly kinder and more moderate in her judgement than some of her contemporaries; Bunsen, for example, was happy to dismiss Ramesses as:

... an unbridled despot, who took advantage of a reign of almost unparalleled length, and of the acquisitions of his father and ancestors, in order to torment his own subjects and strangers to the utmost of his power.[11]

The Egyptologists of today are a more cautious breed and such forceful opinions are now rare, although in 1959 William C. Hayes did class the young Ramesses as 'a brash young man . . . not overburdened with intelligence and singularly lacking in taste . . . [yet with] tremendous energy and personal magnetism'.[12] Over-cautious histories can, of course, make dull reading. Nevertheless Kenneth Kitchen, who has done more than anyone to present a balanced view of Ramesses II to the modern world, is right to advise prudence when reconstructing the pharaohs:

The deeds and attitudes of a Ramesses II cannot just be crudely measured-off against our own supposed social values, as simply boastful or megalomania; they must be compared with what were the norms and ideals in *his* culture, not ours.[13]

How then did Ramesses see himself? What were the norms and ideals of his society? As just one link in the long chain of kings of Egypt he should perhaps have regarded himself as a mere office-holder, completely indistinguishable from his predecessors and successors. Throughout the dynastic age it was recognized that Pharaoh filled an ill-defined but well-understood role which passed directly from king to king. He was the semi-divine conduit which allowed mortals to communicate with the gods and to him fell the awesome responsibility of maintaining *maat* throughout the land. The Egyptian concept of *maat*, or 'truth', is one which modern observers struggle to define; it may perhaps be explained as a continuity of 'rightness' which would ensure that things functioned as they always had done. We might therefore have expected to find Egypt's kings downplaying their own personal achievements; leaving their public buildings, for example, unnamed, and neglecting to commission their own statues. After all, it was the role of the pharaoh that mattered, rather than the individual king. As long as the gods were served correctly they would be happy. Was there any real need to stress the greatness or individuality of Ramesses as opposed to that of his forebears? Did his personal reputation matter that much? Ramesses felt that it did.

Ramesses knew what made a great pharaoh. He (for a great king would always be a 'he') would be a brave warrior, a mighty builder, an educated scribe and an effective priest. His chosen titles 'Strong Bull, Beloved of Right, Truth; Protector of Egypt who curbs the foreign lands' reflected this highly traditional programme and made clear his intention to follow in the footsteps of his father, Seti I. From the very beginning of his reign Ramesses set about proving that he conformed to the ideal of Egyptian kingship. In fact, he determined to prove that he was the greatest of all Egypt's kings. In this ambition he was by no means unusual.

In spite of their acknowledged semi-divine status Egypt's kings were all too human, suffering both from vanity and from something very akin to insecurity. Each ruler, no matter how firmly seated on the golden throne of Horus, felt the need to prove to his people, and of course to his gods, that he personally was capable of fulfilling his pre-ordained duty; that he was indeed the living representative of all the great pharaohs who had gone before. Furthermore, most kings wanted to demonstrate that they were the best. In order to stress their own achievements all kings made full use of the resources at their disposal and the longer-lived, more affluent monarchs were able to ensure that their name and titles were celebrated in stone throughout the land. Every monument, every statue, every cartouche was seen as a re-enforcement of the semi-divine role of the current king. Ramesses, although raised as a future king, was neither descended from a long line of pharaohs nor born to a King's Great Wife (queen consort). Like his father and grandfather before him he was born a commoner, an accident of birth that seems to have made his urge towards self-justification all the stronger.

Exaggeration was considered entirely acceptable under these circum-stances and so we find Egypt's public monuments decorated with unblush-ing hymns of praise to the king which, in our more reticent times, would be considered both immodest and unbecoming. His people fully approved of this less than subtle approach. Did not the revered New Kingdom scribe Amenemope advise his students to 'Publish your good deeds throughout the world so that all may congratulate you'?[14] Pharaoh represented Egypt and by elevating his own profile he lifted the whole country with him. A modest king would not have been fulfilling his proper role. Such a king would not inspire trust.

Many pharaohs, Ramesses included, went one step further. By appro-priating the achievements and monuments of their predecessors they were able to enhance their own reputations at very little cost or effort. A gang of workmen armed with plaster, mallets and chisels could quickly superimpose Ramesses' cartouche over the name of an earlier king and thus, with one hammer-blow, history could be rewritten. By the end of his reign there was scarcely a monument in the Nile Valley that did not bear the cartouche of Ramesses II. This hijacking of history for the greater glory of the current pharaoh was not seen as cheating – were not the living and the dead pharaohs one and the same? – and indeed so strong was the magic associated with the written word that simply rewriting a fact or renaming a statue could cause the new history to become true. Unfortunately this tampering with the past has had a distorting effect upon modern perception of New Kingdom history.

The memory of Seti I has undoubtedly suffered at the hands of the son who happily usurped his monuments. Middle Kingdom monuments, too, were targeted by Ramesses and his masons. Ramesses' principal victim however, was his great role-model Amenhotep III. Amenhotep's reign of almost forty peaceful years had allowed him to build on some of the most prominent sites in Egypt. Ramesses enlarged, rebuilt and largely obliterated many of Amenhotep's Theban monuments, while others of his buildings were dismantled to provide the stone which Ramesses needed for his own projects. Even his statuary was not safe; Ramesses made full use of the many unfinished statues of Amenhotep that littered the Theban temples, and he did not balk at remodelling Amenhotep's head for his own use.[15] This was a mixture of practicality and flattery; Ramesses usurped those he admired and left untouched the sculptures of Hatchepsut and Akhenaten.[16] It is perhaps only just that, not too many years later, some of Ramesses' own sculptures were subjected to the very same abuse.

If Ramesses' monuments had an invaluable role as public propaganda they also fulfilled a more private need. The rules governing life after death were both very clear and – to modern eyes – very harsh. The soul could survive to spend eternity in the Kingdom of Osiris, a peaceful, fertile land remarkably reminiscent of the Nile Valley. However, this would only happen while the discarded earthly body survived. The loss of the body, either through natural decay or deliberate destruction, would immediately extinguish the soul. The deceased would then meet the dreaded Second Death, from which there could be no return. In order to avoid dying the Second Death Ramesses would have taken every possible precaution to ensure that his body survived, but he must have known that mummification followed by interment in a secret royal tomb might not be enough. Already the pyramids of Egypt's first kings had been robbed and the precious royal bodies had been lost. In the early 19th Dynasty the Valley of the Kings appeared both secret and secure, but no monarch knew what troubles might lie ahead. Fortunately, there was a loophole. If the worst happened and the physical body was lost the soul might yet survive in the image, name or even earthly memory of the deceased. By taking steps to ensure that his name and image would survive for ever, Ramesses was preparing to live beyond death.

So intent was Ramesses on replicating his own image, so impatient was he to see results, that he developed a distinct preference for quantity over quality. Size definitely did matter to Ramesses. The royal masons were encouraged to abandon the time-consuming tradition of fine raised relief, a style which lifted the image clear of the background, and adopted instead the cheaper and less demanding sunken relief with the figures incised into the background. The new technique would allow work to progress at a faster pace and, as sunken relief was harder to delete, would effectively foil any subsequent monarchs who might wish to erase or appropriate Ramesses' carvings. This same haste and economy was evident in Ramesses' public buildings which, while outwardly magnificent, were not always constructed to the highest standards. We, with the benefit of hindsight, can see that Ramesses could have afforded to spend more time – if not more gold – over his monuments. He, succeeding after the unexpected death of a comparatively young father and unaware that he was to rule for over sixty years, almost certainly saw things differently.

Far from being the inspired work of talented artists, the royal colossi were exercises in engineering mass produced by workmen of diverse talent supplied with raw materials of variable and occasionally inferior quality. Ramesses commissioned a vast number of statues of himself and the temples of his capital alone housed fifty life-sized or bigger than life-sized images. It is inconceivable that the king would have sat for most, or even any, of these portraits; the royal sculptors would have followed tradition in basing their work on approved models. Similarly the images of the king that adorned his temple walls were not drawn from life. They were never intended to be accurate portraits – there was no ancient equivalent of our modern photograph – and the artists could rely on the magic of the king's written name to convey realism to their work. The king's 'portraits' were in fact pure propaganda, designed to depict Ramesses in one of three traditional roles: the beneficent ruler, the mighty warrior or the living god. Constraints of medium, location and, occasionally, posture could dictate the appearance of a finished piece; the larger statues, for example, were often slightly squat in order to avoid structural problems, while the artists who depicted Ramesses in a semi-prostrate attitude tended to elongate his limbs to make a pleasing horizontal line. Variation in style between the various royal workshops simply added to the artistic differences.

In summary, the official image of Ramesses promoted by the royal artists is something akin to the image of the British monarch as depicted on coins or postage stamps; it is an idealization, instantly recognized and seldom updated. If we suspend our disbelief, and take his statuary at face value, we can see that Ramesses was an entirely traditional king: tall, dignified, physically perfect and forever young. His more personal characteristics include a prominent nose set in a rounded face with high cheek-bones, wide, arched eyebrows, slightly bulging almond-shaped eyes and a small, squarish chin. His somewhat fleshy lips have a permanent regal smile: the 'sneer' which so offended Shelley was to Miss Edwards the sign of 'a godlike serenity, an almost superhuman pride, and immutable will'. Most modern observers agree with her that Ramesses was good-looking: 'Now Ramesses the Great, if he was as much like his portraits as his portraits are like each other, must have been one of the handsomest men, not only of his day, but of all history.'

Better confirmation of the king's appearance can be obtained from his mummified body which is now housed in Cairo Museum. On 1 June 1886, in the presence of a distinguished audience including the Khedive Tewfik, Gaston Maspero took an amazingly brief fifteen minutes to cut open his bandages and reveal the king. Maspero, who was no anatomist, took a few measurements and noted Ramesses' prominent nose 'long, thin, hooked like the noses of the Bourbons and slightly crushed at the tip by the pressure of the bandages', his strong jaw and his prominent ears 'pierced, like those of a woman for the wearing of earrings'. The king was indeed tall for a dynastic Egyptian, standing some 1.733 metres (5 feet 7 inches) high, and as for handsome:

. . . the mask of the mummy allows a fair idea of the face of the living king: an expression of little intelligence, perhaps even slightly brutish, but of pride, of obstinacy and with an air of supreme majesty is still apparent beneath the embalmers' dressing.[17]

Sir Grafton Elliot Smith, able to examine the mummy under less hurried conditions, was struck by the king's long, narrow, oval face dominated by a large beaky nose which had been carefully moulded and stuffed so as to preserve its shape. He felt able to identify in Ramesses' cranial and facial features 'many alien [Asiatic] traits, curiously blended with Egyptian characters',[18] traits which he also recognized in the mummies of Seti I and Ramesses' son Merenptah. All three appeared less typically Egyptian than their 18th Dynasty predecessors. This is not particularly surprising; we might reasonably expect to find some Near Eastern blood flowing through the veins of the Delta families.

Ramesses' fine, silky, white hair had been stained yellow-red during the embalming process. However, modern scientific analysis of his hair-roots has confirmed that in his youth the king was indeed a natural red-head.[19] As today, auburn hair was not particularly common in dynastic Egypt, and Ramesses must have appeared conspicuous amongst his dark-haired compatriots. As a colour, red had slightly unfortunate associations. The 'Red Land', the arid desert which bordered the fertile 'Black Land', was the natural graveyard. Red was the colour of the ambivalent god Seth, brother and enemy of Osiris, uncle and seducer of Horus. Those with auburn hair, and animals with red fur, were therefore considered to have an affinity with Seth. Seth represented confusion and disorder, the very opposite of *maat*. However, far from being shunned, as Christians shun Satan, Seth was seen as a necessary member of the pantheon and Egyptians did not hesitate to name their children after him. Seth dwelled in the eastern Delta town of Avaris, the home town of the Ramesside family. During the 19th Dynasty he was also considered to be the lord of foreign countries, a role which allowed him to be equated with the Hittite god Teshub and the Semitic god Baal.

Given the link between the god Seth and the colour red it is tempting to speculate that red hair was a Ramesside family trait, with Seti (or Seth) I, father of Ramesses, being named with reference to his own auburn tresses. However the Ramesside devotion to the god Seth may simply have been a reflection of their northern roots.

Ramesses may once have been the youthful auburn-haired hero of the temple walls, but by the time of his death all resemblance to the glorious victor of the battle of Kadesh had faded. The old king's face and neck were heavily lined – hardly surprising, given that he had lived for almost a century – and the undertakers had helpfully attempted to smooth out his wrinkles before bandaging his head. Ramesses had suffered badly from the indignities of a prolonged Egyptian old age. The severe arthritis that affected his hip, and the arteriosclerosis in his lower limbs, would have caused circulatory problems and would have prevented him from walking comfortably. Elliot Smith, without the benefit of X-ray analysis, described Ramesses' teeth as 'clean and in an excellent state of preservation: they were only slightly worn'. In fact, although well-spaced and properly aligned, the king's teeth and gums were badly decayed and, in his final years, must have caused him constant pain. As professor of dentistry James E. Harris remarked after X-raying the 19th Dynasty

*Fig 1.1   Seth: the curious animal-
headed god of Avaris, the eastern Delta
home of the Ramesside kings*

pharaohs of Cairo Museum, 'good
dental hygiene would have saved
both rulers [Ramesses and Mer-
enptah] considerable discomfort'.[20]

The physical Ramesses, then,
can be reconstructed with a fair
degree of certainty from his
mummified remains. But can we
advance any further in our quest
to understand the 'real Ramesses'
hidden behind the rhetoric of his
role? Contemporary literature is
stubbornly unhelpful in this matter.
Although we have access to a fair
quantity of official pronouncements, diplomatic letters and
administrative documents all dating
to the Ramesside era, we are completely lacking the private diaries
and personal letters which make
modern biographies so intimate.
Upper-class Egyptian males frequently included a short 'autobi-
ography' – a carefully constructed
hymn of self-praise designed to
impress visitors who might then
leave an offering – on the wall of
their tomb. Unfortunately for
modern historians, kings did not
bother with such small-scale personal writings. Egypt's pharaohs
carved their history on the land, using the blank temple walls as their
noticeboard. Here the monarch's greatest achievements would be
described, and lavishly illustrated, for all to see.

The one incident which it seems Ramesses wanted to promote above
all others was his magnificent 'victory' over the Hittite Empire. This is
less, however, a personal preference than a close adherence to tradition;

scenes of Egyptian triumph had long been recognized as the appropriate decoration for temple walls. The scenes depicting the battle of Kadesh, preserved as text and relief at a number of temples, over-emphasize this battle at the expense of Ramesses' other, more peaceful achievements, and it is not surprising that a vast amount of scholarly research has been dedicated to gaining a complete understanding of the sequence of events.[21] The temple walls show us a young King Ramesses whose courage knows no bounds:

His majesty slew the entire force of the enemy from Hatti . . . as well as all the chiefs of all the countries that had come with him . . . His majesty killed them all; they fell before his horse, and his majesty was alone, none other with him.[22]

Ramesses clearly wants his people and their gods to understand that he has been brave, indeed 'braver than hundreds of thousands all together'. His relief at being able to fulfil one of the most important requirements of a great pharaoh – the successful defence of his country – is obvious. Ramesses extracted maximum publicity from his defeat of a worthy enemy. The fact that his 'great victory' turned out to be nothing of the kind troubled him little. He was the king. The very act of proclaiming and inscribing a great victory would cause it to become history.

Ramesses has left us sufficient evidence to reconstruct the king he wanted to be: noble, brave, physically perfect, pious and, of course, very rich – how else could he afford to leave such magnificence? If we look beyond the obvious we can perhaps detect more personal characteristics. His public actions confirm that he was a monarch anxious to comply with tradition, eager to retain and justify his position. The Ramesside kings, relative newcomers to the throne, could not afford the casual disregard of tradition seen during the disastrous reign of Akhenaten and they made their conservatism obvious at every opportunity. Egypt's state gods would not be neglected during their reigns. Nevertheless Ramesses was not afraid to experiment and he successfully established a new capital city, a bold move given the unfortunate precedent of Amarna.

His famous battle scenes send us a mixed signal. Ramesses was not a great general; he was too impatient, too inexperienced and too trusting to make balanced tactical decisions. His assessment of his own performance is open to interpretation – did he really believe his own hype, or was he merely fulfilling a role? And yet his after-battle publicity plan was superb; even today Ramesses enjoys worldwide renown as one of the great warrior pharaohs. Similarly, while Ramesses may not have displayed the obvious political acumen of Horemheb or Seti I, his foreign and domestic policies brought peace and prosperity to Egypt for many years. Calmly, without emulating the excessive zeal of the Amarna period, he was able to implement a religious strategy designed to restrict the power and influence of the priesthood of Amen.

Ramesses allows us a few, carefully calculated, glimpses into his private life, although even here we are observing a man playing out a pre-ordained role. We are allowed to see that Ramesses is a good family man; a devout and dutiful son who completes his dead father's unfinished monuments (although on a smaller scale than Seti might have hoped) and who reveres his mother during her lifetime. He is without doubt an enthusiastic husband who respects and probably loves his principal wives, and who makes an affectionate father to his scores of children. He is even a friend to animals, and his pet lion features in several temple scenes. It appears that all Egyptians loved Ramesses the Great. His enemies, the despised foreigners whom he vanquished, smote and ritually trampled, would presumably have told a very different tale.

Notes

1 Discussed in some detail with references, in Bianchi, R. S. (1991) 'Graeco-Roman uses and abuses of Ramesside traditions', in Bleiberg, E. and Freed, R. (eds) *Fragments of a Shattered Visage: Proceedings of the International Symposium of Ramesses the Great*, Memphis: 1–8.

2 Genesis 47:11; Exodus 1:11, 12:37; Numbers 33:3.

3 Herodotus, *Histories 2*, 121–3.

4 Diodorus Siculus, *Histories* I.47.

5 This 'classic case of Egyptological obfuscation' is discussed in detail by James, T. G. H. (1994), 'A Poetic Puzzle', *Hommages à Jean Leclant 4*, Cairo: 147–51.

6 Richard Holmes believes that 'Ozymandias' was written soon after Shelley visited the British Museum with his agent Horace Smith. Egyptology was then very much in vogue amongst the English poets; earlier in 1817 Shelley, John Keats and Leigh Hunt had passed an evening writing competitive poetry about the River Nile. Holmes, R. (1974), *Shelley: the pursuit*, London: 410.

7 Harry James has suggested that Shelley may have been reading William Hamilton's travel guide *Aegyptiaca*, published in 1809. This is discussed in detail by James, T. G. H. (1991), 'Ramesses II: appearance and reality', in Bleiberg, E. and Freed, R. (eds) *Fragments of a Shattered Visage; Proceedings of the International Symposium of Ramesses the Great*, Memphis: 38–49.

8 See for example Terence Gray's short 'play for Bible students who know not Egypt' *A Royal Audience* in which Ramesses appears as 'Riyamosis'; Gray, T. (1923), *And in the Tomb Were Found: plays and portraits of old Egypt*, Cambridge, also Bantock, G. (1892), *Ramesses II: A Drama of Ancient Egypt*, London. Ken Kitchen records that the comic strip 'Ramesses' appeared first in the *Bournemouth Evening Echo* and then in the *Southern Evening Echo*; Kitchen K. A. (1982), *Pharaoh Triumphant: the life and times of Ramesses II*, Warminster; 235. Jacq, C. (1995–7), *The Son of Light*; *The Temple of a Million Years*; *The Battle of Kadesh*; *The Lady of Abu Simbel*; *Under the Western Acacia*. See also Gedge, P. (1995–7), *Lady of the Reeds*; *House of Illusions*.

9 Rice, A. (1989), *The Mummy*, London and New York.

10 Edwards, A. B. (1877) *A Thousand Miles up the Nile*, London. This and all subsequent Edwards quotations are taken from the revised 1888 edition, Chapter 15: 262–83.

11 Quoted in Edwards, A. B. (1888), *A Thousand Miles up the Nile*, London. 282–3.

12 Hayes, W. C. (1959), *The Scepter of Egypt 2: the Hyksos Period and the New Kingdom*, Cambridge Mass.

13 Kitchen, K. A. (1982), *Pharaoh Triumphant*, Warminster; 235.

14 *The Instruction of Amenemope*. For a full translation of this text consult Lichtheim, M. (1976), *Ancient Egyptian Literature II: the New Kingdom*, Los Angeles: 146–63.

15 Consult Sourouzian, H. (1995), Les Colosses du IIe pylon du Temple d'Amon-Re à Karnak, remplois ramessides de la XVIIIe dynastie, *Cahiers de Karnak* 10; 505–29.

16 See Yoyotte, J. (1968), *Les Trésors des Pharaohs*, Geneva.

17 Maspero, G. (1889), *Bulletin de l'Institut Egyptien*: 253–5.

18 Smith, G. E. (1912), *The Royal Mummies*, Cairo: 69.

19 Discussed in Clement, J.-L., Le Pareux, A. and Cecaldi, P.-F. (1985) Etude de la chevelure, in Balout, L. and Roubet, C. (eds) *La Momie de Ramses II*, Paris: 212–23.

20 Harris, J. E. and Weeks K. R. (1973), *X-Raying the Pharaohs*, London: 155.

21 See for example Gardiner, A. H. (1960), *The Kadesh Inscriptions of Ramesses II*, Oxford; Kitchen, K. A. (1999), *Rameside Inscriptions Translated and Annotated 2: notes and comments*, Oxford: 3–55.

22 For a full translation of this text consult Kitchen, K. A. (1996), *Ramesside Inscriptions Translated and Annotated 2: Ramesses II Royal Inscriptions*, Oxford: 2–26.

2

A New Beginning:
Life Before Ramesses

When General Horemheb buried old King Ay in an unfinished, hastily prepared tomb in the Western Valley, he confirmed his own right to ascend to the Horus throne of Egypt. As an experienced statesman he must have been all too aware that he was inheriting a country on the verge of acute political crisis.

The decline in Egypt's fortunes had been both swift and, to the Egyptians if not to some of their neighbours, entirely unexpected. The 18th Dynasty, already over 200 years old, had started out as a glorious antidote to the disruptions and foreign rule of the Second Intermediate Period and had developed to witness some of the most successful reigns of the pharaonic age. The Theban god Amen, 'The Hidden One', smiled on the southern kings, allowing a series of mighty warriors to be suitably interspersed by monumental builders and astute diplomats so that by the reign of Amenhotep III Egypt's treasury was brim-full of gold, her granaries were overflowing and her ancient mud-brick cities were dominated by imposing stone-built temples. While the simple, monotonous lives of the 'ordinary' people – the peasants who made up the vast majority of the population – saw very little change from reign to reign, the élite and the middle classes now enjoyed an unprecedented prosperity and security.

With an empire stretching from Nubia to Syria and a sphere of influence extending far further afield, Egypt seemed invincible. Few bothered to challenge her authority and the army was seldom called upon to fight. Instead Egypt's neighbours vied to be her friend, showering her king with lavish gifts of precious metals, jewels and exotica in a practical if somewhat cynical attempt to express their loyalty. An intermittent procession of women – royal brides, their retinues and of course their dowries – started to wend its way towards Memphis as each successive monarch was courted by those anxious to forge a more personal link with their patron. With little competition the Egyptian bureaucracy effectively controlled the Levantine world and the Egyptian court, growing richer by the day, developed a degree of cosmopolitan sophistication never previously seen. The art, literature and even the clothing of this period reflect a spirit of joyful extravagance and a willingness to cast off the conservative austerity of earlier dynasties.

At the heart of the court stood pharaoh, a man of absolute power. State mythology decreed that the king should reign unopposed, his position made unassailable by the support of the gods whom he represented on earth. His semi-divine role was one of contradictions, a combination of the practical and the ritual presented in a display of archaic pomp calculated to inspire reverential fear while obscuring the true down-to-earth nature of his position. It is perhaps not surprising that some of his newer subjects, dazzled by the omnipotent monarch and unable to define his precise political status, started to worship pharaoh as a living god.

In theory the king of Egypt owned all the land and everything in it, including the people. By extension he officially headed the bureaucracy which regulated the priesthood and the civil service and which took responsibility for the safety of the pharaoh. In practice the bureaucracy was controlled by the king's most loyal supporters, a select band of educated statesmen born to long dynasties of career politicians whose sons were trained to follow in their fathers' administrative footsteps. During the Old and Middle Kingdoms a small, tightly controlled bureaucracy had been enough to ensure the smooth running of the country. Now, however, the unprecedented prosperity of the New Kingdom – which generated a massive volume of administrative work – and the development of a professional army, challenged the efficiency of the old structure. The sudden demand for scribes, accountants and administrators led to the emergence of the professional middle classes as an economically significant group. Meanwhile, the bureaucracy, growing uncomfortably over-inflated and difficult to control, began to split into three constituent parts: civil service, priesthood and army.

Much of Egypt's new wealth found its way into the coffers of the gods as successive monarchs made lavish offerings to demonstrate their gratitude for Egypt's golden age. By the mid-18th Dynasty the state cults had developed into influential financial institutions with direct control over a wide portfolio of assets while their managers, or priests, had become accomplished accountants. Richest of all was the priesthood of Amen, a highly professional political organization whose accrued resources allowed a degree of independence from the king and whose god could now provide a subtle challenge to the pomp and ceremony of the monarchy. From the dark depths of his temples, the portals of which were forbidden to all but a favoured few, the once hidden god started to emerge into the sunlight, processing amongst his people before disappearing again into the gloom. The ordinary Egyptians, excluded for hundreds of years from the celebration of state religion, revelled in this contact and it must have seemed that the great Amen himself had descended from the heavens to rule Egypt. The king, in comparison, seemed somewhat diminished.

Increasingly, throughout his reign, Amenhotep III attempted to dissipate the growing power of Amen by patronizing rival theologies. In a dual offensive he both promoted the ancient sun-cults of the north and reasserted his own semi-divine nature in the south. The once insignificant Luxor Temple, now linked to Amen's Karnak Temple by a sphinx-lined processional avenue, was decorated with the tale of the king's own divine conception and birth and dedicated to the celebration of the royal soul. In Nubia, Amenhotep went one step further in establishing a cult to 'Amenhotep, Lord of Nubia', a deified form of himself. Such subtle changes in religious emphasis, however, posed little threat to the steadily increasing wealth and influence of Amen. Consequently Amenhotep's son and successor, Amenhotep IV or Akhenaten, embarked on a more direct line of attack.[1]

To describe the 'heretic king' Akhenaten as an enigma has become an Egyptological commonplace. Argument has raged long and hard over the source of Akhenaten's inspiration. Was he a true religious zealot, a bold monotheistic visionary? Or was his new religion merely an excuse, his reign a calculated if misguided attempt to curb the growing power of Amen? Was Akhenaten ever anything more than an unbalanced, self-obsessed ruler incapable of fulfilling his destiny? Whatever his motivation it is clear that Akhenaten, ostensibly in pursuit of his own religious dream, felt able to distance himself from the traditions and expectations of the Egyptian monarchy and built a new city at Amarna. Turning his back on his inherited obligations, the new king devoted his entire reign to the worship of a single sun god, the Aten. Conveniently for Akhenaten, the new god could only be worshipped by the immediate royal family. Lesser mortals were now compelled to address their formal worship via the king and queen.

The mysteries of the new god were celebrated in a lengthy poem, the Great Hymn to the Aten, supposedly written by the king himself:

Glorious, you rise on the horizon of heaven, O living Aten, creator of life. When you have arisen on the eastern horizon you fill every land with your beauty. You are gorgeous, great and radiant, high over every land. Your rays embrace all the lands that you have made . . . Though you are far away, your rays are upon the earth. Though you are seen, your movement is not. When you set on the western horizon the land is dark, like death.[2]

Akhenaten's attraction to an obscure cult – assuming his attraction to be genuine religious feeling – was not in itself remarkable. Egypt's official deities routinely passed through cycles of popularity and obscurity and even the great Amen, now hailed as the king of the gods, was a relative newcomer to the pantheon who owed his meteoric rise to the patronage of the Theban kings. It would be a mistake to see the king of Egypt as the defender of the faith as, quite simply, there was no one faith. Rather, the king should be regarded as the defender of Egypt's ancient traditions. To him fell the duty of maintaining the archaic rituals which had proved so effective in ensuring Egypt's prosperity in the past. His role as chief priest of all cults was a matter of administration rather than devotion – a duty to ensure that the rituals were performed, rather than to perform them himself – and it was quite acceptable for him to delegate these rites. The idea of 'religion', separated from all other aspects of daily life, is very much a modern one. As religion was effectively the science of ancient Egypt, providing explanations for phenomena which would otherwise have been inexplicable, it is perhaps not too far-fetched to see pharaoh as the head of a vast laboratory, responsible for ensuring that all procedures are carried out correctly and so enabling his country to operate smoothly.[3]

Akhenaten, then, was free to indulge his devotion to the Aten. He was even free to adjust the divine hierarchy by honouring the Aten above all others. He was not, however, free to turn his back on Egypt's other gods. Such a move was a blatant rejection of the most important aspect of his kingship. No one knew exactly what would happen if the gods were not accorded their regular rituals; no one really wanted to find out. Akhenaten was embarking on an unknown path fraught with danger for both himself and his country. And yet, such was his conviction that within five years of his accession he had taken the unprecedented move of disbanding the state cults and closing their temples, ensuring that, officially at least, only the Aten could be worshipped in Egypt.

Atenism could never be a comforting religion for a people who, accustomed to a multitude of anthropomorphic deities blessed with all the foibles and quirks of human behaviour, were suddenly faced with one characterless, emotionless symbol whose light shone only for the king and his immediate family. This may have mattered less than we might suppose. The rituals of the state gods had always been the preserve of the monarch and there is little evidence to suggest that, outside Akhenaten's new city of Amarna, there was any change in private beliefs. It would be wrong to compare the enforced Aten worship of the New Kingdom with, say, the compulsory Catholicism of the Spanish Inquisition, or the determined Protestantism of Elizabethan England. Instead Akhenaten's abrupt closure of the old temples was the ancient equivalent of the take-over of a state bank. The assets which the temples held, and the considerable income derived from these assets, were all redirected to the cult of the Aten which was closely controlled by Akhenaten himself. As an added bonus, the king was now freed from his obligation to make regular offerings to the traditional gods and, of course, he had no need to continue expensive building works at Karnak.

A new god needed a new city. Amarna, ancient Akhetaten, was designed to serve as the home of the sun god and here, after a flurry of rapid and somewhat shoddy building works, the royal family retreated to devote themselves to the Aten. Once he had settled in Middle Egypt Akhenaten became increasingly reluctant to leave his city, rejecting the mobile style of kingship which had seen his forebears spending much of their year travelling up and down the Nile in favour of a settled life. Amarna because a permanent court, and Akhenaten and his advisors grew to all intents and purposes invisible to the vast majority of the people. The Egyptian bureaucracy, now over-centralized and bereft of a strong ruler, began a slow but steady decline.

The Amarna court was both insular and self-obsessed. Akhenaten showed little interest in events outside his own secure world, seeming oblivious to the shifts in power which, already by the end of his father's reign, were starting to destabilize the Near East. King Ahmose, in pursuing the hated Hyksos invaders from the Nile Delta into Canaan in order to establish a protective 'buffer-zone', had established a tradition of military supremacy in the Near East. Tuthmosis I and Tuthmosis III continued this policy with gusto, experiencing advances and retreats, until the battle of Meggido left Egypt in full control of Palestine and much of Syria. Thus, almost by accident, was the Egyptian empire born. Now, as Akhenaten worshipped, and was worshipped, in peace the Near Eastern situation rapidly grew much worse.

The emergence of a powerful and potentially dangerous entity in Asia Minor was treated as a matter of almost complete indifference at Amarna. The origins of the Indo-European-speaking Hittites remain obscure, although it seems likely that they had settled on the central Anatolian plateau (modern Turkey) towards the end of the 3rd millennium BC. Initially, the Hittites (based at Hatti) had played an aggressive role in Near Eastern politics but internal problems had caused them to withdraw temporarily from the international scene. Now they were back, with a vengeance! Suppiluliumas, ruler of the new Hittite empire, was Akhenaten's immediate opposite: a determined soldier and shrewd politician who kept a keen eye on his neighbours' affairs. Mitanni (situated in what is now northern Syria, eastern Turkey and northern Iraq), once Egypt's most powerful Near Eastern ally and Hatti's fiercest rival, had been greatly weakened by political in-fighting. Suppiluliumas now intervened to back the rebel government in exile against the ruling king Tushratta. Tushratta, brother-in-law of Akhenaten, was left to struggle alone, and ultimately unsuccessfully, against the enemy while Akhenaten, far from offering his kinsman support, turned his back on Mitanni and established instead a friendly if not over-effusive correspondence with Suppiluliumas. The campaign ended with Tushratta dead, Mitanni split into two separate, ineffective, kingdoms, and the Hittites in possession of Syrian lands as far south as the River Orontes. Now the Egyptians and the Hittites shared a common border.

Many of Akhenaten's Syrian vassals, receiving no support from their overlord and no doubt realizing where their best interests lay, had already transferred their allegiance to Suppiluliumas so that the Hittite sphere of influence now extended over most of Egypt's eastern territories. Others, sensing the weakness of Egypt's control, indulged in minor rebellions and inter-city feuding. Egypt not only lost the tribute paid by these vassals; denied access to the Levantine ports she was unable to import the high quality timber which was desperately needed in the Nile valley. At the same time Nubia, always alert to signs of weak rule, had started to push against Egypt's authority in the south. While it would be wrong to see Akhenaten as a religious pacifist – there is evidence of limited military campaigning during his reign, and it seems that he may even have been planning action against the Hittites shortly before his death – it is clear that pharaoh took little personal interest in foreign affairs. His reactions to the appeals of his vassals were unpredictable and often bizarre. He might issue an urgent, undignified summons to a respected ambassador, or might ignore the same ambassador for many months. Tales of foreign delegations being ordered to stand for hours in the glare of the hot Amarna sun did little to enhance his diplomatic reputation. Isolated at Amarna, Akhenaten felt himself invulnerable, and the military action that he did sanction was simply far too little, far too late.

Akhenaten ruled Egypt for seventeen years – a long time given that the average New Kingdom adult, having escaped the perils associated with birth, infancy and childhood, might reasonably expect to live for some 30–40 years, but nowhere near long enough to ensure that his theological reforms became permanently absorbed into the system. A religion based so closely on the identification of a single god with a particular king had always been doomed to fail, and Akhenaten's death signalled the death of monotheism in dynastic Egypt.

The religious experiment was to prove an expensive one. Seventeen years of royal neglect had left Egypt weak and vulnerable, her foreign policy in tatters and her internal economy corrupted. A strong pharaoh cast in the traditional 18th Dynasty mould of Ahmose or Tuthmosis III might perhaps have been able to bring an abrupt halt to the economic and military decline. However Egypt was now faced with a succession of short-lived rulers who died before they could complete any programme of restoration or, indeed, before they could father an heir. Four royal deaths, two of them untimely, in less than one generation were hardly conducive to political stability. Such an unfortunate chain of events suggested all too clearly that the dynasty had lost the support of the gods.

The death of the pharaoh was always an unsettling time, raising as it did a series of uncomfortable questions plus more pressing practical problems. At its most basic level the loss of the chief administrator left a void at the very heart of government. The king needed to be replaced, and quickly, as a vacant throne might prove too tempting to political opportunists. Spiritually, the ending of such a prominent life brought Egypt into unwelcome contact with the inexplicable and frightening mysteries of death, serving as a reminder of mortality to all. For those who cared to think the unthinkable, the all-too-human victory of death over semi-divine life called into question the validity of the theology which underpinned the institution of the Egyptian monarch. Religious tradition had consistently decreed that the king was no mere mortal, that he was a demi-god, the only living link between heaven and earth. How then could such an august being die?

The theory of divine kingship was riddled with contradictions and inconsistencies which the developing myths and legends of New King-dom theology could not fully address. It seems almost inconceivable to modern, dispassionate observers that these theological flaws were not obvious to the educated dynastic Egyptians. Perhaps they were, although comparison with contemporary religions suggests that those who adhere to a particular system of beliefs are often the last to appreciate its faults. However, no matter how awkward the reasoning, how vague the official explanations and how nagging the residual doubts, such heresies were never published. Religion had to be perceived as providing an adequate explanation of the mortal death of the king, for one thing was very clear – Egypt could not function without her pharaoh. The social, administrative and religious infrastructures were all based on the assump-tion that there would be a king on the throne. Accepting this the Egyptian people never, in over thirty centuries of dynastic rule, attempted to replace their pharaoh with a more democratic form of government. A king, no matter how incompetent, how unconventional or even at times how foreign, was always better than no king at all.

Ideally, a son should succeed his father as the god Horus had followed his father Osiris to the throne of Egypt. Akhenaten, therefore, was succeeded by his son Smenkhkare.[4] Unfortunately Smenkhkare proved to be an ephemeral king, outliving his father by only a couple of years. His brief reign had little impact on the historical or archaeological record, and his final resting place has never been confirmed.

As Tutankhaten succeeded his elder brother Smenkhkare, Egypt's luck seemed at last to have turned. The new king, a healthy, malleable boy with a young and presumably fertile wife, seemed set for exactly the kind of lengthy and conventional reign which would allow the dynasty time to recover from its unfortunate aberration. Tutankhaten may have been lacking in political experience but he had the good sense to heed his inherited advisors who, having served through the Amarna period, were all too well aware of the problems which now beset both the monarchy and the country. If the situation was to be retrieved, some serious backtracking was needed. Almost immediately the decision was taken to draw a firm line between the new king and his two immediate predecessors. In spite of his youth Tutankhaten was henceforth to be promoted as an old-fashioned New Kingdom monarch; an ideal combination of brave warrior, wise administrator and conscientious priest who would serve as a worthy successor to the crowns of Ahmose. By stressing his own personal orthodoxy while hinting at his own divinity, by identifying the religious experiment as an official failure, and by making good the damage of his father's reign, the new king would prove his worth and Egypt would be renewed. This policy was proclaimed from Memphis and set in stone at Karnak:

Now when His Majesty rose as king the temples and cities of the gods and goddesses, from Elephantine down to the marshes of the Delta, had decayed. Their shrines had fallen into desolation and had become ruins overgrown with weeds . . . The land was in chaos and the gods had turned their backs on it . . . But after many days His Majesty rose upon the throne of his father and ruled over the land of Horus. The Black Land and the Red Land fell under his supervision and everyone bowed before his might.[5]

The Aten, once all powerful, was to be demoted and it was Tutankhaten, now renamed Tutankh-amen 'Living Image of Amen' as an obvious means of emphasizing his orthodox devotion, who was to be credited with re-establishing the traditional state gods and reopening their temples.

Internally Egypt was to be enhanced by a programme of monumental building, while her position on the international stage was to be re-enforced by diplomacy and, where diplomacy failed, by the army under the command of General Horemheb. Unfortunately all this promise came to nothing. After only nine years as king Tutankhamen met a premature death, and with his passing came the end of Akhenaten's line.

Tutankhamen was followed on the throne by his mentor, Ay. We may still see the new pharaoh, at the very moment of his inheritance, immortalized on the wall of Tutankhamen's tomb (KV 62). Ay has donned the leopard-skin cloak of a priest to perform the 'Opening of the Mouth' ceremony before the dead Tutankhamen, a ritual which was traditionally the responsibility of the heir to the deceased and which

Fig 2.1   King Ay, dressed in the leopard skin of a priest, performs the opening of the mouth ceremony in the tomb of Tutankhamen

therefore confirmed Ay's right to rule. Ay appears glowing with health and vigour, he exudes confidence in his new role. However, Egyptian art is often deliberately deceptive. The new pharaoh was no youngster. The brother-in-law of Amenhotep III and probable father of Queen Nefertiti, Ay had served under Amenhotep III, Akhenaten, Smenkhkare and Tutankhamen and was already, even in modern terms, an old man. Even the most optimistic could never have regarded him as anything other than a temporary monarch. Furthermore, he too was lacking a son to inherit the throne and his imminent death would invariably precipitate another crisis. Although it is rare to find any evidence of discontent within the secret workings of the royal palace, it seems that King Ay may not have been universally welcomed:

My husband has died and I do not have a son. But, they say, you have many sons. If you would give me one of your sons he would become my husband. I could never choose one of my servants and make him my husband.[6]

The cuneiform letter quoted above allows us a rare opportunity of peeping behind the diplomatic scenes as a succession crisis develops. The message is deceptively simple. A recently widowed queen of Egypt, lacking a male child to inherit the throne and apparently unable to find any suitably regal suitor in her own country, has written to the king of the Hittites asking that he should send one of his sons as a bridegroom. By marrying the royal widow this son would automatically become the next pharaoh.

The recipient of the letter, the wily and experienced Hittite King Suppiluliumas, was rightly suspicious of the queen's proposal. Such a request was both unprecedented and totally contrary to Egyptian tradition. While Hittite princesses were regularly sent as brides to foreign courts, everyone knew that Egyptian princesses were never permitted to marry even the friendliest of foreigners. However, in spite of his political acumen, Suppiluliumas was fatally tempted. Egypt, even in her weakened state, was a glittering prize, far too good to be missed. After some hesitation, and some discreet investigations by the Hittite ambassador, Prince Zananza was selected and despatched to his wedding. The unfortunate Zananza was ambushed and murdered before he even set foot in Egypt and relations between Egypt and Hatti sank to an all-time low.

The name of the letter writer has not been preserved but, assuming that the document is a genuine appeal for help and not merely a cunning attempt to draw the Hittites to the brink of war, its date suggests that she must have been Queen Ankhesenamen, widow of Tutankhamen and daughter of Akhenaten and Nefertiti.

But when was the letter written? Did Ankhesenamen really have strenuous objections to Ay, her grandfather, becoming pharaoh? Or did she look ahead, seeing beyond the temporary monarch to the time when Egypt would once again be in urgent need of a king? Certainly it is tempting to interpret Ankhesenamen's fatal letter to Suppiluliumas as an attempt to prevent the increasingly powerful General Horemheb, rather than Ay, from seizing the throne. This is our last sighting of Ankhesenamen; the abrupt disappearance of so prominent a lady has been interpreted by many as evidence of foul play at court.

Four years after his accession Ay, too, was lying cold in his tomb (WV 23). Egypt's new monarch, Horemheb, was an experienced politician with a strong military background and a record of distinguished service under his two immediate predecessors. Good luck, or astute political manoeuvring, had allowed him to maintain a low profile throughout the Amarna period and in consequence Egypt's new king was not tainted with the Aten heresies which contaminated so many of his contemporaries.[7] A beautiful, life-sized grey granite sculpture recovered from Memphis and now housed in the Metropolitan Museum, New York, shows us Horemheb the statesman during the reign of Tutankhamen. The 'King's Deputy, Fan-bearer on the King's Right and Great Troop-Commander' Horemheb is seated with his legs crossed in the traditional scribal pose. On his lap is an unrolled papyrus scroll engraved with a hymn to Thoth, while the base of the statue bears prayers dedicated to Thoth, Ptah and Osiris. Horemheb's interest in justice is already apparent; here he praises Thoth for his role as the 'vizier who settles law-cases, and who brings peace to disorder'.[8]

Horemheb's numerous titles, his impressive statue and, above all, the well-appointed tomb in the Memphite cemetery which provides us with details of his successful military career under Tutankhamen, combine to confirm his role as a man of great wealth and influence.[9] His parentage, however, remains a mystery and there is no evidence to indicate that he was born an immediate member of the Theban royal family. Horemheb did enjoy royal connections, but these came late in life via his second marriage. Queen Mutnodjmet, consort of Horemheb, is almost certainly to be identified with the Lady Mutnodjmet, sister of Queen Nefertiti and daughter of Ay, who appears as a slender young girl in some of the scenes which decorate the tombs of the Amarna nobles. It is perhaps not stretching credibility too far to imagine the elderly Ay marrying his intended successor to his daughter and thereby confirming the adoption of Horemheb as his intended heir.

It may seem curious that a king who sought to distance himself from the irregularities of the Amarna court should consider such a marriage, but the advantages of linking himself to the previous monarch presumably outweighed the disadvantages of marrying Akhenaten's sister-in-law. Marriage with the daughter of a vanquished foe had long been the prerogative of a victorious king; tradition held that Narmer, the southern warrior who united Egypt at the start of the dynastic age, had consolidated his position by marriage with a northern princess. Similar diplomatic marriages were conducted in the west in relatively modern times; Henry VII, for example, confirmed his hold on the English throne by marrying Elizabeth of York, the daughter of his defeated rival.

The new king was crowned by Amen – assisted by his earthly representative – at Thebes. *The Horus King*, Strong Bull, Skilled in Plans; *He of the Two Ladies*, Great in Marvels in the Temple of Karnak; *The Golden Horus* Who is Pleased with Truth and Who Causes the Two Lands to Come into Existence; *King of Upper and Lower Egypt*, Lord of the Two Lands, Djeserkheperure Setepenre; *Son of Re*, Horemheb, beloved of Amen, started his reign where Tutankhamen had left off. Already Amarna had been abandoned. Now Memphis, rather than Thebes, was to serve as Egypt's principal city. The civil service, which took responsibility for the collection of taxes in kind, had grown lazy and inefficient through years of neglect, with extortion and bribery now the only means of doing business. Horemheb made a public pledge to 'protect the whole land . . . repelling wrong doing and destroying falsehood'.[10] The bureaucracy was to be purged of all corruption while the legal system was strengthened by the establishment of a network of local courts and judges, making justice accessible to the common people. Punishment for those who disobeyed Horemheb's laws was both swift and severe; any official who attempted to exploit his position was threatened with exile or facial mutilation.

Horemheb used his military experience to reorganize the demoralized army into two separate divisions, north and south, each under its own commander. The troops were employed to crush a rebellion in Nubia and there was a morale-boosting campaign to Syria, although the new king, in spite of his own military background, made internal rather than international politics his overriding concern. As the temples to the Aten were dismantled block by block monumental building works recommenced at Karnak and Memphis and the traditional priesthoods were restored to some, but by no means all, of their former powers. In an echo of Tutankhamen's policy decree Horemheb:

Sought out the precincts of the gods which were in ruins in this land and set them in order even as they were since the days of antiquity, and instituted for them regular offerings . . . He equipped them with ordinary priests and lectors from the pick of the army, and opened up for them fields and herds equipped with all services . . .[11]

The new pharaoh, too wise to allow any single cult to rise to prominence, did not share Tutankhamen's particular devotion to Amen and instead paid public homage to a variety of gods including Horus, his namesake. At the quarry site of Gebel Silsila (38 miles or 61 kilometres to the north of modern Aswan) he continued 18th Dynasty tradition by starting to build – but not finishing – an impressive rock-cut chapel or *speos* dedicated to seven deities; the local crocodile-headed Sobek, Amen, Mut, Khonsu, Tawaret, Thoth and the deified Horemheb himself.

Quietly and effectively, Horemheb laid the foundations for a renewed Egyptian prosperity whilst systematically erasing all trace of the unortho-dox Amarna period. This is generally regarded as an impersonal, political cleansing rather than a frenzied hate campaign; we have little evidence to suggest that Horemheb bore a personal grudge against Akhenaten and his god, although the dismantling and subsequent reconstruction, upside-down and mutilated, of Queen Nefertiti's Theban *Ben-ben* temple within his own Karnak gateway hints at more complex feelings towards his sister-in-law. Could Horemheb's apparent dislike of Nefertiti have stemmed from his bad relationship with her daughter Ankhesenamen? Ultimately, however, Horemheb was too closely identified with the economic and military decline which ended the 18th Dynasty to escape entirely from the Amarna shadow. Manetho chose to classify Horemheb, whom he knew as Oros, as the last king of the ailing 18th Dynasty and it was Horemheb's protégé and successor, Ramesses I, a man with no personal links with the Amarna period, who was to be celebrated as the founder of the 19th.

Like his three immediate predecessors Horemheb had no son to follow him on to the throne and he too looked to the army for an heir, a sensible decision which would ensure that his successor would enjoy the full support of the military. Horemheb selected an ex-officer turned adminis-trator called Paramessu, or Ramesses, son of the Commander of Troops Seti. This Ramesses, a near-contemporary of Horemheb, had proved his abilities through many years of loyal service, first as a soldier where he rose to the position of General, and then as one of Egypt's two Viziers. In many ways his career mirrored that of Horemheb before him, but there was one important difference: Ramesses and his wife Sitre already had a living son and a living grandson, and therefore had the potential to found a dynasty. When Ramesses died after less than two years as king, Horemheb's judgement was vindicated. The throne passed smoothly to Ramesses' son Seti and Egypt was spared the doubts and uncertainties that had plagued her immediate past. Meanwhile, it now fell to Ramesses to bury Horemheb.

Horemheb's original Memphite tomb, although grand enough for a commoner, was hardly suitable for a royal burial. To replace it Horemheb commissioned a magnificent decorated tomb in the Valley of the Kings (KV 57). This tomb, with its long, steep corridors, multiple flights of steps and columned halls, was the most impressive to be excavated in the main Valley for over a hundred years. Unfortunately, its elaborate painted walls were still unfinished when Horemheb's death forced the workmen to down tools. The tomb, sealed, desecrated, restored and re-desecrated in antiquity, was rediscovered by a team of British archaeologists in 1908. Arthur Weigall was present as the excavators 'wriggled

Fig 2.2   General Horemheb kneels before Osiris in his Memphite tomb

and crawled' along the hot, dark, rubbish-filled passageways, eventually reaching the devastated burial chamber:

There is something peculiarly sensational in the examining of a tomb which has not been entered for such thousands of years, but it must be left to the imaginative reader to infuse a touch of that feeling of the dramatic into these words . . . In some of the tombs which have been opened the freshness of the objects has caused one to exclaim at the inaction of the years; but here, where vivid and well-preserved wall-paintings looked down upon a jumbled collection of smashed fragments of wood and bones, one felt how hardly the Powers deal with the dead. How far away seemed the great fight between Amon [sic] and Aton [sic]; how futile the task which Horemheb accomplished so gloriously![12]

Horemheb's body has never been recovered.

The cult of the deified Horemheb flourished for a time at Memphis where his unused tomb and its chapel served as a focus for worship during the Ramesside era, particularly during the reign of Ramesses II. Tia, sister of Ramesses II, even had her family tomb annexed to that of Horemheb, a sure sign of the religious importance attached to the site. Devotion to the memory of Horemheb was perhaps a practical means of repaying the immense debt owed by the Ramesside family to their late patron, although this devotion had a strictly limited application. No delicacy of feeling, for example, prevented Ramesses I from erasing Horemheb's name from his Karnak gateway and replacing it with his own. Nevertheless, this lingering sense of gratitude may explain why later, when the decision was taken to rewrite Egyptian history eliminating all trace of the Amarna kings, Horemheb was allowed to retain his reign. The revised line of succession was now to pass directly from Amenhotep III to Horemheb himself, and Akhenaten, Smenkhkare, Tutankhamen and Ay were all to be forgotten. Thus the commoner-kings of the Ramesside dynasty could, with a clear conscience, trace their kingship back to the glorious kings of old, without reference to the embarrassment of the Amarna Period.

The Horus King, Strong Bull, Flourishing in Kingship; *He of the Two Ladies*, Who Arises in the Kingship like Atum; *The Golden Horus* Who Establishes *Maat* Throughout the Land; *King of Upper and Lower Egypt*, Lord of the Two Lands, Menpehtyre; *Son of Re*, Ramesses I, was highly conscious of his role as the founder of a new dynasty. His chosen titles, stark in their simplicity, deliberately mirrored those used by Ahmose, heroic founder of the 18th Dynasty, some two hundred and fifty years before. Ramesses, ably aided by his son Seti, clearly intended to become a pharaoh in the classical mould reintroduced by Horemheb; once again Egypt was to be ruled by a brave soldier and an extensive builder. However, while the 18th Dynasty had been Theban kings the 19th were northerners, and proud of it. Their very names spoke of their northern origins. As we have already seen, Seti, 'Man of Seth', indicates a family loyalty to the god Seth of Avaris while the name Ramesses 'Born of the god Re' shows a devotion to the ancient cult of Re at Heliopolis. As a northerner, Ramesses felt no personal debt of allegiance to either Thebes or Amen although he was happy to accept Amen in his now-traditional role as patron god of royalty. Throughout the Ramesside era, while Karnak remained an important religious complex, the site of extensive building works dedicated to Amen and his family, and while the Theban west bank retained its role as the royal necropolis, there was to be increased political and religious activity in the north.

Just as Ahmose had needed to fight for his throne, so Ramesses knew that he would need to use force if he wished to regain his eastern territories. A new pharaoh – particularly one with no royal lineage – had to prove himself to his foreign subjects; any sign of weakness following a change of ruler was invariably interpreted as the signal to revolt. Ramesses acted swiftly. A period of intense military training supervised by Crown Prince Seti was followed by a sudden, successful raid on Canaan which, while contributing little in terms of land gained, sent a clear warning to the potentially disloyal Levantine states.

Meanwhile, back home, much of the vandalism and neglect of the Amarna period was still apparent. A nationwide plan of restoration was clearly needed. Building works had already started at Karnak where there were ambitious designs to convert an open court built by Horemheb into a magnificent hall of columns – a hypostyle hall – dedicated to Amen. All too soon, however, disaster struck. The elderly king fell ill and died a mere sixteen months into his reign.

Ramesses had planned to build himself a magnificent tomb in the Valley of the Kings (KV16). Here he might lie close to his friend and predecessor Horemheb. But, given the king's advanced age, the construction of his tomb had always been a race against time. Now time had won and, with the king dead, only two steep stairways linked by a corridor and leading to a single room had been hewn out of the rock. The unfinished room would of necessity have to serve as a royal burial chamber. The walls, after a hurried coating of plaster, were painted to show the king and his gods, with Osiris allowed a prominent position. The red granite sarcophagus too was painted rather than carved with inscriptions which, due to their hasty preparation, included a number of unfortunate errors. Finally the king, having passed seventy days at the embalming house, was laid to rest by his son, Seti I.

In spite of stringent security, none could be guaranteed eternal rest in the Valley. When Ramesses' tomb was rediscovered by Belzoni's workmen on 11 October 1817 it had already been thoroughly looted:

I found the tomb just opened, and entered to see how far it was practicable to examine it. Having proceeded through a passage thirty-two feet long and eight feet wide, I descended a staircase of twenty-eight feet, and reached a tolerably large and well-painted room . . . The ceiling was in good preservation, but not in the best style. We found a sarcophagus of granite, with two mummies in it, and in a corner a statue standing erect, six feet six inches high, and beautifully cut out of sycamore wood . . . The sarcophagus was covered with hieroglyphics merely painted, or outlined: it faces south-east by east.[13]

The sarcophagus had been damaged by thieves who had levered off its lid in their search for jewels and amulets. The bodies which Belzoni found within the sarcophagus were, however, later burials. Ramesses had already been removed for safe keeping by the New Kingdom priests and officials who were responsible for guarding the mummies of the pharaohs. His body has never been recovered, and it is just possible that his was the mummy which Miss Amelia Edwards famously declined to buy and which a pair of her acquaintances, having made the purchase and 'unable to bear the perfume of their ancient Egyptian, drowned the dear departed at the end of a week'.[14] Ramesses' massive sarcophagus still lies in its tomb, surrounded by the forest of wooden beams now needed to support the weakened ceiling.

As Horemheb had planned, Seti I inherited the throne of his father with the minimum of bureaucratic disruption. Seti, an experienced soldier and administrator, had been well schooled for his destiny, serving first as Vizier then as co-regent during his father's reign. At the time of his accession he was in his mid-thirties, already married and the father of a healthy son of some eight or nine years of age. Marriages between families of similar social and professional classes were the preferred unions throughout the dynastic age and so Seti's wife, Tuya or Mut-Tuya, came from a similar upper-class military background to his own, being the daughter of the Lieutenant of Chariotry, Raia, and his wife Ruia. The couple eventually produced at least three children including a son who died in infancy, a daughter Tia and a second son named Ramesses after his grandfather.

Seti now ruled Egypt as *The Horus King*, Strong Bull Arising in Thebes, Who Causes the Two Lands to Live; *He of the Two Ladies*, Bringer of Renaissance Who Protects Egypt and Curbs Foreign Lands; *The Golden Horus* Strong-in-Years, Great-of-Victories; *King of Upper and Lower Egypt*, Lord of the Two Lands, Menmaatre; *Son of Re*, Seti, Beloved of Ptah. Once again Egypt was blessed with a king eager to emulate the more successful New Kingdom pharaohs. Seti's chosen regal names were based on those of his most illustrious 18th Dynasty predecessors, the mighty warrior Tuthmosis III 'Strong Bull Appearing in Thebes' Menkheperre, and the monumental builder Amenhotep III, Nebmaatre 'heir of Re'.

Seti immediately resumed his father's aggressive foreign policy and the summer of his regnal Year 1 saw the new king leading the Egyptian army in a brief campaign to reassert control over the Sinai land bridge linking Egypt to Canaan. The Shoshu bedouin, whose activities were threatening the security of this all-important trade route, had fatally underestimated the determination of their new king:

Now, as for this king he rejoices at the beginning of battle. He delights to enter a fight and his heart is gratified at the sight of blood. He cuts off the heads of the dissidents. More than the day of rejoicing he loves the moment of crushing the enemy. His majesty slays them at one stroke. He leaves them no heirs, and whoever escapes his hand is brought as prisoner to Egypt.[15]

Later in the same year he returned to Canaan, travelling further north to suppress disturbances in the Jordan Valley. A stela celebrating this glorious achievement was erected in the garrison city of Beth-Shan, and

Seti returned home in triumph with the province of Canaan secure and his own reputation greatly enhanced.

Over the next few years Seti returned to Canaan and the northern province of Upi, reaffirming Egypt's control and advancing inland as far as Damascus before securing the ports of Tyre, Sidon, Byblos and Simyra. Such local victories, although invariably presented as great triumphs, did little to test the strength of Egypt's troops. Seti clearly had his sights set on a challenge to the might of the Hittite Empire, a challenge which, if successful, would earn him a place amongst the greatest of Egypt's warrior kings. Already the two super-powers shared a common border, and the temptation to push northwards into Hittite territory must have been great. However, before the situation could advance beyond a minor skirmish – a skirmish which, although brief, had allowed the Egyptians to appreciate just how formidable their new enemy could be – a potentially serious Libyan problem diverted Seti's attention westwards. The Egyptian army marched home to defend the western Delta in a brief, satisfyingly successful campaign during which the fourteen-year-old Prince Ramesses, already titled 'Commander-in-Chief of the Army', was allowed to experience his first battle.

With his western border secure Seti was free to resume military manoeuvres to the east. Ramesses, now a seasoned campaigner, was allowed to accompany his father on a mission to subdue Amurru and recapture the important Syrian city of Kadesh (modern Tell Nebi Mend) on the River Orontes. However, the momentum had been broken and although the army was able to erect a triumphal stela in Kadesh the promised trial of strength against the Hittites never came. Seti had had time to reflect on his position, and instead of bloodshed and potential defeat he decided that there was to be peace with honour. An agreement was reached, a formal treaty may have been signed, and Kadesh and Amurru eventually reverted to Hittite control while Egypt was permitted to retain her hold on the seaports which would allow her once again to import timber. Again Seti returned home in triumph, with Egypt's military reputation almost fully restored to its pre-Amarna glories.

To the south, Seti's authority went largely unopposed. In Year 8 rumours of a planned insurrection in the remote land of Kush, beyond the Third Cataract, had met with such a quick response that few subsequently cared to challenge the authority of pharaoh. Seti's army took only one week to march through the southern oases, crushing the rebellion and returning with hundreds of captives. Five years later a minor revolt in Lower Nubia allowed Prince Ramesses to take sole command of Egypt's troops for the first time. Ramesses was in little danger and the sight of the charging Egyptians was enough to cause the rebels to run away. Nevertheless, Ramesses felt it appropriate to mark his glorious victory by building a small rock-cut temple at Beit el-Wali. Here, alongside images of the old Syrian and Libyan campaigns, he displayed scenes of weeping Nubians, and of vanquished Nubians offering tribute to their conqueror.[16]

Concerned that the uninterrupted supply of gold be maintained and even increased, Year 9 found Seti on a personal tour of inspection visiting the gold-workers in the eastern desert. Establishing a much-needed well for the benefit of travellers and quarrymen (and, of course, for the increased efficiency of the mining operation), he took the opportunity to dedicate a small sandstone temple where he could marvel at his own kindness:

When His Majesty had travelled many miles, he halted in order to take counsel with his heart. He said: 'How painful is a road without water! What are travellers to do to relieve their parched throats? . . . Woe to the man who thirsts in the wilderness. Now I will plan for them. I will provide the means to sustain them, so that they may bless my name in the future . . . For I am indeed considerate and compassionate towards travellers.[17]

Nor was the welfare of the stonemasons neglected. An inscription at Silsila records how in Year 6 Seti had improved the rations, a highly popular move which allowed each man a daily portion of bread, roast meat, assorted vegetables plus two monthly sacks of grain. Three years later Prince Ramesses served as his father's assistant as he visited the Aswan quarries on a personal quest for high-grade granite suitable for the production of colossal statues.

Egypt's ever-increasing wealth allowed the king to finance a portfolio of ambitious building projects. The Temple of Re at Heliopolis, the Temple of Ptah at Memphis and, of course, the Temple of Amen at Karnak all benefited from the king's generosity. At the same time Seti embarked on the construction of a more private building, a magnificent summer palace in his eastern Delta homeland, close to the old Hyksos city of Avaris.

The remarkable hypostyle hall at Karnak was henceforth to be known as the temple 'Glorious is Seti in the Domain of Amen', with no reference to its original begetter, Ramesses I, whose image was restricted to the top of the northern half of the west wall. Construction work had finished by now and the builders had given way to the artists who were to decorate the walls and columns in the elegant raised relief which characterized all of Seti's monuments. Working from north to south the interior walls were carved with scenes of temple ritual designed to glorify Amen. The exterior walls of the hall – vast, blank surfaces visible to all and therefore ideally suited to propaganda messages – were in contrast decorated with a series of vivid battle scenes showing the triumphal Seti in all his military glory. Here Canaanites, Syrians and Libyans would fall before Seti for all eternity.

The tableaux on the north wall allow us a glimpse of the valiant young Ramesses fighting by his father's side. In one scene Ramesses helps Seti to kill a Libyan while in another he walks behind his father's chariot. Wherever he appears, however, his figure is a late addition clumsily carved into plaster concealing a pre-existing image. Initially it seemed that the figure of Ramesses must have been substituted as a replacement for the image of an older, now dead, brother; the ruthless excision of the names and images of the newly dead, and their replacement with those of the living, was a common enough practice at this time. However, research by the Oriental Institute of the University of Chicago has revealed the deleted figure to have been a commoner, the Troop Captain and Fan Bearer Mehy. There is therefore no reason to believe that Ramesses was at any time second in line to his father's throne, while suggestions that Ramesses may have murdered an elder brother (named Mehy?) in order to guarantee his own inheritance may be dismissed.[18] Although his prominent position indicates that Mehy may well have been a favourite of Seti we have no reason to think that he was ever a serious contender for the throne. It seems that Ramesses, seeking to insert himself in a conspicuous position in his father's battle scene, simply removed the unfortunate Troop Captain who was standing in his way.

On the west bank, opposite the Karnak Temple, work had started on the construction of the king's mortuary temple at Gurna. At the same time the more secretive excavation of the king's tomb continued deep in the Valley of the Kings (KV 17). New Kingdom tradition decreed that Seti should furnish himself with a hidden burial chamber to house his body plus a conspicuous mortuary temple, built some distance away, which could serve as a temple dedicated jointly to the god Amen and the living Seti during his lifetime and as a more specialized temple dedicated to the cult of the deified king at his death. These two elements, temple and burial chamber, although physically separate, were complementary halves of the same tomb. The magnificent mortuary temple, carefully situated on the processional way between the Karnak temple of Amen and the Deir el-Bahari cult centre, incorporated a small chapel for Ramesses I who had died before he could complete his own provisions for eternity. It was to be decorated in the same time-consuming raised relief used in the hypostyle hall. Eventually Seti, too, would die before he could finalize his funerary preparations, and it would be left to Ramesses II to finish his father's work.

There was one other site, however, which could with some justification claim to be the proper graveyard of the kings of Egypt. Abydos, some 80 miles (128 kilometres) downstream of Thebes, had long been recognized as the burial place of the dead god Osiris. Osiris, once king of the living, had been betrayed and brutally murdered by his brother Seth. His mummified body was now understood to rest beneath the Umm el-Qa'ab, the actual burial ground of Egypt's earliest kings. The Egyptians had always believed that proximity in death could have beneficial results; this is why so many courtiers chose to be buried close to the pyramids and tombs of their masters. Interment near to the tomb of Osiris was therefore seen as a highly desirable but somewhat impractical option for the masses. Instead, from the Middle Kingdom onwards, Abydos became an established place of pilgrimage with many Egyptians visiting the site to dedicate either statues or *mahat* – mud-brick cenotaphs holding limestone stelae which could act as dummy burials. The statues were placed in the cult temple of Osiris while the *mahat* were set up overlooking the processional way that linked the temple of Osiris to his tomb.

Kings, too, established *mahat* at Abydos, although their monuments were on a far larger scale. The royal link with Osiris was a particularly strong one as Osiris, in his role as 'Foremost of Westerners', was recognized as the king of the Afterlife and as such represented the dead counterpart of both Amen-Re (the living king of the gods) and of pharaoh himself (the living king of Egypt). Just as the living king was associated with Horus, so the dead king effectively became Osiris. Already, during the Middle Kingdom, Senwosret III had provided himself with an Abydene cenotaph temple which may even have replaced his Dahshur pyramid as his final burial place. Ahmose continued this tradition by building a cenotaph for his grandmother Tetisheri, and other 18th Dynasty kings followed suit, although the majority of their monuments are now lost. The most impressive surviving *mahat* are the temples built by the kings of the early 19th Dynasty. This is not particularly surprising. As association with Osiris was a means of strengthening the right to rule we might expect to find a dynasty of *arrivistes* attempting to reinforce their claim to the throne by stating a conspicuous allegiance to Osiris. It is probably no coincidence that the best-known King List is to be found in Seti's Abydos temple. Here is detailed a seemingly unbroken line of kings from Menes, legendary founder of the 1st Dynasty, down to Seti himself. Seti, the living king, is shown adoring the cartouches of the ancestors with the 'Eldest King's Son, Heir Apparent' Prince Ramesses by his side.

Seti built a small *mahat* for his father, Ramesses I, and an enormous one for himself. He also allowed his son to start building his own smaller cenotaph. Ramesses II subsequently completed both monuments; a rare example of Ramesses settling for second best. Seti's cenotaph temple can be seen as the direct counterpart of his mortuary temple at Gurna with one important difference: at Thebes, Amen, his wife Mut and his son Khonsu were the primary deities while at Abydos the family of Osiris took over this role. Uniquely, the Abydos temple has seven sanctuaries dedicated to Osiris, Isis, Horus, Amen-Re, Re-Harakhty, Ptah and the deified Seti. At both Gurna and Abydos daily prayers and offerings would be made for the beneficial survival of the dead king.

Just as the Theban mortuary complex had two elements, the temple and the tomb, so at Abydos Seti built not only a dummy mortuary temple, but also a dummy tomb. Immediately to the west of his temple he excavated a subterranean structure with a central hall whose granite roof was supported by giant granite pillars. This structure is today known as the Osireion. Although the Osireion never housed the king's body, a room opening from the central hall was designed with the shape and decoration of an enormous sarcophagus. A channel surrounding the hall effectively provided a ground-water moat, allowing the hall to represent the mound of creation. Access to the underground chamber was via a long, sloping corridor running at right-angles to the hall, reflecting the traditional design of the 18th Dynasty Theban royal tombs.

Seti, who would have learned about the troubled successions of Tutankhamen, Ay and Horemheb from his father, was well aware of his duty to leave an obvious and conspicuous heir. In his case the matter was relatively simple. As Seti had succeeded his father Ramesses I, so Prince Ramesses, the only surviving son of Queen Tuya, would eventually follow Seti and rule Egypt. Nevertheless, in ancient Egypt it never hurt to state the obvious and so the young Ramesses, at approximately ten years of age, had been promoted to the rank of First King's Son, or Crown Prince. Later, having served his apprenticeship and proved himself worthy, he was installed as regent to assist Seti in his rule. Ramesses, now formally Usermaatre Ramesses, himself described this gratifying sequence of events on the wall of his father's Abydos temple:

It was Menmaatre [Seti] who nurtured me, and the All-Lord himself advanced me when I was a child until I could start to rule. Already when I was in the egg he had given the land to me. The officials kissed the ground before me when I was installed as the Eldest Son . . . and when I reported concerning the affairs of the Two Lands as commander of the infantry and of the chariotry. When my father rose up before the people (when I was still a child in his arms) he said of me: 'raise him as a king so that I may see his beauty while I still live'. He summoned the chamberlains to place the diadems on my brow. He equipped me with private attendants and with female royal attendants who were like unto the great beauties of the palace. He selected for me women throughout the land . . . harem women and female companions.[19]

The co-regency, a 12th Dynasty tradition, had been revived during the New Kingdom as a means of strengthening the succession. In theory any form of joint reign should have been impossible in a land where divine kingship was believed to pass from father to son only at death, so that the son became the living Horus at the very second his father became the dead Osiris. However, in this as in many other instances, the Egyptians

*Fig 2.3   Ramesses as a young man
displaying the characteristic 'side-lock of
youth' hairstyle and the finger raised to
the lips*

were prepared to overlook theological inconsistencies in favour of
practical advantages. Despite a
number of obvious difficulties –
Was there a major and a minor
king? Who had ultimate authority?
And how was the joint reign to be
dated? – the co-regency was seen
as a good thing. Not only did it
make the succession crystal clear, it
allowed the older pharaoh to fade
into a semi-retirement while the
younger king learned his trade.
Ramesses I had already used the
convention of the co-regency as a
means of confirming Seti's right to
rule.

Some kings were not above
inventing a co-regency with their
predecessor to add a spurious air of
legitimacy to an otherwise dubious
claim to the throne; the female
king Hatchepsut, for example, attempted to justify her otherwise inexplicable accession on the (false) grounds that it had been sanctioned by her
father and co-regent Tuthmosis I. At the other end of the spectrum many
joint reigns, those where the more junior monarch shared the regnal
years of the senior, have left little or no trace in the archaeological record.
The co-regency of Seti I and Ramesses II, well publicized from the
outset, appears to be an entirely genuine association, with Ramesses'
pleasure at being crowned co-regent matched only by his excitement
at receiving a houseful of beautiful women. Even so, we must allow
for the usual Ramesside exaggeration. Ramesses was presumably not
raised to rule 'from the egg', as he here claimed, as he was born the
commoner son of a commoner. Nor, indeed, was this in any way a
partnership of equals. Even after his coronation, when he was permitted to use his own titles and write his name in a cartouche, Ramesses
was very much the junior or deputy monarch; he did not, for example,

start to count his own regnal years until he became sole ruler. Now he devoted himself to learning his trade, serving as his father's deputy.

After ten to sixteen years on the throne, and probably no more than four years of co-regency, Seti died at Avaris.[20] Ramesses, also resident in the Delta, waited for his father's body to be released from the embalming house and then sailed south with the mummy, to Thebes. Here Ramesses confirmed his right to rule as Seti, suitably preserved and bandaged, was interred in the longest, deepest and most beautifully decorated tomb in the Valley of the Kings (KV 17). Almost three thousand years later this tomb was rediscovered by Belzoni and his workmen on 16 October 1817 when:

Fig 2.4   Seti I embraced by the god Horus on a pillar within his tomb, KV 17

I recommenced my excavations in the valley of Beban el Malook [Valley of the Kings], and pointed out the fortunate spot, which has paid me for all the trouble I took in my researches. I may call this a fortunate day, one of the best perhaps of my life . . .

Seti's tomb consisted of an impressive sequence of stairways, passageways and pillared rooms leading to a vaulted burial chamber whose walls stood some twenty feet high and whose meticulously plotted astronomical ceiling was an unprecedented treasure. Beyond the crypt a curious passage ran downwards into the unstable, underlying shale. Although local rumours maintain that this dangerous, impassable corridor leads to vast deposits of gold and jewels, it would more realistically appear to be a failed attempt to reach ground water and so create the equivalent of the ground-water moat incorporated in Seti's Abydos cenotaph. This was the first royal tomb to be completely decorated in all its passages and chàmbers, and the fine style of the raised and painted relief is highly reminiscent of that used at Seti's Abydos temple. To some, the atmosphere within the torch-lit painted tomb was one of suppressed horror:

Immediately on entering the tomb, the visitor finds himself actually transported into a new world. The almost joyous pictures of the Sakkara and Beni-Hassan tombs have altogether disappeared. The defunct is no more to be seen at home, in the middle of his family . . . All this has become, so to speak, fantastic and chimerical. Even the gods themselves assume strange forms. Long serpents glide hither and thither around the rooms, or stand erect against the doorways. Some convicted malefactors are being decapitated and others are precipitated into the flames. Well might a visitor feel a kind of horror creeping over him if he did not realise that, underneath all these strange representations lies the most consoling of all dogmas, that which vouchsafes eternal happiness to the soul after the many trials of life.[21]

Inevitably the tomb had been looted in antiquity, but the painted walls remained substantially intact at the time of discovery and the king's body had been salvaged, restored and stored by the priest who guarded the secrets of the necropolis. Today Seti rests in Cairo Museum where his beautifully preserved head, unfortunately detached from his more battered body, represents one of the finest examples of the dynastic embalmer's art.

The walls of KV 17 were soon targeted by thieves who were able to chisel out sections of the paintings for sale on the illegal antiquities market. Belzoni, contributing to the damage by taking 'squeezes' of the walls, had been able to recover a few of the original grave goods including hundreds of wooden *shabti* figures, provided to do the work of the dead king in the Afterlife, and the remains of an embalmed bull. The massive anthropoid alabaster sarcophagus or outer coffin, decorated with scenes and verses from the *Book of Gates*, was a thing of great beauty:

[the coffin] merits the most particular attention, not having its equal in the world, and being such as we had no idea could exist. It is a sarcophagus of the finest alabaster nine feet five inches long, and three feet seven inches wide. Its thickness is only two inches; and it is transparent, when a light is placed in the

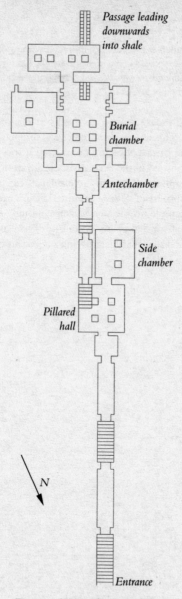

Passage leading
downwards
into shale

Burial
chamber

Antechamber

Side
chamber

Pillared
hall

N

Entrance

Fig 2.5   KV 17: the tomb of Seti I

inside of it. It is minutely sculptured within and without with seven hundred figures, which do not exceed seven inches in height and represent, as I suppose, the whole of the funeral procession and ceremonies relating to the deceased, united with several emblems, etc.

Belzoni, working pre-1822, had no means of reading the hieroglyphs within his tombs. This remarkable artifact was shipped to England where the trustees of the British Museum considered it too expensive to purchase. It is now housed in the Soane Museum, London.

Usermaatre Ramesses II became sole ruler of Egypt in 1279, on day 27 of the third month of *Shemu* (summer). By Year 2 Ramesses had decided that his simple pre-nomen was not enough; he was now to be known as Usermaatre Setepenre [Strong-in-Truth-is-Re, Chosen-of-Re], a name which signified his growing interest in the sun cult of Re of Heliopolis.

Notes

1 Many books have been written on the subject of Akhenaten and his god. See for example Aldred, C. (1988), *Akhenaten, King of Egypt*, London; Redford, D. B. (1993), *Akhenaten: the heretic king*, Princeton.

2 Extract from the Great Hymn to the Aten, translation by Steven Snape. For alternative translations of this poem consult Gardiner, A. (1961), *Egypt of the Pharaohs*, Oxford: 225–7; Lichtheim, M. (1976), *Ancient Egyptian Literature 2: the New Kingdom*, Los Angeles: 96–100; Simpson, W. K. (ed) (1973), *The Literature of Ancient Egypt*, New Haven and London: 289–95.

3 In an alternative analogy, the temples of Egypt have been compared to 'the power station in which society produces the energy it needs to function and survive': Quirke, S. (1992), *Ancient Egyptian Religion*, London: 70.

4 It is by no means universally accepted that Smenkhkare and Tutankhaten (or Tutankhamen as he was later known) were the sons of Akhenaten and his wife Kiya, or indeed that they were brothers. For a summary of the arguments concerning the parentage of the two princes, and for further references on this subject, consult Tyldesley, J. A. (1998), *Nefertiti: Egypt's sun queen*, London: Chapter 6.

5 Extract from the restoration stela of Tutankhamen at Karnak. For a full translation of this text consult Davies, B. G. (1995), *Egyptian Historical Records of the Later Eighteenth Dynasty, Fascicle VI*, Warminster: 30-3.

6 Translation after H. G. Guterbock, as quoted in Schulman, A. R. (1978), 'Ankhesenamun, Nofretity and the Amka Affair', *Journal of the American Research Center in Egypt* 15: 43–8. This article discusses the identity of the letter writer in detail.

7 It has been suggested that Horemheb may have served under Akhenaten as Paatenemheb, a high-ranking soldier. While it seems unlikely that Horemheb enjoyed a meteoric rise through the ranks from nobody to general during the reign of Tutankhamen, this suggestion of an earlier career is based on nothing more substantial than the similarity of the names and titles borne by the two soldiers. For details of Horemheb's career see Hari, R. (1964), *Haremhab et la reine Moutnedjemet*, Geneva.

8 Winlock, H. E. (1924), 'A Statue of Horemheb Before his Accession', *Journal of Egyptian Archaeology* 10: 1–5.

9 This tomb was rediscovered in 1975 by a joint Anglo-Dutch expedition led by G. T. Martin. Reliefs and statues from the tomb had already made their

way on to the antiquities market, suggesting that the tomb had been known to the locals for some time. See Martin, G. T. (1989), *The Memphite Tomb of Horemheb, Commander in Chief of Tutankhamun*, London. Appendix I contains a summary of Horemheb's life as a commoner.

10 From the decree of Horemheb at Karnak. For a full translation of this text consult Davies, B. G. (1995), *Egyptian Historical Records of the Later Eighteenth Dynasty, Fascicle VI*, Warminster: 77–83.

11 Extract from the coronation decree of Horemheb. For a full translation with commentary see Gardiner, A. (1953), 'The Coronation of King Haremhab', *Journal of Egyptian Archaeology* 39: 13–31.

12 Weigall, A. (1911), *The Treasury of Ancient Egypt*, Edinburgh and London: 235.

13 This and all subsequent Belzoni quotations are taken from Belzoni, G. B. (1820), *Narrative of the Operations and Recent Discoveries within the Pyramids, Temples, Tombs and Excavations, in Egypt and Nubia*, London.

14 Edwards, A. B. (1888 revised edition), *A Thousand Miles up the Nile*, London: 451.

15 Extract from the Karnak battle inscriptions of Seti. For a full discussion of Seti's eastern campaigns consult Hasel, M. G. (1998), *Domination and resistance: Egyptian military activity in the southern Levant 1300–1185 BC*, Leiden: 119–24.

16 See Ricke, H., Hughes, G. and Wente, E. R. (1967), *The Beit-el-Wali Temples of Ramesses II*, Chicago.

17 Extract from the dedication inscription of Seti I at el-Kanais. For a full translation of this text see Lichtheim, M. (1976), *Ancient Egyptian Literature 2: the New Kingdom*, Los Angeles: 52–7.

18 See, for example, Breasted, J. H. (1937), *The History of Egypt*, New York: 418–19: '[This scene is] evidence of the bitter conflict of the two princes involving of course the harem and the officials of the court and a whole lost romance of court intrigue may still be traced by the trained eye on the north wall of the Karnak hypostyle.'

19 For a full translation and commentary on this inscription see Murnane, W. J. (1977), *Ancient Egyptian Coregencies*, Chicago: 58.

20 The precise date of Seti's death, and Ramesses' immediate actions are discussed with full references in Kitchen, K. A. (1999), *Ramesside Inscriptions Translated and Annotated 2: notes and commentaries*, Oxford: 191–7.

21 Mariette-Bay, A. (1890), *The Monuments of Upper Egypt*, translated by Al. Mariette, London: 264–5.

3

Ramesses the Warrior

Pirates! Egypt's ships and her northernmost towns suddenly found themselves under serious threat from seaborne invaders who, originally
tempted by the cargo-laden vessels criss-crossing the Mediterranean,
were now landing to wreak havoc along the Delta coast. The pirates, or
Sherden people, hailed from the lawless coast of Ionia (the south-west
corner of Turkey) and being fishermen by trade were accomplished
sailors. Their attacks on Egypt were an offence against *maat* which clearly
could not be tolerated and so Ramesses, while still co-regent, was
entrusted with their elimination. Posting troops and ships at strategic
points along the coast, Ramesses waited patiently. Eventually the Sherden
appeared, were taken by surprise and captured. As skilled mercenaries
they made a useful addition to pharaoh's army. Wielding their distinctive
straight swords, and protected by horned helmets and round shields, they
were to play an important part in the battle of Kadesh.

But why was the Nile Delta experiencing an unprecedented plague
of pirates? The answer lies in the lure of the sophisticated trade networks
which were now linking the lands and islands of the eastern Mediterranean
to trading centres near and far.

The stereotypical image of dynastic Egypt is that of a country content
to stand aloof from all others. This is in many ways a valid representation,
particularly during the earlier centuries of dynastic history. Her geography
made Egypt a neat, self-contained unit so that, although in theory pharaoh
ruled the entire world, in practice he knew that he reigned over a single
country whose sharply defined natural borders provided the ideal defence
against unwelcome guests: to the east and west were inhospitable desert
zones, to the north was the Mediterranean Sea and to the south was the
First Nile Cataract which made it difficult to sail beyond Aswan. The
bountiful River Nile provided all life's necessities and many of her
luxuries – although there was a regrettable shortage of trees – and there

was no real need for anyone to venture abroad. To say that the Egyptians appreciated their good luck would be an understatement. The dynastic Egyptians were the ultimate patriots, for hundreds of years believing themselves, their land, their gods and their traditions to be far superior to any other. The outside world was both unknown and distrusted, while foreigners, those who by an unfortunate accident of birth were compelled to live in the inferior lands beyond Egypt, were either to be pitied or despised. In spite of this extreme nationalism the ancient Egyptians cannot be considered racists as we use the term today. Dynastic Egypt was a mixed-race society which did not discriminate on the basis of skin colour or religious belief. The important difference was a simple one drawn between those who lived in Egypt, spoke Egyptian and followed Egyptian customs and those, for whatever reason, who did not.

Egypt's geography encouraged an innate conservatism that manifested itself in a highly distinctive and decidedly self-referential culture. The visual arts proved particularly resistant to change with Egypt's painters and sculptors looking backwards rather than outwards, rejecting foreign influences and seeking instead inspiration from their country's past. The early development of the 'canon of proportion', a means of ensuring that the appearance of the depicted human body remained constant throughout the pharaonic age, did nothing to lessen this impression of artistic stagnation, so that to the untrained eye the artistic style of the Old Kingdom does not differ markedly from that of the New. However, it would be entirely wrong to project from this limited evidence a dynastic Egypt existing in total cultural isolation.

Temple and tomb walls may well persuade us that a pure, all-Egyptian lifestyle managed to survive uncontaminated by outside influences for thousands of years, but it would be a mistake to base our understanding of daily life in ancient Egypt on these scenes alone. The vivid tomb vignettes were never intended to be an accurate representation of the present and should not be read as such. They were instead idealized religious images, designed to predict the traditional joys of life after death, which would, by their very presence in the tomb, enhance the chances of the deceased experiencing these joys. In these scenes there is precious little realism: the principal players show no signs of disease, ugliness, hunger or pain and only in the minor figures do we see variation away from this ideal. Instead we see the beautiful rich adhering to a tightly

*Fig 3.1   The traditional enemies of New Kingdom Egypt: a Nubian and an
Asiatic are bound and kneel before pharaoh's might*

prescribed formula; clothed in shining white linen, garlanded and spark-
ling with jewels, they enjoy life to the full in the perpetual sunshine of
the Kingdom of Osiris. In their rigid adherence to an idealized past these
images are conforming to a universal pattern; religious tradition of all
cultures is notoriously slow to reflect contemporary fashions so that even
in our own modern society priests, nuns and monks adopt anachronistic
medieval garments.

By the time Ramesses came to the throne Egypt was undeniably part
of a wider eastern Mediterranean landscape and there were significant
numbers of foreigners making a success of life under pharaoh. Some,
recognizing the opportunities provided by a prosperous country, had
chosen their own destiny and had emigrated to Egypt bringing with
them their own skills and traditions. Already northern Memphis was
home to a large population of Canaanite merchants and could boast
an impressive temple dedicated to the Canaanite deity Baal. These
newcomers were tolerated if not actively welcomed, and were soon
marrying into the native Egyptian families. Less desirable were the
Bedouin nomads who regularly infiltrated the eastern Delta from Sinai
and who were generally regarded as low-life trouble to be avoided at all
costs.

Others arrived in Egypt on an involuntary basis. Throughout
Ramesses' reign there was a constant influx of foreign captives of varied
origins: prisoners-of-war seized during one of pharaoh's many glorious

campaigns; the men, women and children snatched as the human spoils of war; civilian 'tribute' donated by Egypt's vassal states; slaves bought and sold on the international slave-market for profit; labourers conscripted to work on pharaoh's monuments; brides sent as gifts to the royal harem. The long-established policy of transporting vast numbers of the 'enemy' to Egypt had proved a useful means of averting manpower shortages while, of course, acting as a strong warning to client states who might be tempted to rebel. It is doubtful whether Ramesses would have completed his ambitious building programme without the 'help' of foreign workers.

Egyptian texts let us know the worst fate, short of death, which could befall a convicted criminal or prisoner-of-war: he could be sent to break rocks in the harsh gold mines of Kush. Although both Seti and Ramesses took a highly publicized interest in the welfare of their Egyptian work-force, making periodic tours of mines and quarries and establishing wells and adjusting rations as and when necessary, they showed little or no concern over the fate of their guest workers who seem to have been regarded as simply unworthy of notice. Many of these died in the pursuit of pharaoh's goals. Not all captives, however, faced the rigours of manual labour. The educated, and those who had mastered a trade or profession, were encouraged to use their skills for the good of Egypt and often found work in the temples, palaces and civil service. Escape for many of these more privileged prisoners would have been unwelcome, and many slaves soon found that they had exchanged an existence of constant uncertainty and hardship in Canaan for a secure life in the land of plenty. The Sherden were by no means the first to recognize the advantages of a life of legitimate Egyptian employment.

Some 'foreign' workers were Egyptian born and bred, although, having retained their own cultures and languages, they were not regarded as such by their fully Egyptian neighbours. The Nile Delta was home to many Semitic-speaking peoples who, having settled in Egypt from the end of the Old Kingdom onwards, now found themselves vulnerable to attack from the administrators responsible for filling pharaoh's work-gangs:

There arose up a new king over Egypt, which knew not Joseph, and he said unto his people 'Behold! The people of the children of Israel are more and mightier than we are . . .' Therefore they did set over them taskmasters to afflict them with their burdens. And they built for the Pharaoh treasure cities, Pithom and Raamses [Pi-Ramesse] . . . And the Egyptians made the children of Israel to serve with rigour. And they made their lives bitter with hard bondage, in mortar and in brick, and in all manner of service in the field . . .[1]

The story of the preservation of Moses in pharaoh's palace, his exile and his return to free the Israelites from bondage is recorded in the Bible. Here, too, we learn of the fate of the Egyptian troops sent to recapture the valuable, vanishing work-force:

And Moses stretched out his hand over the sea; and the Lord caused the sea to go back by a strong east wind all that night, and made the sea dry land, and all the waters were divided. And the children of Israel went into the midst of the sea upon the dry ground: and the waters were a wall unto them on their right hand, and on their left. And the Egyptians pursued, and went in after them to the midst of the sea, even all Pharaoh's horses, his chariots and his horsemen . . . And Moses stretched forth his hand over the sea, and the sea returned to his strength . . . and the waters returned and covered the chariots and the horsemen, and all the hosts of Pharaoh that came into the sea after them; there remained not so much as one of them.[2]

The body of King Merenptah, successor to Ramesses, was, when recovered from the Valley of the Kings, coated in salt. At first this was interpreted as absolute proof that Merenptah had drowned in the Red Sea, or in the Reed Lake, while chasing Moses and the Israelites from Egypt. Today it is realized that this salty deposit is an unexpected and unexplained side-effect of the mummification process. If the biblical story is to be regarded as a true one, rather than as an inspirational tale, who is the unnamed pharaoh? Most experts would agree that it must be Ramesses, with the Exodus far less dramatic and of far less significance to the Egyptians than the Bible would suggest, occurring some time during the first half of his reign.[3] The Egyptian texts make no mention of a time of plagues and runaway workers, nor indeed of parting waters and drowned soldiers, but we would not expect them to; defeat, however minor, did not feature in Egypt's official history.

Although the native Egyptians continued to vaunt the superiority of their own culture they were not averse to adopting and adapting practical foreign ideas such as the compound bow, horse-drawn chariot and body armour which had been introduced by the Second Intermediate Period Hyksos invaders. Advanced foreign techniques of glass manufacture, metalworking and weaving all found their way into the Egyptian repertoire while improved strains of livestock were eagerly welcomed. Alien gods were absorbed into the Egyptian pantheon with ease; the Canaanite warrior god Resheph and the naked goddess Astarte proved particularly popular and cults to these deities were established up and down the Nile. Unfortunately the more mundane perishable imports – a jar of olive oil, a flagon of fine wine or a bolt of exotic cloth – are likely to leave little or no trace in the archaeological record and so are in danger of passing unnoticed today.

If we take Ramesses, Seti and many of their New Kingdom predecessors at their word, we would have to believe that Egypt's sole point of contact with her neighbours was the field of battle. War, both thrilling and glamorous and with recognized religious undertones, is amply documented on the exterior temple walls. Here, time and time again, we are treated to scenes of the king vanquishing the enemy and thus fulfilling his duty to defeat the forces of chaos and preserve *maat*. The noble pharaoh rides in a chariot driven by fiery steeds; the fearless pharaoh leads his nervous troops into the thick of the fighting; the unyielding pharaoh beats his cringing enemies to death with a club. The Egyptians, of course, always win their wars and the ignoble foe are inevitably forced to grovel at pharaoh's feet. Lest anyone should be in any doubt over the nature of the victory, piles of amputated enemy right hands, or heaps of uncircumcised foreign penises, bear grisly witness to the extent of the battlefield slaughter.

Many of these battle scenes are based on real events which have been wildly exaggerated to enhance the reputation of the king and his country. Others are purely symbolic, designed to confirm the divine right of the king to rule. Only a few, such as the relatively modest reports of Tuthmosis III, conform to our own strict standards of historical reporting and so may be classified as fairly accurate records of battles won with honour. Ramesses' own campaigns, as detailed on the walls of his various temples, undoubtedly fall into the first category. These are not, when stripped of all hyperbole, over-impressive achievements: Ramesses accompanied his father to fight against the Asiatics and Libyans; he quelled occasional resurrections in Nubia; he campaigned in Canaan and Syria, pitting the might of the Egyptian army against individual city-states and he fought, but did not necessarily win, a famous battle against the Hittites.

The Egyptian temple wall was a fortress wall designed to repel chaos and protect the peace, or *maat*, within. The defence of the land was very much a religious duty of the pharaoh, and all victories would be presented to the great god of the temple. It is therefore not surprising that conventional New Kingdom monarchs preferred to ornament their temples with scenes of battle, blood and gore rather than scenes of peace and cooperation. Only one king, Hatchepsut, who had no battle scenes to display, was happy to substitute a successful trading mission for a scene of carnage on the walls of her Deir el-Bahari mortuary temple. Here a cartoon-like strip of drawings shows the mission sailing south to the exotic land of Punt, a long-established trading centre most probably situated on the Eritrean/Ethiopian coast. We see the arrival of the ships, and the negotiations with the Puntites who accept a rather poor collection of beads and weapons in exchange for a vast array of luxury items. The Egyptians return home in triumph, burdened with the weight of a small orchard of incense trees planted, in order to preserve their roots, in baskets suspended between two carrying poles. Myrrh, frankincense, ebony, ivory, gold, cattle and even a troop of monkeys are all unloaded and some foreigners, Puntites and Nubians, disembark to kneel before the king. Hatchepsut offers the best of these goods to her divine father, Amen, just as a victorious male king might dedicate his military triumph to the glory of Amen.

A precursor of the battle scene, where the king dominates the action against a background of fighting men, chariots and horses, is the scene where the larger-than-life-sized king stands alone to uphold the honour of Egypt. Our earliest view of Egypt's pharaoh in action – the pre-dynastic King Narmer whose image is preserved on a stone palette (now known as the Narmer Palette) housed in Cairo Museum – shows the king fighting and vanquishing an unidentified bearded enemy who grovels at his feet. This image of the king as the ritual slayer of Egypt's foes was to prove a constant theme recurring time and time again as the centuries progressed. Even those who had never fought in battle were keen to exploit its symbolism and so we find the least militaristic of the New Kingdom pharaohs, Amenhotep III and his son Akhenaten, depicted in the act of smiting the enemy. From the security of his Amarna court

Akhenaten was able to trample over his foes at will; his Great Palace included a pavement painted with images of bound foreign captives plus the archetypal 'nine bows', the symbolic representation of the enemies of Egypt. In defiance of tradition which decreed smiting to be a king's game, Akhenaten's consort, Nefertiti, was also occasionally permitted to wield a mace and despatch a female foe. We simply do not know whether these violent scenes should be taken literally; was the king occasionally expected to bludgeon a token enemy in order to confirm his right to rule? Their message, however, is clear. Pharaoh triumphant sacrifices his enemy to the greater glory of Egypt and her gods. The defeated enemy invariably adopts an attitude of total submission; he knows that it would be futile to struggle against his fate.

The same three enemies, the Nubians from the south, the Libyans from the west and the Asiatics from the east, appear again and again to suffer humiliation at the hands of the noble Egyptians. The Nubians, or *Nehesy*, the most ancient and most accessible of these traditional foes, could not be considered a serious threat to Egypt's security as, for most of the dynastic age, they were kept firmly under the Egyptian thumb. Nubia's natural resources had always attracted her northern neighbours. During the Old Kingdom, trading missions travelled to Nubia in order to exploit her gold and to deal in the exotic products, such as ebony, ivory, incense and even dwarfs which were being imported from further south.

As the pharaonic age developed, Nubia experienced increasing militarization, with forts strategically placed to control both the population and the all-important trade routes. The Middle Kingdom saw Egypt's southern empire extending as far as the Second Cataract, and by the time Ramesses came to the throne Nubia was effectively a province of Egypt ruled by an Egyptian-appointed viceroy. This did not, however, prevent Ramesses from continuing to depict southerners as the archetypal enemy. They were to continue in this unenviable role even when Egypt herself was ruled by the Nubian (Kushite) pharaohs of the 25th Dynasty.

The Nubians are invariably shown with the distinctive facial features, curly hair and dark skin of black Africans. In contrast, the tribes given the generic name of Libyans (traditionally the *Tjehenu* or *Tjemeh*; during the New Kingdom there are also the *Meshwesh* and *Libu*) have a fair or yellow skin and small goatee beards. From the New Kingdom onwards

Libyans appear dressed in a long, open-fronted coat and wear a side-lock and ostrich feathers in their hair. The Tjehenu were enemies of long standing, and were perceived as a constant threat to Egypt's western border. The broken predynastic Battlefield Palette (now in the collections of the Ashmolean Museum, Oxford, and the British Museum, London) shows an unnamed king of Egypt taking the form of a fierce lion to maul a group of unfortunate westerners.

The third group of enemies, the Asiatics, are given the same red-brown skin as their Egyptian contemporaries but they display distinctive non-Egyptian profiles and sport beards. The earliest Asiatics appear with long braided hair and are dressed in kilts and cloaks, but by the time of Ramesses they have adopted a long, colourful robe, a distinctive fringed shawl and a curious haircut in which the top of the head is shaved but the back hair grows long. Asiatics, too, cringe bound and submissive before the might of pharaoh, a conventional image which gives a deliberately misleading impression of the complex relationship which existed between Egypt and her eastern neighbours throughout the New Kingdom.

Although the Old and Middle Kingdoms had witnessed occasional Egyptian campaigns against specific fortified Canaanite towns, it was only during the New Kingdom, following Ahmose's expulsion of the Hyksos, that the Asiatics developed into full-blown enemies. Even then, periods of enmity were interspersed with periods of peace and mutually beneficial trade. From the very dawn of the dynastic age Egypt had enjoyed good trading relations with Syria–Palestine, although occasional instability in the Levant could cause this relationship to falter. Egyptian luxury goods – stone palettes and vessels displaying Egyptian seal impressions – have been recovered from Early Bronze Age Canaanite sites, while Canaanite amphorae, presumably used to transport and store wine and olive oil, have been found in many of the 1st Dynasty royal tombs at Abydos. So important was this trade to the Canaanites that the collapse of the Old Kingdom brought about the immediate failure of the Canaanite economy and a temporary abandonment of urban life in the southern Levant.

Egypt never attempted to absorb her eastern territories as she had Nubia; there was no equivalent of the Nubian viceroy and indeed little formal organization of the eastern empire. Instead the region remained divided into a series of independent city states whose kings, chiefs and headmen were allowed to retain their titles if not their power. The people of Canaan continued to serve their traditional masters who were in turn expected to prove their allegiance to pharaoh by plentiful 'gifts' of tribute accompanied by repeated declarations of loyalty. Disloyal vassals quickly disappeared from the scene. The young children of these local rulers were sent to Egypt where they either entered the royal school or the royal harem. Those sons who returned home to take up their thrones did so brainwashed into the Egyptian way of thought. Their sisters remained in Egypt, hostages in all but name.

Enough New Kingdom royal correspondence has survived to confirm that the exchange of letters and luxury goods between royal courts was a routine occurrence. Monarchs of equally high standing – the kings of Egypt, Mitanni, Hatti and Babylon – wrote personal, somewhat inconsequential letters and presented each other with generous, carefully calculated gifts which they fully expected to see reciprocated. These royal pen-friends seldom met, although the occasional diplomatic marriage invariably involved a foreign princess travelling to Egypt. Lesser rulers, those eager to curry favour with their political master, composed more formal missives accompanied by endless protestations of their own loyalty, denouncements of their neighbours' disloyalty and payment of copious 'tribute' intended to soften the heart of pharaoh. It seems that a lesser monarch's 'gift' was very much a superior monarch's 'tax'; there was almost certainly an element of compulsion attached to these voluntary offerings whatever their donors chose to pretend. Innumerable envoys, burdened with messages and valuable gifts, braved bandits and inhospitable terrain – 'the road is very long, the water supply cut off and the weather hot'[4] – to ensure that this royal exchange network did not falter. It seems that everyone regarded Egypt as a land of inexhaustible riches, and foreign kings were never shy of asking for favours. Thus we find Tushratta of Mitanni, perhaps the most greedy of the royal correspondents, writing unself-consciously to his brother-in-law Amenhotep III:

May my brother treat me ten times better than he did my father . . . May my brother send me in very great quantities gold that has not been worked, and may my brother send me much more gold than he sent to my father. For in my brother's country gold is as plentiful as dirt.[5]

Egypt was physically linked to her eastern neighbours by the north Sinai land-bridge which allowed the import and export of goods and people. Crossing the land-bridge by donkey train was, however, an inconvenient method of transporting a large or heavy load. Strings of valuable donkeys, vulnerable to attack by brigands, travel slowly and require frequent stops for food, water and rest. A donkey may carry up to its own body-weight but an overloaded donkey forced to travel too far, too fast in the desert sun will invariably collapse.[6] Most traders sensibly preferred to transport their bulky cargo by sea and so, as we might expect, the New Kingdom Mediterranean swarmed with merchant boats; not mighty ocean-going vessels but relatively small sailing ships, owned privately or by the state or temple, whose mixed cargoes might include royal consignments. It was these boats, and their lucrative freight, that had attracted the attention of the Sherden pirates.

In Egypt, too, bulky merchandise was transported by boat:

The merchants sail downstream and upstream, always busy, carrying goods from one city to another and supplying him who has nothing.[7]

The Nile made life very easy for Egypt's sailors. Travelling southwards they only had to raise a sail to take advantage of the prevailing wind, while boats sailing north enjoyed the benefit of the current. The Egyptians were not, however, accustomed to long sea voyages and their sailors had a tendency to feel nervous when out of sight of land. The Egyptian navy, although occasionally called upon to repel sea-borne invaders, was generally used as a means of transporting troops and equipment relatively short distances.

Sea routes leave very little material trace for modern historians to discover. Fortunately we have enough evidence to show that sea-trade with Syria–Palestine was already well established during the Old Kingdom. Documents dating to the 4th Dynasty reign of King Snefru detail ships sailing between Egypt and the highly Egyptianized independent Phoenician port of Byblos, a route which seems confirmed by an almost unbroken sequence of Old Kingdom Egyptian royal gifts recorded in the temple of the Mistress of Byblos. Byblos, close to the great forests of Lebanon, was the best source of timber for Egypt. By the 18th Dynasty trading relations in the eastern Mediterranean world had become both extensive and sophisticated. While a ship commissioned to collect a single, specific cargo might take a direct route, the major trade mechanism was an anti-clockwise sea route, dictated by the Mediterranean tides.

A private merchant ship leaving the independent Syrian port of Ugarit (modern Ras Shamra) on the first leg of its circular journey might be laden with a varied cargo originating from as far east as Afghanistan, including precious tin carried via the overland route through Mesopotamia. Sailing westwards to Cyprus the vessel might pause to pick up copper, fine ceramics and opium before following the coast, island hopping perhaps to Mycenaean Greece or to Late Minoan Crete where a cargo of fine olive oil and wine could be collected. From Crete the crew would face their most hazardous journey: a sea crossing during which they would lose sight of the coast and so be unable to predict exactly where the boat might land. Sailing southwards the boat would sight the north African coast and then turn eastwards until it reached the mouth of the River Nile. From here it could sail down to the port of Memphis where it would unload, pick up a supply of Egyptian and African goods, and then set off again along the Levantine coast. No wonder the pirates were tempted!

The Ulu Burun wreck, the world's oldest known shipwreck, provides impressive confirmation of this extensive international trade. The 50-foot vessel sank to a depth of 150 feet (45 metres) off the coast of Turkey some time during the Late Bronze Age (14th century BC; most probably during the reign of Seti I). Discovered by a local sponge diver in 1982, it has been investigated by a team of marine archaeologists from the Institute of Nautical Archaeology, Texas, led by Dr George Bass. Analysis of the wreck and her treasures is still in progress, but so far she has yielded a mixed cargo of valuables originating from at least seven separate cultures including six tons of Cyprus copper (which Dr Bass estimates would have been enough, when converted to bronze, to manufacture 300 helmets, 300 corselets, 3,000 spearheads and 3,000 swords[8]), tin from either Turkey or Afghanistan, distinctive Canaanite vessels, Baltic amber beads, Syrian ivory, African ostrich eggs and Egyptian artifacts, including a golden scarab bearing the titles of Queen Nefertiti. We have no reason to believe that the boat was unusual in carrying such a diverse and precious load. A collection of weapons included in the hold may well have been provided to protect the vessel and its crew against the dreaded pirates.

Not long after his successful neutralization of the Sherden pirate threat Ramesses established a defensive line along Egypt's north-western frontier. To date the remains of three of his forts have been discovered to the west of the modern city of Alexandria, at Gharbaniyat, el-Alamein and Zawiyet Umm el-Rakham, with a further two in the western Delta at Tell Abqa'in and Kom el-Hisn. It seems likely that these represent the remains of a more substantial chain of forts built one day's march apart and stretching to protect the Delta edge and western coast from Memphis to Umm el-Rakham. This was not an innovation. Egypt's interests in Nubia had long been protected by a series of fortified towns while the eastern Delta had been, from the time of Amenemhat I (12th Dynasty) onwards, guarded by a line of fortresses known as the Walls of the Prince. Unfortunately the Walls of the Prince are now known only from contemporary documents. A similar chain of forts protected the Way of Horus, the 140 miles of inhospitable desert road crossing northern Sinai and linking Egypt to southern Canaan. The Way of Horus forts served as combined garrisons and customs/administration houses. They provided protection, water and provisions for those passing on legitimate business between Canaan and Egypt while discouraging the uncontrolled migration of Asiatics. At Sile, the most westerly and most important link in the chain, all parties crossing the border were required to register by name, town of origin and intended destination, and all foreigners wishing to enter Egypt needed either an entry permit or a bribe.

Ramesses' western forts had a dual purpose. Standing an impressive 40 feet (12 metres) tall they dominated the coastline, serving as a welcome landmark and providing both provisions and protection for boats *en route* from Crete to Memphis. However, the primary purpose of the forts was to offer a defence against overland invasion from the west. Ramesses was growing increasingly concerned over the behaviour of the Libyan nomads who were showing a disturbing tendency to migrate eastwards and settle in the prosperous Delta. Egypt's subsequent history was to prove Ramesses' fear justified; his son Merenptah and his namesake Ramesses III were both to do battle with Libyan invaders. Now Ramesses built his forts around the wells and water holes which might otherwise have allowed the Libyans free access into Egypt.

Egypt's soldiers took a pessimistic view of foreign postings and the New Kingdom satirical Papyrus Anastasi outlined the horrors and depri- vations that a private must expect to encounter away from the security of the Nile Valley:

Come let me tell you the woes of the soldier . . . He is called up to go to Syria. He is not permitted to rest. There are no clothes and no sandals. The weapons of war are assembled at the fort of Sile. He has to march uphill, through the mountains. He drinks water only every third day, and then it is tainted and smells of salt. His body is racked with sickness. The enemy comes and surrounds him with weapons, and life ebbs away from him . . . When the army is victorious the captives are handed over to pharaoh and must be escorted to Egypt. The foreign woman faints on the march; the soldier is forced to support her. While he is supporting the woman he drops his pack and it is stolen. His own wife and children are back home in the village; he dies and does not reach it. If he survives he is worn out through marching . . .[9]

This is, of course, a highly biased account. Papyrus Anastasi was a school- book written specifically to encourage young men to become professional scribes and as such did not hesitate to exaggerate the uncongenial nature of all other professions. Most garrison postings during Ramesses' reign were not really so dreadful even if they were lengthy, occasionally lasting as long as six years. Nubia was both pacified and Egyptianized, and the presence of the River Nile allowed the comforting illusion of being close to home. Syro-Palestine was potentially more dangerous as war with the Hittites or their allies was an ever-present threat. In times of peace, however, the cities of the Levant, just as sophisticated as those of Egypt itself, must have offered the Egyptian soldier a range of possible diversions.

The worst posting in the empire must have been to the new fort at Zawiyet Umm el-Rakham, a place with none of the compensations of Nubia or Syro-Palestine.[10] Umm el-Rakham, situated close to the modern city of Mersa Matrouh and almost 200 miles (320 kilometres) to the west of Alexandria, is the most remote and best preserved of Ramesses' northern forts, lying a good week's march to the west of the Delta; a hot and dusty tramp through potentially dangerous territory. The natives seem to have been unrelentingly hostile desert nomads – no evenings spent fraternizing in jolly taverns here – who moved around the desert

1. Belzoni and his workmen remove the 'Younger Memnon', a colossal statue of Ramesses II, from the Ramesseum, Thebes.

2. The 'Younger Memnon' now housed in the British Museum, London.

3. Tuthmosis III, Egypt's warrior king.

4. The Colossi of Memnon; gigantic statues of Amenhotep III that may have inspired the colossal statuary of Ramesses II.

5. A colossal head of Amenhotep III.

6. Queen Tiy; wife of Amenhotep III and mother of Akhenaten.

7. Ramesses II shown as a young man hunting.

8. Queen Tuya; wife of Seti I and mother of Ramesses II.

9. The mortuary temple of Seti I at Gurna, Thebes.

10. Colossal statue of Ramesses II at Karnak.

11. The Ramesseum, mortuary temple of Ramesses II.

12. The broken head of Ramesses II in his mortuary temple.

13. Ramesses II smiting the traditional enemies of Egypt: a Nubian, an Asiatic
and a Libyan.

at will. In contrast, the Egyptian garrison probably ventured outside the thick perimeter walls with a good deal of trepidation, and only for good reason. The size of the fort – almost 20,000 square metres in area and defended by a mud-brick wall some 5 metres thick whose single gate was protected by two limestone-clad towers – gives some indication of the perceived seriousness of the Libyan threat. The outer wall alone contained some 1,600,000 mud bricks, each so large that one man could carry no more than two at a time.

Umm el-Rakham's role as a trading station, most probably the initial landing place of boats sailing from Crete, has been confirmed by the discovery of warehouses holding a large number of non-Egyptian storage vessels, including Canaanite amphorae and Aegean stirrup jars. It seems that the garrison was able to deal with the merchants who, on their way to the lucrative markets at Memphis, could be persuaded to leave the soldiers a few creature comforts such as olive oil, wine and opium. Care was evidently taken to make the foreign sailors feel welcome; alongside the Egyptian temple and three chapels dedicated to cults of the deified Ramesses II, the fort housed a curious building consisting of three parallel chambers each with a central standing stone – a possible Canaanite temple.

Having taken steps to avert the possibility of a Libyan invasion, Ramesses turned his attention eastwards. He had determined to succeed where his father had failed, and to recapture the city-state of Kadesh. Kadesh, strategically placed at the tip of the Lebanese Mountain range so as to enjoy full control over access to the south, was protected in an elbow made by the northwards-flowing River Orontes and an eastwards-flowing tributary. A man-made channel cut between the two rivers made the fortified city into a triangular island. To Ramesses, Kadesh was unfinished business. He had been present as Seti's campaign ended in an unsatisfactory truce which allowed the Hittites to retain control over both Kadesh and Amurru. For Egypt this was a less than satisfactory outcome and Ramesses had taken advantage of the lull in hostilities to prepare his soldiers for further action.

Now the Egyptian army was ready to give battle. The summer of his regnal Year 4 saw Ramesses embarking on a 'Campaign of Victory', marching along the coast of Palestine to confirm his hold over Canaan and the Phoenician ports before turning inland to Amurru. Benteshina,

ruler of Amurru, was easily persuaded to change his allegiance from Hatti
to Egypt and Ramesses returned home in triumph leaving a division of
élite soldiers garrisoned in Amurru, ideally placed for a future attack on
Kadesh. Meanwhile Benteshina wrote to his former master in Hatti to
explain the change in his circumstances. This did not go down well.
King Muwatallis, grandson of the great Suppiluliumas, was not prepared
to take this insult lightly and in a sacred oath to the gods of Hatti he
vowed to regain his lost territories. Calling on his allies and vassals he
started to assemble a magnificent army: according to the Egyptian records
he was able to command an impressive 2,500 chariots and 37,000 foot-
soldiers, including trained infantrymen, mercenaries and pirates:

Now the vile enemy from Hatti had gathered together all the foreign lands as
far as the end of the sea. The entire land of Hatti had come, and the lands
of Nahrin, Arzawa, Dardany, Keshkesh, Masa, Pidasa, Irun, Karkisha, Luka,
Kizzuwadna, Carchemesh, Ugarit . . . Their chiefs were with him, together
with their infantry and chariotry, making a great number never before seen.
They covered the mountains and filled the valleys and were like locusts in their
numbers. He left no silver in his land but stripped the country of all its wealth
which he gave to the foreign countries in order to bribe them to fight with
him.[11]

In the spring of Year 5 Ramesses again left Egypt, riding eastwards at
the head of an impressive army of some 20,000 men subdivided into four
divisions of 5,000, each a mixture of infantry and chariotry and each
marching under the standard of a protective god; Amen (soldiers recruited
from Thebes), Re or Pre (Heliopolis), Ptah (Memphis) and Seth or
Sutekh (north-east Delta region). The troops, horses and chariots, accompanied by pack animals and ox-drawn carts laden with the necessary
provisions, weapons, and tents plus an assortment of camp followers,
including high-ranking ministers and members of the royal family, took
one month to pass along the coastal road through Canaan and south
Syria and, making use of the Bekaa Valley, to approach Kadesh from the
south. Meanwhile the élite force left behind in the previous year's
campaign had started to march from Amurru in order to rendezvous at
Kadesh.[12]

Ramesses and his troops eventually reached the Wood of Labwi, some

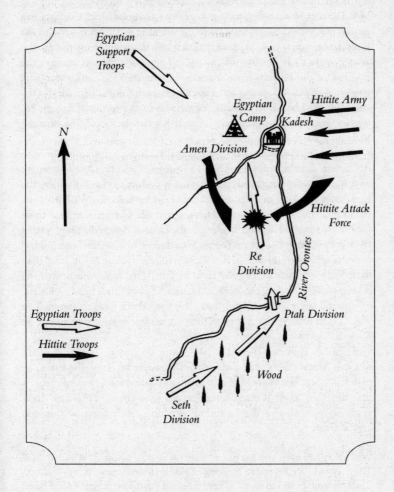

Fig 3.2 Sketch plan of the battle of Kadesh showing the positions of the Egyptian and Hittite forces

ten miles to the south of Kadesh. Here, as they prepared to ford the broad River Orontes, they had some unexpected good luck. The Egyptian guards discovered two Shosu Bedouin skulking in the trees around the Egyptian camp. These Bedouin, apparently deserters from the Hittite army, swore their loyalty to Ramesses. They were able to confirm the position of the Hittites who, mentally unprepared for battle, were still cowering some 120 miles (200 kilometres) to the north of Kadesh: 'the enemy from Hatti is in the land of Khaleb to the north of Tunip. He was too frightened to proceed southwards when he heard that Pharaoh had come northwards'.

Clearly the Bedouin, who were actually Hittite spies, knew how to devise a story which would appeal to Ramesses' vanity. On the strength of this dubious information, and making no effort to check the tale, the inexperienced king decided to head straight for Kadesh. With luck, he could take the city before the Hittites arrived. The army split into its four divisions and Ramesses, riding at the head of Amen division, forded the river and marched across the plain to make camp on the high ground to the north-west of Kadesh. Re division followed close behind and Ptah then Seth were left to ford the river in turn. This tactic meant that the divisions were strung out over a distance of some miles but, with the enemy still several days' march away this should not have mattered. The plan was to reunite the troops in time for a surprise morning assault on Kadesh.

Then, as Ramesses rested in the camp of Amen, as Re marched towards Amen and as Ptah and then Seth prepared to cross the river, the plan fell apart. The capture of two further Hittite spies – spies so obvious that this time even Ramesses recognized who they were – and their confessions, encouraged by a sound thrashing, made the true situation crystal clear:

When they had been brought before pharaoh his majesty asked 'Who are you?' They replied 'We belong to the king of Hatti. He has sent us to spy on you.' Then his majesty said to them 'Where is he, the enemy from Hatti? I had heard that he was in the land of Khaleb, north of Tunip.' They replied to his majesty 'Lo, the king of Hatti has already arrived, together with the many countries who are supporting him ... They are armed with their infantry and their chariots. They have their weapons of war at the ready. They are more numerous than the grains of sand on the beach. Behold, they stand equipped and ready for battle behind the old city of Kadesh.'

Muwatallis and his troops had already reached the eastern side of Kadesh and were poised for an immediate ambush. The Egyptians, with their four divisions spread out on either side of the Orontes, were in a highly vulnerable position. As the full horror of the situation dawned Ramesses summoned his senior officers to an urgent council of war during which he managed to place all blame for the catastrophe squarely on the shoulders of his subordinates. They in turn blamed the faulty Egyptian intelligence service which had unaccountably failed to detect the presence of a mighty army less than two miles away. The fleetest messengers, and the Vizier, were quickly despatched to summon the missing divisions, and the vulnerable royal family were sent to a position of safety away from the army camp. Suddenly the Hittites, having crossed the Orontes to the south of Kadesh, launched a fierce chariot attack on Re division.

The soldiers of Re, isolated and taken completely by surprise, forgot all their training, scattered and fled northwards, leading the enemy straight to the Egyptian camp. Now it was Amen division's turn to be taken by surprise; many of the soldiers took one look at the approaching chariots, panicked and ran away. Ramesses soon found himself alone, surrounded by the vile Hittites. Only the great god Amen, and the loyal shield-bearer Menna, who rode beside pharaoh in the royal chariot, could help the king of Egypt now. None can tell what happened next better than Ramesses himself:

There was no officer with me, no charioteer, no soldier. My infantry and my chariotry had run away before the enemy and no one stood firm to fight with them. I prayed: 'What is happening, Amen my father? Is it right for a father to ignore his son? Are my deeds something for you to ignore? . . . I know that Amen will help me more than a million troops, more than a hundred thousand charioteers, more then ten thousand brothers and sons . . .'

Although I prayed in a distant land my prayer was heard in Thebes. Amen came when I called to him; he gave me his hand and I rejoiced . . . I found that my heart grew stout and my breast swelled with joy. Everything which I attempted I succeeded . . . I was before the enemy like Seth in his moment. I found the enemy chariots scattering before my horses. Not one of them could fight me. Their hearts quaked with fear when they saw me and their arms went limp so they could not shoot. They did not have the heart to hold their spears. I made them plunge into the water like crocodiles. They fell on their faces, one on top of another. I slaughtered them at my will . . . Those who fell down did not rise . . .

I raised my voice to shout to my soldiers 'Be of brave heart, my troops. Behold I am victorious, me alone! For Amen is my helper, his hand is with me . . . But you have all been cowards. Not one of you has stood fast by my side as I fought . . .'

Ramesses shows no qualms over sacrificing the reputation of his own troops – who stand condemned by their own general's words as both cowardly and ill–disciplined – in order to enhance his own valour. Perhaps even he realized that the story as written might not be totally credible; this may be why he added a coda swearing to the truth of his tale: 'As I live, as Re loves me, as my father Atum favours me, everything that my majesty has told I did in truth.'

What really happened? Muwatallis had not committed his full infantry to the ambush on Re division; had he done so, the result would have been a foregone conclusion and Ramesses would have suffered the humiliation of becoming the first New Kingdom monarch to be captured by the enemy. The bulk of the Hittite army waited instead with Muwatallis on the east bank of the Orontes, relying on the surprise chariot attack to wipe out a quarter of Ramesses' divided army. The timely and totally unexpected arrival of the Egyptian élite troops – who are not mentioned in the texts but who can be seen arriving in a relief scene – came as a complete shock to the Hittites. Thus reinforced, Ramesses was able to push back the Hittite chariots who, perhaps wondering how many other Egyptian divisions were about to appear as from nowhere, suddenly turned tail and fled, swimming back across the Orontes to their colleagues on the eastern bank. As the Hittites struggled in the water Ptah division finally arrived, led by the Vizier, and the deserters of Re and Amen sheepishly returned to stand by their king. Seth division arrived even later, and the Egyptian camp settled down for the night.

The morning dawned to witness more bloodshed. It is not quite clear what happened the next day, as the temple texts are somewhat ambiguous. Was Ramesses again called upon to demonstrate his exceptional valour against the Hittites? Or did he punish his own cowardly troops until they 'sprawled before my horses, and lay dead in heaps in their own blood'?[13] The two greatest armies that Syria had ever seen, now ranked on opposite banks of the Orontes, may not have welcomed an open battle; this was not at all their usual kind of warfare. The Hittites preferred to ambush their enemies, relying on surprise tactics rather than superior military prowess. The Egyptians, too, accustomed to subduing one relatively weak city state at a time, had never before been called upon to meet a large, well-disciplined army face to face. Both sides had already suffered serious losses; Re and Amen divisions had borne the brunt of the Hittite attack while many of the Hittite charioteers, including members of the Hittite royal family, had failed to make it back across the Orontes. Both Ramesses and Muwatallis must have felt as if they were staring disaster in the face.

Eventually, so Ramesses tells us, the cowardly Hittite king sent a letter to the Egyptian camp pleading for peace. Negotiators were summoned and a truce was agreed, although Ramesses, still claiming an Egyptian victory and doubtless remembering the inadequate terms imposed on his father some fifteen years earlier, refused to sign a formal treaty. Ramesses returned home to enjoy his personal triumph, which was to be retold many times in prose, as an epic poem and in relief carving; the people could see their king's victory at Karnak where it filled the south exterior wall of the hypostyle hall (but was later reduced to allow the depiction of other military triumphs), the Ramesseum (twice in the forecourts), Luxor (three times), Abu Simbel, Derr and Abydos where it was featured on the north and west exterior temple walls. We even have three papyrus copies of the tale written in hieroglyphs and a cuneiform letter written from Ramesses to King Hattusilis III, successor to Muwatallis.

So much for the Egyptian version of events. The Hittite records, recovered from Bogazkoy, tell of a very different battle ending with a humiliated Ramesses forced to retreat from Kadesh in ignominious defeat. The known facts do tend to support this Hittite version. Ramesses' departure, without a signed treaty, allowed the Hittites to reinforce their hold on Kadesh and regain control of Amurru, deposing the unfortunate Benteshina who was marched off to Hatti to explain himself. The Hittites then pushed further south through the Bekaa Valley to secure the Egyptian territory of Upi which was placed under the control of the king's brother Hattusilis. Soon Egypt's sphere of influence was once again restricted to Canaan.

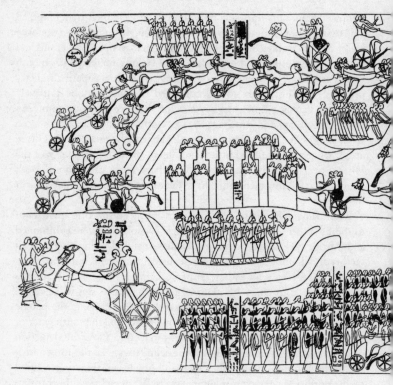

*Fig. 3.3   The battle of Kadesh. The city lies protected in a bend of the River
Orontes. Ramesses, far larger than his fellow soldiers, leads the charge into the
Hittite chariots*

The battle of Kadesh did not see the end of Ramesses' eastern campaigns. On the contrary the Kadesh debacle, and the subsequent unchallenged loss of Upi, seem to have inspired several local rulers to try their
luck against the demoralized Egyptians. Canaanite 'tribute' was suddenly
remarkably slow in arriving in Egypt, while increased Bedouin activity
disturbed the peace of the Egyptian vassals. Ramesses was forced to
embark on a series of missions in order to reassert his authority, attempting
to make good some of his losses by military action in Canaan, Syria and

Amurru. These campaigns are recorded on the walls of the Karnak temple where the lack of regnal years makes their precise order difficult to determine. It seems that Years 8 and 9 saw Ramesses campaigning in Galilee before marching eastwards to reach and occupy the cities of Dapur and Tunip which had been lost to Egypt for over 120 years. A further campaign in Phoenicia, including a return visit to Dapur, occurred in Year 10 while Syria was targeted intermittently between years 10 and 18.

The successful siege of Dapur is recorded in detail both at Luxor and at the Ramesseum. Dapur, a heavily fortified city, is situated on a hill and protected by an inner and outer wall with towers so that the Egyptian soldiers are forced to attack from below. The Hittite defenders stand on the walls and towers and use their bows and arrows to shoot down at the Egyptians. Rocks and spears rain down on the Egyptian heads, while the occasional enemy falls head-first to the ground, dead. The Egyptians have evidently developed a good technique for dealing with sieges, and have equipped themselves with ladders and battering rams. Prominent amongst the soldiers, Ramesses again displays exceptional bravery (some might say exceptional folly) by refusing to wear protective clothing: 'His majesty took up his coat-of-mail to wear it [only after] he had already spent two hours standing and attacking the city of the Hittite foe, in front of his troops and chariotry, [without] a coat of mail on him. Only then did his majesty come back to pick up his coat-of-mail again, to put it on . . .'[14]

In Hatti, meanwhile, things were not going well. The constant skir-mishes with Ramesses were starting to take their toll on an army which really needed to concentrate its resources on a far more dangerous opponent. The Assyrians, a new and highly aggressive enemy who had already stripped Mitanni of its last vestiges of power and influence, were now starting to threaten the Hittite territories in north Syria. Soon the Hittite and Assyrian empires would share a common border. At the same time Hatti was experiencing a full-blown dynastic crisis. King Muwatallis had died unexpectedly leaving his unpopular young son Urhi-Teshub to take the throne as Mursilis III. Urhi-Teshub, who as the son of a secondary wife was not necessarily the obvious heir to his father, managed to cling on to power for seven years before his more popular uncle Hattusilis staged a successful coup. The deposed king was banished to Syria where, fuelled by an understandable hatred of Hattusilis, he attempted to make trouble for his uncle. Exile in Cyprus followed before Urhi-Teshub sought refuge at the Egyptian court where he continued with his one-man anti-Hattusilis crusade. Hattusilis demanded the immediate return of his errant nephew, but Ramesses refused. War seemed imminent but, now threatened on two fronts, the Hittite king sought a better solution.

King Hattusilis was an experienced diplomat. Having already con-cluded a successful peace treaty with Kadashman-Turgu, King of Babylon, he focused his diplomatic skills on Egypt. Egypt and Hatti were by no means traditional enemies. Indeed, until the end of the Amarna Age they had been on friendly terms. Surely a formal peace treaty between the two superpowers would prove mutually beneficial? Egypt's annual Syrian campaigns were proving a pointless waste of resources for both sides; a town like Dapur would submit easily to an Egyptian siege, only to revert back to Hittite control as soon as the Egyptian army marched away. Peace with Egypt would free Hatti to concentrate on the Assyrian threat and would, of course, avert the danger of Ramesses backing Urhi-Teshub in a campaign to reclaim the Hittite throne.

Regnal Year 21 – some sixteen years after the ill-fated battle of Kadesh – saw the arrival of the Hittite diplomat Tili-Teshub bearing a letter from the Hittite king. Ramesses and his advisors entered into lengthy negotiations and eventually terms were agreed. The peace treaty, inscribed on two matching silver tablets, was settled. In an agreement intended to last beyond the death of either monarch the two nations were now pledged to respect each other's territories and to defend each other against enemy attack. Above all, peace was to be maintained; a peace which would allow the Hittites to turn their attention to the Assyrian threat. An interesting clause, perhaps a reference to the Urhi-Teshub problem, bound Ramesses to ensure that Hattusilis' son would succeed him on the Hittite throne. The witnesses to the treaty were to be the massed gods of Egypt and Hatti: 'As for him who shall keep these terms written on this silver tablet . . . the thousand gods of Hatti and the thousand gods of Egypt will cause him to flourish and will make him live, together with his household, his land and his servants.'[15]

The sealing of the treaty brought an end to eastern hostilities. Amurru and Kadesh were now irretrievably lost to the Hittites but the Syrian territories would remain Egyptian and there would be free access to the important port of Ugarit. Ramesses never relaxed his firm control over his eastern vassals and his reign saw the start of a deliberate policy of remodelling which was to continue into the early 20th Dynasty. Canaanite cities deemed to be of little or no economic use were now abandoned, while others, considered to be of economic or strategic importance, were strengthened to serve as Egyptian outposts. The more important cities housed permanent garrisons containing large numbers of Egyptian soldiers and Nubian police. To facilitate their roles as administrative centres they were endowed with large Egyptian-style public buildings known today as the 'Egyptian governor's residency'.

The Hittite and Egyptian courts were suddenly on the most friendly of terms, with the two royal families exchanging a series of personal letters and gifts. The queen of the Hittites was by tradition accorded a more prominent role in affairs of state than her Egyptian counterpart; she held her own royal seal and was allowed to make independent sacrifices to the state gods. As a matter of routine she received copies of all correspondence addressed to her husband. Now, as Hattusilis started to write to Ramesses, his queen, Pudukhepa, automatically started to write to her new 'sister' Nefertari whom she addressed as 'Naptera'. Nefertari's reply, although undeniably polite, was disappointingly dull:

Thus says Naptera, the Great Queen of Egypt, to Pudukhepa, the Great Queen of Hatti, my sister:

All goes well with me, your sister, and all goes well with my country. May all go well with you, too, my sister, and with your country may all go well also. I have noted that you, my sister, have written to enquire after my well being. And that you have written to me about the new relationship of good peace and brotherhood in which the Great King of Egypt now stands with his brother the Great King of Hatti.

Re and the Weather-God will uphold the treaty and Re will ensure that it is a prosperous peace, and he will make excellent the brotherhood between the Great King of Egypt and the Great King of Hatti, his brother, for ever. And now I am in friendship with my sister, the Great Queen of Hatti now and for ever.[16]

Difficulties of translation, and disappointed expectations, caused occasional hiccoughs in this most diplomatic of correspondence. On one occasion Hattusilis complained that Ramesses was adopting an arrogant tone in his letters, treating the king of the Hittites as an underling rather than as an equal. Ramesses was swift to deny this accusation, soothing his hurt feelings with a series of magnificent gifts including medicines and a skilled physician. Egypt's doctors were appreciated throughout the Mediterranean world, although even they occasionally failed. When Hattusilis later requested a physician who could cure his sister's sterility Ramesses sent a blunt reply:

As for Matanazi, my brother's sister, the king your brother knows her. Fifty years old, you say? Never! She is certainly sixty! No one can produce medicine to make her fertile. But, of course, if Re and the Weather-God should wish it

... I will send a good magician and an able physician and they will prepare some fertility drugs for her anyway.[17]

Ramesses occasionally felt that the gifts supplied by his brother king were below par – on one occasion he grumbled that Hattusilis had sent him only one disabled slave. Now Hattusilis redeemed himself by offering the ultimate gift: his eldest daughter as a bride.

Notes

1 Exodus 1: 8–14.
2 Exodus 14: 21–28.
3 The precise interpretation of the biblical story has, naturally, been a topic of great debate amongst Egyptologists; see for example Naville, E. (1924), 'The Geography of the Exodus', *Journal of Egyptian Archaeology* 10: 18–39, where the author makes a spirited defence of his own position by attacking the position held by such luminaries as Dr (later Sir) Alan Gardiner and Professor Peet.
4 Amarna Letter 7. For a full translation of this and all other Amarna Letters quoted in this chapter consult Moran, W. L. (1992), *The Amarna Letters*, Baltimore and London.
5 Amarna Letter 19.
6 The most efficient means of desert transport, the camel, was not commonly used in Egypt until after the Ramesside age. The development of the camel train is discussed, with further references, in Artzy, M. (1994), 'Incense, camels and collared rim jars: desert trade routes and maritime outlets in the second millennium', *Oxford Journal of Archaeology* 13(2): 121–47.
7 Gardiner, A. H. (1937), *Late Egyptian Miscellanies*, Brussels: 103.
8 The seven cultures are Assyrian, Canaanite, Cypriot, Egyptian, Kassite (Babylonian), Mycenaean Greek and Nubian. For further details of the cargo consult Bass, G. F. (1987), 'Oldest Known Shipwreck Reveals Splendors of the Bronze Age', *National Geographic* 172:6: 693–733.
9 This papyrus is also known as Papyrus Lansing. For a full translation and commentary consult Lichtheim, M. (1976), *Ancient Egyptian Literature 2: the New Kingdom*, Los Angeles: 168–75.
10 This site is now being excavated by a team from Liverpool University led by Dr Steven Snape. For details of Umm el-Rakham see Habachi, L. (1980), 'The Military posts of Ramesses II on the coastal road and the western part of the Delta', *Bulletin de l'Institut Français d'Archéologie Orientale* 80: 13–33; Snape, S. R. (1995), 'Walls, wells and wandering merchants; Egyptian control of Marmarica in the Late Bronze Age', *Proceedings of the Seventh International Congress of Egyptologists* (C. J. Eyre, ed.), Leuven; 1081–4.
11 This and all subsequent extracts from the Kadesh battle inscriptions are based on the translation given in Lichtheim, M. (1976), *Ancient Egyptian Literature 2: the New Kingdom*, Los Angeles: 58–72. Lichtheim provides a full commen-

tary on the bulletin and the poem, with references. For an alternative interpretation of the complete text consult Kitchen, K. A. (1996), *Ramesside Inscriptions Translated and Annotated 2: Ramesses II Royal Inscriptions*, Oxford, 2–26. For further commentary see Kitchen, K. A. (1999), *Ramesside Royal Inscriptions Translated and Annotated 2: Notes and Comments*, Oxford: 3–55.

12 For a popular, highly illustrated account of the battle of Kadesh, based on the work of Hans Goedicke, see Healey, M. (1993), *Qadesh 1300 BC: clash of the warrior kings*, Wellingborough. For a more scholarly account consult Breasted, J. H. (1903), *The Battle of Kadesh*, Chicago; Goedicke, H. ed (1985), *Perspectives on the Battle of Kadesh*, Baltimore.

13 The suggestion that the next morning was spent punishing the Egyptian deserters is made in Goedicke, H. (1985), 'The "Battle of Kadesh" a reassessment', in H. Goedicke (ed) *Perspectives on the Battle of Kadesh*, Baltimore: 77–121.

14 Kitchen, K. A. (1982), *Pharaoh Triumphant*, Warminster: 69.

15 Kitchen, K. A. (1982), *Pharaoh Triumphant*, Warminster: 79.

16 For details of the letters sent from the Egyptian royal family to Hatti consult Edel, E. (1994), *Die Agyptisch Hethitische Korrespondenz aus Boghazkoi I–III*, Opladen.

17 After Kitchen, K. A. (1982), *Pharaoh Triumphant*, Warminster: 92. This is one of the many sources which combined to form the basis of the tale of the travelling statue of the healing god Khons-the-Planmaker discussed in Chapter 1.

4

Ramesses the God

Soon after the death of his father, possibly while Seti's body still rested with the embalmers, Ramesses made an important announcement. Egypt was to be blessed with a new and most impressive capital. Seti's summer palace, situated close to the old Hyksos capital of Avaris (some 60 miles or 100 kilometres to the north-east of modern Cairo) allowed the northern pharaohs to retain a link with their cherished heartland, while its proximity to the eastern border made it a useful military base. Now the palace was to be rebuilt as the focus of a magnificent city. The new city was to be named Pi-Ramesse Aa-nakhtu, the 'House of Ramesses-Great-of-Victories', as a lasting tribute to its founder.

Pi-Ramesse was destined to become the principal royal residence although, heeding the warning offered by the disastrously isolated Amarna court, Ramesses never abandoned the tradition of the peripatetic pharaoh. Particularly during the earlier years of his reign, he spent a great deal of time travelling up and down the Nile, making personal visits to every corner of his realm in order to reassure – and perhaps warn – his people that wherever they lived, their king was never far away. Now, as the builders set to work at Avaris, he made full use of the northern palaces at Memphis and Heliopolis. Memphis, founded soon after the unification of Upper and Lower Egypt, was the long-serving administrative centre of Lower Egypt. A crowded, cosmopolitan port situated at the apex of the Nile Delta, Memphis had grown wealthy through trade and boasted among its enviable amenities a flourishing dockyard, a sizeable army barracks and an impressive temple complex dedicated to the creator god Ptah. Just outside Memphis were the ancient royal cemeteries of Giza and Sakkara, home to the pyramids, the mastaba tombs and the catacombs of the sacred Apis bulls.

Heliopolis had an equally venerable pedigree. As the ancient cult centre of the solar deity Re, the temple of Heliopolis was revered throughout Egypt. Here, in the temple courtyard, grew the holy *ished* or persea tree. Tradition held that Seshat, goddess of recording, would write the names of each new pharaoh on the leaves of the tree, thereby granting him a lengthy and successful reign. A schist statue, recovered from a disposal pit at the Karnak Temple and now housed in Cairo Museum, shows us the young Ramesses soon after his coronation. He lies semi-prostrate, dressed in a simple kilt and a head-cloth, and is offering a box or chest to his god. The inscription on the base of the statue assures us that 'his [Ramesses'] achievements are confirmed hundreds of thousands of times on the leaves of the sacred *ished* tree'.[1] Unfortunately, city, temple and, of course, tree are now vanished, the masonry of ancient Heliopolis having been absorbed into the buildings of medieval Cairo.

After seventy days at the embalming house it was time for Seti to sail southwards on his final journey to Thebes. Seti had died in June but it was mid-September before Ramesses, having paused for ceremonies at both Memphis and Heliopolis, could inter his father in the Valley of the Kings. This timing was fortuitous. September was the time of the Theban Opet festival, the greatest festival in the calendar of Amen. Religious processions were very much a feature of Theban life, indeed the city was divided by a series of processional ways, sphinx-lined paved avenues linking the various temples of the east and west bank. Now Ramesses led the celebrations as the hidden Amen, his wife Mut and their son Khonsu emerged from the gloom of their sanctuaries to be carried, discreetly veiled in their shrines, down to the River Nile. Here each embarked on his or her own barge to sail or be towed upstream to the Luxor Temple. A flotilla of small boats accompanied the divine barges, while an assortment of priests, musicians, dancers, acrobats, soldiers and excited members of the public crowded along the river bank, eager to catch a glimpse of their gods. Amen was to spend twenty-three days at Luxor, during which time his identity would merge with that of Ramesses as both king and god experienced a renewal of divine power.

While at Thebes Ramesses – with the help of the oracle – decided who was to fill the position of High Priest of Amen, vacant since the death of the previous incumbent, Nebneteru. The High Priest of Amen was a man of immense political influence with control over an impressive array of assets. Amen, having made a quick recovery from the ignominy

of the Amarna period, once again owned an impressive port-folio of agricultural land, boats, mines, quarries, cattle, peasants and prisoners-of-war distributed throughout Egypt; it has been estimated that during the New Kingdom the temple of Amen at Karnak employed more than 81,000 individuals each year.[2] With Thebes an inconvenient 470 miles (750 kilometres) to the south of Pi-Ramesse, it was vital that the correct, pro-Ramesses man was chosen as High Priest. Nebneteru had proved to be a loyal member of the Ramesside faction; his son Paser had become Theban Vizier under Seti and continued in this role under Ramesses. Eventually Nebwennef, High Priest of Thinis and Dendera, was chosen as his replacement although the appoint-ment was, for the time being, to be kept secret. There were other minor adjustments to the hierarchy as Ramesses sought to insert his own men into the key positions.

The precise role played by the oracle in these proceedings is not clear. During the New Kingdom the oracle was developed as a means of allowing the gods to communi-cate directly with the people. Being omniscient the oracle provided a convenient means of solving life's baffling mysteries although its

Fig 4.1   The god Amen, patron deity of Thebes

scope was slightly limited by the fact that the god could only answer 'yes' or 'no'; questions, as in some modern party games, had to take the form of 'Did Isis steal my necklace?' As the god processed along the sacred avenues of Thebes, borne aloft in his sacred barque or boat carried on the shoulders of his priests, he would pause to allow the people to pose their questions. His reply would be indicated by a forward or backward movement of the divine barque. If time permitted it was possible to read out a list of suspects, and the oracle would indicate the guilty party by once again causing the barque to move. Ramesses, as pharaoh, had no need to consult the oracle; he could communicate directly with the gods. He was not the first New Kingdom monarch, however, to use the oracle to add strength to his decisions. The system was, of course, open to a great deal of abuse and it seems safe to assume that the oracle never dared to challenge a decision made by the king.

Thebes, officially named Waset, but often simply called *Niwt* or 'The City', was the administrative centre of Upper Egypt and the official residence of the king's southern deputy, the Vizier Paser. More importantly, it was the home of the great warrior god Amen and his family. The Karnak Temple complex dominated the east bank of the river; indeed, much of Middle Kingdom Thebes had been sacrificed to its expansion and now lay buried beneath the impressive New Kingdom stone-built extensions. On the opposite bank stood the mortuary temples of the New Kingdom pharaohs and, hidden away in the western mountains, the secret royal tombs. The incessant building works – the excavation of the tombs and the embellishment of the temples – called for a constant supply of workmen who resided alongside the civil servants, priests, sailors and townsfolk, making Thebes a vibrant, bustling city. Although much of the residential area was centred around the temples the settlement spanned the river, with royal palaces on the east bank.[3] Unfortunately much of the non-religious architecture, built at a lower level than the temples and therefore beneath the modern water-table, is now lost to us.

His lengthy stay at Thebes allowed Ramesses time to inspect the ongoing work at the Karnak Temple complex *Ipet-isut*, or 'The Most Select of Places'. Here, perhaps influenced by his first Opet procession, he was to build an avenue of 120 ram-headed sphinxes (the ram being one of the sacred animals of Amen) linking the Temple of Amen to the river quay and so allowing Amen easy access to his barge. Between their front paws his sphinxes guarded the image of Ramesses, the mediator between man and god. Subsequent work at Karnak included the dedication of a temple to 'Amen-who-hears-prayers', and the erection of a monumental eastern gateway flanked by two obelisks. However the decoration of the hypostyle or columned hall was now his most pressing concern.

The magnificent hall first envisaged by Ramesses I and then adopted by Seti was now, predictably, to be known as the temple 'Glorious is Ramesses II in the Domain of Amen'. Building work had already been finished and the hall boasted a forest of 134 columns in the style of papyrus plants arranged in sixteen rows, the twelve columns in the two central rows standing 79 feet (24 metres) high while the outer columns, sixty-one on each side, stood 40 feet (12 metres) tall. Dim light filtered through the high, barred clerestory windows creating an atmosphere of mystery, a cool, dark, calm contrast to the heat, light and bustle of the secular world. This hall, its columns once famously described as 'enormous, like the gnarled shafts of ancient space rockets arranged on some unbelievable launch-pad for simultaneous blast-off'[4] is classed by many as one of the unofficial wonders of the ancient world. The earliest tourists came to marvel at the sheer size of the columns:

. . . The enormous columns of the great hall, the lofty obelisks, and the towering masses of the pylons inspire in the beholder a feeling of reverential wonder at the greatness of the minds which thought on such a scale. The dominant feeling with anyone who explores these ruins is the *bigness* of it all. Big, not only in its conception, but in the overcoming of seemingly insurmountable difficulties of construction.[5]

Seti's workmen were already well on with the decoration of the walls and columns. The exterior was eventually to be embellished with scenes of battle, including the ubiquitous Kadesh triumph, plus a copy of the Hittite peace treaty, while the interior was, as tradition dictated, to show scenes of a more religious nature, including the divine coronation of Ramesses. Now the workmen, busily carving the interior surfaces in the delicate raised relief favoured during Seti's lifetime, were ordered to adopt the faster, less elegant sunken relief which characterizes almost all of Ramesses' monuments.

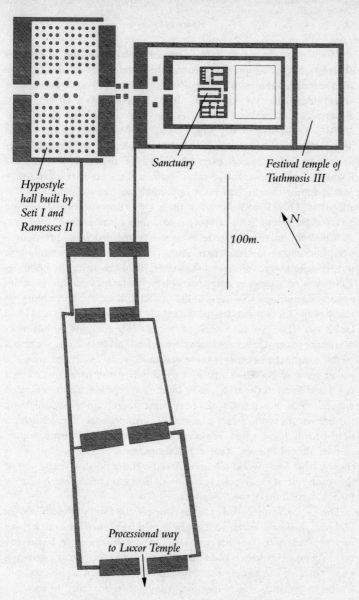

Hypostyle
hall built by
Seti I and
Ramesses II

Sanctuary

Festival temple of
Tuthmosis III

N

100m.

Processional way
to Luxor Temple

Fig 4.2   The Temple of Amen at Karnak during the 19th Dynasty

This abrupt change in style seems somewhat shocking to modern observers, but the temptation to equate the raised relief with good artistry and the sunken relief with bad is one which should be resisted as a modern value judgement. To Ramesses, artistic standards were of secondary importance; his priority was to see the work completed in his own lifetime, if possible in a way which would prevent others from usurping his carvings. In this aim he succeeded. However, the difference in styles must have been obvious, even when covered in layers of paint, and Ramesses later returned to re-carve sections of the raised relief so that it would appear that he had been responsible for the decoration of the entire hall. That his intention was to usurp rather than enhance is indicated by the alteration of Seti's cartouches to those of Ramesses.

When considered alongside Ramesses' early change of pre-nomen from Usermaatre to Usermaatre Setepenre, the abrupt discontinuity in style of reliefs which followed Ramesses' involvement in the buildings – either as co-regent or immediately after his father's death – provides today's Egyptologists with a means of establishing the chronology of many of the monuments started during the reign of Seti and completed by his son.[6] The Nubian temple of Beit el-Wali, founded by Ramesses during the reign of Seti, provides a classic case. This temple was decorated in three distinct phases; first there was raised relief associated with the earlier form of Ramesses' name (carved during the period when Seti ruled and dictated the style); then came sunken relief, again associated with the earlier pre-nomen (carved at a time when Ramesses was allowed to supervise the work, either as co-regent or immediately after his father's death); finally there was sunken relief, plus the later form of the pre-nomen (carved after Ramesses' Year 2 change of name).[7] The Karnak reliefs show us that Seti's workmen decorated the entire north side and part of the south side of the hypostyle hall, with Ramesses taking responsibility for the decoration of the remainder.

The Luxor Temple, dedicated to Amen in the form of the ithyphallic god Min, had been substantially rebuilt by Amenhotep III so that there was now little of the original early 18th Dynasty structure left. Tutankhamen, Ay and Horemheb had built at Luxor, and such was the growing importance of the temple that Horemheb had chosen to be crowned within its precincts. Here, too, Seti had planned but failed to finish an impressive project: a pylon and forecourt garnished by mighty obelisks and colossal statues. These, inevitably, were taken over by Rameses II with the work being largely completed by Year 3. With Seti's founding role forgotten the public face of the pylon was once again destined to show scenes of the famous battle of Kadesh. Passing through the gateway the scenes changed to show images of Ramesses and his consort before various gods; we see Ramesses offering *maat* to Amen-Re, Ramesses offering to Min, and Ramesses and Queen Nefertari before Amen-Re. Nefertari, delicately carved in the style of the earliest Rameside reliefs, shakes her sistra and offers a prayer for the preservation of her husband:

Playing the sistra before thy beautiful face I sing of love . . . I play the sistra before thy beautiful face; I propriate thee for thy goodness sake; may thou protect thy son whom thou lovest and with whom thou art pleased, the Lord of the two Lands, User-Maat-Re Setepenre, given life like Re, eternally.[8]

Two red granite obelisks were erected in front of the pylon; one of these was removed in 1835 and now stands in the Place de la Concorde, Paris, while the other remains *in situ*.

The forecourt – a peristyle court surrounded by a double row of seventy-four papyrus-style columns – included a triple shrine to the Theban triad Amen, Mut and Khonsu, which, originally built by Hatchepsut and Tuthmosis III as a barque station, was now substantially rebuilt by Ramesses. Here the three gods would rest after their journey from Karnak during the Opet festival, and here the oracle would make pronouncements. Within the forecourt there were yet more colossal statues of Ramesses. The building's inscription, carved on the inner or back face of the eastern pylon and along the eastern wall of the forecourt, is unfortunately fragmented and partially obscured by the 13th-century mosque of Abu'l Haggag. However, enough text is visible to show that Ramesses, scholar and scribe, had conducted his own research, delving into the temple archives in order to ensure that his building met with all the correct theological requirements:

As for this goodly god [the king] he is a scribe, accomplished in learning and in knowledge like Thoth . . . Now his majesty did research in the library, and he opened and read the writings of the House of Life. He thus learned the secrets of heaven and the mysteries of earth. He found that Thebes, the Eye of

Re, was a Primaeval Mound which arose in the beginning, since this land had existed . . . The king spoke, giving instructions to conduct the work . . .'

Meanwhile, over on the west bank, Seti's mortuary temple remained to be completed. On the architrave above the portico Ramesses claims to have both 'renewed' and 'erected' his father's monument. Here he is exaggerating: the evidence of the carved relief suggests that he did little more than finish it. The western sections of the temple are decorated in the name and style of Seti and it is only in the porch of the hypostyle hall that we first encounter the cartouche of Ramesses with raised relief and the early form of his name. This is followed by areas of sunken relief with the early pre-nomen – work done around the time of Seti's death – and finally areas of sunken relief combined with the later form of Ramesses' name which must have been carved during Ramesses' solo reign.

No time was too early to make the necessary provisions for death. The site had been chosen for Ramesses' tomb in the Valley of the Kings and now work was to start on his mortuary temple, the 'Mansion of Millions of Years, United-with-Thebes'. This temple, which the Greeks called the 'Memnonium' or the 'Tomb of Ozymandias', is today known as the Ramesseum. It was to lie on the edge of the desert between the 18th Dynasty temples of Amenhotep II and Tuthmosis IV, and was to be orientated towards the Luxor Temple on the opposite bank. The Ramesseum would eventually become the centre of worship for the cult of the dead and deified Ramesses II associated with Amen. This would not be the only cult centre for the dead Ramesses – the Abydos temple was also intended to fulfil this function, and there were to be cult temples at Pi-Ramesse, Memphis and Heliopolis – but the Theban temple, closely linked to the actual tomb of Ramesses, would be the most important.

Unfortunately, the Ramesseum has been badly damaged by both man (treasure seekers ancient and modern) and nature (earthquakes), the resulting picturesque ruins making it a popular picnic spot for tourists at the turn of the century. Enough has survived, however, to show that Ramesses' architect, Penre, was not afraid to experiment. The sandstone mortuary temple incorporated many of the features of the Karnak Temple. Abandoning the practice of fronting the temple with a series of open courtyards Ramesses made his presence felt with a huge pylon which was, naturally, decorated with scenes of the victorious pharaoh. Behind this came two open-air colonnaded courts, the first dominated by the massive 'Re of the Rulers', the famous Ozymandias colossus which had its own chapel. A ramp led upwards to the second court where the eastern and western porticoes were lined with colossal images of Ramesses in the guise of the mummified Osiris. Here was found the 'Younger Memnon', one of a pair of statues whose head and upper body Belzoni transported to the British Museum in 1817. Beyond the two courts lay a forty-eight-columned hypostyle hall with a raised central aisle allowing the provision of clerestory windows, and beyond this again were a series of lesser halls including a room with an astronomical ceiling. Here we see Seshat recording the length of Ramesses' reign on the leaves of the *ished* tree, prompting speculation that this may have been the temple archive and library. Finally came the barque hall, a small square room with support for the portable barque of Amen, and the sanctuary which housed the image of the god.

To the south of the first court, and connected to it by a gateway, was a small palace complete with audience chamber, throne room and balcony or 'window of appearances' which allowed the palace to communicate with the temple. Here the king and his court could live while visiting Thebes for the celebration of the many local festivals. A double shrine, dedicated jointly to the queen mother Tuya and queen consort Nefertari, was to be found to the north of the hypostyle hall, while the temple proper was surrounded by mud-brick subsidiary buildings such as administrative offices and accommodation provided for the temple officials. The entire complex was protected by a thick mud-brick wall. The storage facilities within the compound were impressive; the twenty vaulted granaries could, if completely filled, hold enough grain to feed over a thousand families for three years.[10]

In October Ramesses left Thebes, sailing northwards on Day 23, 3rd month of Inundation, Year I. His first stop was Abydos. Here Seti's unfinished temple was not progressing according to plan, and the whole site had a general air of neglect and decay. The new king was dismayed by what he saw:

He found the buildings in the cemetery belonging to the former kings, their tombs which are in Abydos, falling gradually into ruins, part of them still under

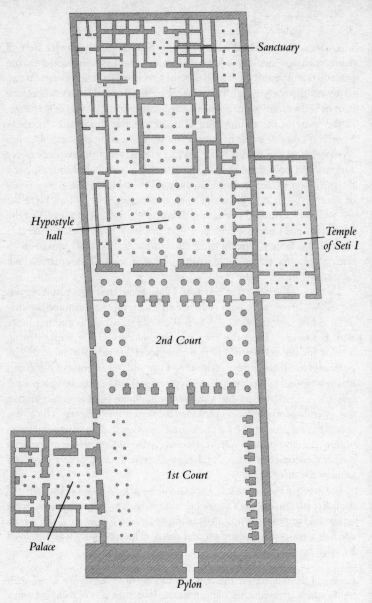

Fig 4.3   *The Ramesseum: mortuary temple of Ramesses II*

construction and part covered with earth ... What was barely started had already crumbled back into dust. No one continued the building work ... after the owners had departed to heaven. No son renewed his father's monuments in the cemetery. Indeed, the temple of Men–Maat–Re [Seti I] had its front and its back under construction when he went to heaven. No one completed its monuments, its pillars not set up on the terracing, its statue lay on the ground ... Its offerings had come to an end ...[11]

It was accepted that, just as a good son would maintain his father's monuments, so a good pharaoh would respect the monuments of his earthly ancestors and a divine son would preserve the monuments of the gods. By so doing, his own monuments would surely be protected in the future. Many 18th Dynasty rulers had taken pride in restoring the relics of earlier kings; Hatchepsut had used her restorations as a means of justifying her right to rule, while Tuthmosis IV attributed his unexpected succession to his actions, while a mere prince, in freeing the Sphinx from a blanket of sand. This commitment to the preservation of the monuments of the past did not, of course, sit easily with the policy of usurping and restyling the same ancient monuments to the glory of the present king, but Ramesses was not a man to allow such scruples to interrupt his rhetoric. The Abydos dedication text recorded on the wall of Seti's temple therefore continues with Ramesses summoning his ministers:

I have considered that it is a worthy deed to benefit those who have passed away. Compassion is a blessing, and it is good that a son should be concerned enough to care about his father. I am determined to confer benefits so that it will be said for ever 'It is his son who perpetuates his name'. So may my father Osiris favour me with the long lifespan of his son Horus ... May it benefit me, just as it was beneficial to him who made me ...

By his own admission Ramesses was prompted to take action in order to glorify his own name rather than to preserve the memory of his dead father. And take action he certainly did. The chief of works received his instructions and construction started again. Soon the back of the building was finished and a portico, two courts and a pylon were added to complete the temple. *Maat*, very obviously, had been brought to chaos and Ramesses was pleased with his work.

The condition of Ramesses' own Abydos temple is not mentioned in the lengthy text quoted above; did the king realize that the workmen who had so callously abandoned his father's temple were in fact busily labouring on his own?[12] Ramesses' temple was similar in plan to that of Seti, but built on a smaller scale. He may even have excavated a dummy tomb to parallel the Osireion; although the area behind his temple is currently unexcavated there is some evidence for a substantial subterranean structure with granite elements.[13] Work seems to have been well under way in the temple proper and here, too, we see a change from raised relief which is found in the rooms at the back of the temple where we also find the earlier pre-nomen of Ramesses, to sunken relief which appears at the front where Ramesses is named Usermaatre Setepenre.

Here, at Abydos, Ramesses summoned Nebwennef and told him of his promotion: 'You are now High Priest of Amen. His treasury and granary are under your seal. You are chief over his domain and all his foundations are under your authority.' The new pontiff was presented with two gold signet rings and a staff of office and sent southwards, to Thebes. Ramesses, meanwhile, resumed his journey northwards to the palace of Memphis.

Ramesses was soon off again on his travels. Sailing southwards he embarked on a tour of Nubia with the aim of reviewing his resources, examining supplies of stone and assessing the efficiency of the gold mines. His major building projects were by now progressing well and Thebes, Luxor, Pi-Ramesse and Memphis all echoed to the sounds of hammer and chisel. Smaller temples up and down the Nile were starting to benefit from the king's generosity, while surveyors were busily marking out plots in Nubia. At the ill-fated city of Amarna labourers were demolishing the last remaining buildings and transporting the stone across the river where it was to be used to enhance the city of Hermopolis Magna (modern el-Ashmunein), home of the god Thoth. Now it was time to consider the financial position. Even to a man of Ramesses' vast wealth, construction on such a massive scale was going to prove a serious drain on resources. Cost-cutting measures such as the use of sunken relief, inferior building techniques and the use of forced foreign labour were all in place, but there was an incessant demand for expensive building materials.

Ramesses had received reports that the eastern deserts were particularly rich in gold, but that a shortage of water in the Wadi Allaki was making these sites very difficult to work. Too many labourers, and too many valuable donkeys, were dying on the long march to the mines. Other kings, Seti included, had attempted to build a much-needed well, but all had failed. Seti's well had been abandoned when it was some 120 cubits (approximately 180 feet or 54 metres) deep. Undaunted, Ramesses summoned his ministers to discuss the matter. With great diplomacy they were able to convince him that:

You are like Re in all that you have done, whatever your heart desires comes to pass. If you desire something overnight, comes the dawn and it happens immediately! We have seen so many of your wonderful deeds since you became king of Both Lands . . . If you say to the water 'Come from the mountain', then the water flood shall come forth promptly after your word, because you are Re in person, the dawning sun in his true form . . .[14]

Persuaded by this irresistible line of reasoning Ramesses issued his men with precise instructions and yes! Water was found a mere 12 cubits beneath the sand and rock. The new well was of course named 'The Well, Ramesses II Valiant-in-Deeds'. The gold fields could now be exploited and the exchequer grew richer.

Ramesses' mastery over the natural world was confirmed in Year 8 when, while travelling in the desert near Heliopolis, he was able to identify a massive block of precious quartzite 'the like of which had never been found since the beginning of time'. This was carved into a colossal figure some 67 feet (20 metres) high and erected at Pi-Ramesse. Next he discovered a second quarry yielding red quartzite, again highly suitable for the manufacture of statues to grace Memphis, Heliopolis and Pi-Ramesse. This impressive achievement mirrored events during Year 9 of his father's reign when, with Ramesses assisting, Seti had astounded his entourage by detecting a useful source of granite at Aswan: 'Then his majesty discovered a new quarry for statues of black granite whose crowns would be of red quartzite from the red mountain. Never had their like been seen since the time of Re . . .'[15] Clearly the Ramesside kings took a very 'hands-on' approach to prospecting.

The new city of Pi-Ramesse, like the primeval mound, was surrounded by water. To the west and north flowed the Pelusiac branch of the Nile,

known as the 'Waters of Re', while to the south and east was an artificial
canal, the 'Waters of Avaris', which fed a lake, the 'Waters of the
Residence'. Further south a second lake allowed the development of a
port within easy reach of both the eastern Mediterranean and southern
Egypt. Thus the city was provided not only with a source of drinking
water but also with a means of transport, sanitation, irrigation and defence.
Beyond the city there was abundant fertile land, with desert to the east.
Everyone who came to Pi-Ramesse was impressed by its beauty and its
abundance.

... It is a beautiful place which, although resembling Thebes, has no equal ...
Life in the residence is good; the fields are filled with all kinds of good produce
so that each day is blessed with good food. Its canals teem with fish and its
marshland is filled with birds ... from the fields come fruit flavoured with
honey. The granaries overflow with barley and wheat ...[16]

It seems almost inconceivable that such a splendid city could disappear
without trace but this is exactly what happened to Pi-Ramesse. Although
the city outlived its founder, continuing in use throughout the 20th
Dynasty, its fate was sealed when the Pelusiac branch of the Nile started
to silt up. Gradually the Nile changed its course to flow further north,
rendering the port of Pi-Ramesse useless and effectively isolating the city
from the main highway of Egypt. Eventually, during the 21st Dynasty,
the decision was taken to abandon Pi-Ramesse and establish a royal city
at nearby Tanis. Much of the old city was dismantled, its valuable masonry
transported to Tanis for reuse. The mud-brick buildings were simply
abandoned, and slowly subsided into mounds of fertile soil. With the
passage of time more modern buildings, fields and irrigation canals
obscured the archaeological site until Pi-Ramesse was just a name preserved in the monuments of Ramesses and in the Bible.

    With all trace of the city obliterated, Egyptologists debated long and
hard over its exact location. To many, Tanis, with its many Ramesside
monuments, seemed the obvious choice. Others favoured Pelusium,
Bubastis or Sile. It is now generally agreed that the old Hyksos capital
of Avaris was located at modern Tell ed-Daba, with Pi-Ramesse close
by at du Qantir. Although excavations are now in progress at this site,
the extent of the destruction and the encroachment of modern cultivation

make it unlikely that we will ever have a detailed plan of the ancient capital.

Ramesses had greatly extended the old summer palace until, together with its associated administrative and religious buildings, harem, kitchens, treasury and storehouses, it became a compact inner city covering an area of some four square miles. The thick mud-brick walls of the palace were by now embellished with limestone columns and brightly coloured faience tiles so that the entire building sparkled in the fierce Egyptian sun. The public throne room, appropriately decorated with tiles showing bound captives, lions eating prisoners and humble vassals paying tribute to their lord, was designed to strike awe into visitors. The private women's quarters, decorated with light floral motifs and aquatic scenes of fish and marsh fowl, were altogether more relaxing. The abundant supply of water allowed Pi-Ramesse to become a garden city, planted with pomegranate and date orchards and vineyards. Around the royal palace were ornamental gardens, a lake and even a zoo; lion, giraffe and elephant bones have all been discovered in the remains of the grounds. Beyond the palace were offices, storehouses, shops, workshops and, of course, the suburbs housing the general population. A large industrial complex included a huge bronze foundry, a glaze-works and the warehouses and docks of a thriving port.

Its position close to Egypt's eastern border ensured that Pi-Ramesse became an important army camp. Here was based a chariot garrison, an army training ground and stables large enough to house almost 500 horses plus their grooms. Here too were extensive army workshops where weapons were manufactured and chariots were repaired. Some of the weaponry was manufactured to Hittite design, and it would appear that, following the peace treaty of Year 21, Hittite workmen settled in the Delta where their expertise was exploited for the greater efficiency of pharaoh's army. Pottery of Mycenaean, Cypriot, Hittite and Levantine origin confirms the cosmopolitan nature of Ramesses' city.

As at all dynastic cities, the most magnificent buildings, constructed from the most durable materials, were the temples. Papyrus Anastasi II tells us that the new city was divided into four regions, with the house of Amen to the west, Seth [or Sutekh] to the south, Astarte to the east and Wadjet, goddess of Lower Egypt, to the north.[17] In addition there were important temples to the northern gods Ptah of Memphis and

Re-Herakhty of Heliopolis. Excavation has confirmed this general geography. The temple of Seth was indeed based in the south, in the old Hyksos city of Avaris. Seth had been the patron deity of the Hyksos, and a stela commemorating the foundation of his temple in 'Year 400, fourth day of the fourth month of the inundation season of the King of Upper and Lower Egypt, Seth, great of courage, son of Re, chosen one, beloved of Re-Herakhty', was erected at Pi-Ramesse and eventually recovered from Tanis. The top of the stela, a copy of a text originally commissioned by Horemheb, shows Ramesses offering wine to his father, Seth, confirming his commitment to the god of his homeland.

The temples of Re and Amen faced each other to the north of the royal palace while the temples of Ptah and Sekhmet-Wadjet were to be found in the northern part of the city. Between the temple of Amen and the temple of Ptah stood the great 'Halls of Jubilee', the venue for the celebration of the king's *heb-sed* ceremony. The Halls, a magnificent complex including two columned chambers built using recycled stone from older buildings, was fronted by a spectacular granite gateway and three pairs of obelisks. The stable area, to the east of the city, included a sanctuary dedicated to the Syrian warrior goddess Astarte, who had become the patron deity of the royal horses.

These temples were in a very literal sense believed to be the houses of the gods, and as such they followed the same basic plan as all Egyptian homes. Areas accessible to the general public led to more private regions and finally to the hidden sanctuary where the god in the form of a statue lived isolated from contact with the uninitiated and impure. At the same time the Egyptian temple, protected from day-to-day city life by its thick enclosure wall, was intended to be a representation of the universe at the very moment of creation, a creation that was re-enacted daily by the rising sun. Within the wall was an ideal, pure world where the god could participate in the cosmic or reproductive cycles. The pylon, or gateway, hid the temple, but allowed a favoured few entry to the interior. With most temples orientated on an east–west axis at right-angles to the River Nile the rising sun would shine through the pylon, which in outline resembled the hieroglyph for 'horizon', and illuminate the pathway to the sanctuary. As the priests approached their god they moved from light into darkness, and the ground rose slightly to represent the primeval mound emerging from the lake of chaos. At the same time the ceiling gently sloped to create a more intimate, enclosed space. Here, on the first mound, the sun god had stood as existence came into being. Papyriform columns, such as those found in the hypostyle hall at Karnak, were imagined to be growing from the lake and holding up the star-spangled sky.

The temples were, to the vast majority of the population, secret structures whose gates seldom opened and whose gods rarely ventured beyond the safety of their own shrines. The outer temple walls and gateways, decorated with scenes of the triumphant pharaoh defeating the enemies of Egypt, were all that the man or woman in the street could reasonably expect to see of the buildings which dominated his or her city, although during festivals the great wooden gates might be opened to allow access to the first open court. The chambers beyond this were unknown territory.

If the state gods remained hidden, and the king rarely appeared before his people, colossal images of Ramesses were everywhere. Ramesses commissioned at least fifty self-portraits to grace his new capital, and all were life-sized or larger. These statues, each of them named, were placed either in front of the temple pylon or within the first, public, temple court. Unfortunately almost all of these figures are now irredeemably fragmented, but we know from literary sources that Ramesses variously towered over the people of Pi-Ramesse as 'Montu [god of war] in the Two Lands'; 'The God'; 'Appearing Among The Gods'; 'Beloved of Atum'; 'Son of Rulers'; 'Ruler of Rulers'; 'Ramesses II Effective for Amen/Atum/Seth/Re'.

These statues were not merely enormous works of art. Highly visible to the ordinary people, each figure, like the king it represented, was seen as an intermediary standing partway between mortal man and the remote gods of the state pantheon. The colossi therefore became the focus of royal cults, developing their own hereditary priesthoods and supporting a full complement of cult officials including female singers and musicians. Citizens of all classes dedicated stelae to these statue cults. In theory the people were expressing their devotion not to the king himself, but to the office of kingship personified in the form of his colossal image. In practice it seems likely that many of the uneducated citizens, unaware of the complexities of Egyptian theology, were simply worshipping the statue.[18]

Ramesses, by erecting his colossi, was providing his people with a simple, accessible focus for their religious feelings which official religion denied them. Furthermore, he was providing them with a means of expressing – most publicly – their loyalty to the crown. In this he was following well-established tradition. Amenhotep III had been particularly partial to colossal statues and had erected the four largest figures so far known; a pair of huge Amenhoteps stood before the temple of Amen at Karnak, while his most famous pair, the so-called 'Colossi of Memnon' still sit in lonely splendour before his now vanished mortuary temple. That these colossi were intended as objects of worship is clear; an 18th Dynasty relief carved at Aswan shows the sculptor Men worshipping a seated statue of Amenhotep III, while his sculptor son Bak offers before a statue of Akhenaten (who is now erased from the scene).

Although much of Ramesses' attention was focused on the building of Pi-Ramesse, Memphis, too, benefited greatly from his generosity. Here he made substantial improvements to the Temple of Ptah, a temple founded by Amenhotep III and embellished by Seti I, which soon rivalled in size, beauty and possibly plan the complex of Amen at Thebes. Memphis was now dominated by giant images of the king, and at least eleven colossi – whole or in pieces – have been recovered from the environs of the Ptah Temple. These were statues built on a truly impressive scale; it has been estimated that the largest known example, represented by a massive fist now housed in the British Museum, would have stood some 70 feet (21 metres) tall. Of the two most complete a 35-feet (10.5 metres) granite figure now stands in Ramesses Square, Cairo, where it dominates the entrance to the railway station, while a 42-feet (12.5 metres) limestone Ramesses lies flat on its back in its own museum at Memphis. A third statue, rediscovered in large fragments in 1962, was restored in 1986 by an American team of conservators and sent on temporary loan to Memphis, Tennessee, where it formed the centrepiece of an exhibition dedicated to the life and times of Ramesses the Great. Even with all the advantages of modern technology, including heavy duty transport trucks, forklift trucks and a crane, it proved a difficult and delicate task to transport and then lift the 24-feet (7 metres), 47-ton figure.[19]

Ramesses' workmen were armed only with saws (firstly copper, then bronze), drills, chisels and ball-shaped hard-stone hammers. His statues and obelisks were cut laboriously from the living rock by teams of workers who bounced their hammer-stones again and again against the rock surface to dent it. Once the required shape had been substantially formed the colossus was dragged to the canal and loaded on to a barge. Pliny, like all classical authors, was deeply impressed by the size of Egypt's sculptures, and described in some detail the technique used for loading an obelisk:

A canal was dug from the River Nile to the spot where the obelisk lay and two broad vessels, loaded with blocks of similar stone a foot square – the cargo of each amounting to double the size and consequently double the weight of the obelisk – was put beneath it. The extremities of the obelisk remained supported by the opposite sides of the canal. The blocks of stone were removed and the vessels, being gradually lightened, received their burden.[20]

The barge was towed first to the Nile, and then to its intended destination. Here the removal of the figure from the barge, and the erection of the sculpture, posed major engineering problems. The exact method used has not yet been confirmed, but it is likely to have involved the construction of an earth bank which would allow the figure to be raised and then dropped, base forward, into position. The whole process was both laborious and time consuming; no wonder Ramesses preferred to adapt the monuments of his predecessors!

Cult statues need not be colossal. One beautiful granite statue, a 'mere' 7.5 feet (2.31 metres) tall, shows Ramesses in the form of a plump child crouching before the Semitic god Hauron who in turn takes the form of the Egyptian falcon god Horus.[21] Ramesses appears as a typical boy. He is naked, has his hair dressed in the 'side-lock of youth' and holds his right index finger to his mouth. In his left hand he holds the plant which symbolizes Upper Egypt. Only the sun disc and cobra at his brow betray his exalted status. His figure, however, if read as a series of hieroglyphs, is a visual pun on his name: *Ra* the sun god is represented by the solar disk; Ramesses assumes the attitude of *mes*, the hieroglyphic symbol for child; *su* the plant is held in his hand. The cult of this statue long outlived Ramesses; having started life at Pi-Ramesse it was eventually recovered from a Late Period mud-brick shrine within the temple enclosure of King Psusennes I at Tanis, and is now housed in Cairo Museum.

Group statues – statues showing Ramesses in association with one or more gods – were manufactured as objects of worship to be placed in the sanctuaries and side chapels of the major temples, thus firmly associating the mortal king with the worship of the divine gods.[22] It is probably no accident that in many of the surviving examples the king is frequently better modelled, and more substantial, than his divine companions so that he effectively dominates the group. In many of the groups recovered from Pi-Ramesse the deity even bears Ramesses' name, being labelled 'X of Ramesses', as in, for example, 'Ptah of Ramesses'. This direct association of Ramesses and god is found at other Ramesside cities, so that at Memphis we again encounter 'Ptah of Ramesses', at Hermopolis 'Thoth of Ramesses' and at Karnak 'Atum', 'Re', 'Amen' and 'Ptah of Ramesses'. These gods were worshipped alongside, rather than instead of, the more traditional Ptah, Amen, Atum and Re. The precise meaning of the phrase 'of Ramesses' is not obvious, although it might simply indicate that the god was a resident of or welcome visitor to Pi-Ramesse (Ramesses being used as an abbreviation of Pi-Ramesse) or indeed that Ramesses, rather than the temple, owned the figure? Art historians have suggested other, more subtle interpretations: did they allow Ramesses to merge his identity more firmly with that of the particular god shown? Or did they allow him to assume the more specific role of Re in his role of senior creator god (as Re had created the gods, so Ramesses created the statues of the gods)? This identification of Ramesses with the sun god was extended further when, towards the end of his reign, he started to use the epithet 'Great Soul of Re-Herakhty', an epithet which was also added to the name of Pi-Ramesse.

A thin line separated mortal and divine kings. A dead king was undeniably divine. The colossal statue of a living king might be considered divine. Now, in Nubia, the living king himself was to become divine. Amenhotep III and Ramesses, kings who constantly hinted at their own divine status within Egypt's official borders, were far more forthcoming in Nubia where both were accepted as gods.[23] The explanation for this difference in styles is nowhere stated, but it seems to have been accepted that the unsophisticated colonials, incapable of appreciating the subtle nuances of Egyptian theology, would prefer the simplicity of a living god. Nubia, far from the restrictive influence of the state clergy, would be an ideal place to conduct a theological experiment.

Ramesses, of course, is likely to have followed the lead set by his great role-model Amenhotep III (an element of 'anything he can do, I can do better'), while both kings would have found that their enhanced status helped them maintain control over their far-flung territories. The living Amenhotep III was worshipped at Soleb as 'Amenhotep, Lord of Nubia', while a companion temple dedicated to his consort, Queen Tiy, was erected at Sedeinga.

Nubia was by now resigned to her role as the southernmost province of Egypt. There had been little or no trouble since the valiant Prince Ramesses had marched to subdue the rebellion recorded on the walls of the Beit el-Wali temple, and only once during Ramesses' reign was it to prove necessary to send troops southwards. Some time around Year 21 a minor rebellion was crushed by an Egyptian army whose leaders included the royal princes Sethemwia (8th son) and Merenptah (13th son). The result was a foregone conclusion. Seven thousand rebels were captured and the triumph was commemorated on the main gate of Amara West (now known as 'Ramesses the Town') where they served as a reminder to all of pharaoh's might. With little need to increase Nubia's defences, Ramesses turned his attention to temple building. His temples, functioning as administrative and economic centres, would have the right to gather and store the enviable resources of his southern lands.

Nubia was to see at least seven new Ramesses II temples plus several older foundations re-embellished in the Rameside style. Local geography, Ramesses' newly acquired divinity, the inclination of the southern architects and the skills of the local workforces combined to ensure that many of the new temples took the form of the *speos*, with the sanctuary cut deep into the living rock. All were ornamented with a high number of colossal figures which were often integrated into the temple architecture, so that, for example, pillars were faced with colossal figures of the king.

The new temples demonstrate an interesting progression as Ramesses gradually moves from mortal king to full divinity. The most northerly, Beit el-Wali, founded during the reign of Seti when Ramesses was undeniably mortal, was dedicated to Amen-Re. At Aksha, near the Second Cataract, a temple started by Seti was re-dedicated to the colossal 'Ramesses II, Great God, Lord of Nubia' while at Derr the 'Temple of Ramesses II in the Domain of Re' was dedicated to both Ramesses and

Re-Herakhty. The two final Nubian temples were built under the supervision of the forceful Vizier Setau, and by now Ramesses' exalted status was to be made obvious to all. At Wadi es-Sebua, a temple site first used by Amenhotep III, the temple of 'Ramesses Beloved of Amen in the Domain of Amen' was built between Years 35 and 50 using a workforce snatched during a raid on the Libyan oases. This practical method of obtaining cheap labour had been employed by Ramesses I and Seti when building at Buhen. Here at es-Sebua we see Ramesses taking his place at the centre of the divine family while the mortal Ramesses worships himself. Ramesses also appears in the form of the colossal sphinx wearing the double crown; 'Sebua' is the Arabic word for lion. A parallel temple was built at Gerf Hussein where Ramesses II was linked with Ptah.

Ramesses' most celebrated Nubian monuments are the two temples built on the west bank of the Nile at Abu Simbel, some 40 miles (64 kilometres) to the north of the Second Cataract and 175 miles (280 kilometres) to the south of Aswan. The temples were started early in his reign and were dedicated during Year 24, although they were not completely finished until some time after Year 35. Abu Simbel was a remote spot, far from any sizeable settlement, and it seems that Ramesses was inspired by the local geography which would allow him to cut neighbouring temples into sandstone cliffs set at an angle to each other so that just twice each year (20 February and 20 October), the rising sun would penetrate the gloom of the Great Temple to illuminate the four statues seated in the niche at the back of the sanctuary. The French Egyptologist Christiane Desroches Noblecourt has taken this astronomical interpretation a step further, suggesting that the orientation of the two temples and their relationship with the nearby Nile was deliberately engineered to link the regular conjunction of the sun and Sirius, the Dog Star, to both the gods of the temple and the rising of the Nile at the time of inundation.[24]

Old and Middle Kingdom graffiti suggest that the site was already considered to be a sacred one, and Horemheb had built a shrine not far away. Egyptian temples, of course, did not rely on the presence of a congregation, but it is curious that no housing associated with the site has been discovered; we have not even recovered the settlement of those who built the monument, or indeed their graves. This is by no means an unusual situation; the settlements associated with Beit el-Wali, Gerf Hussein, Wadi es-Sebua and Derr have never been found. It seems that, as at Wadi es-Sebua and Buhen, many of the labourers were prisoners-of-war. The king's agent Asha-Hebsed, charged with over-seeing the workforce, left details of the labourers carved on the Abu Simbel cliff face:

Behold, His majesty's mind was alert to discover every good opportunity for conferring benefits on his father, the god Horus of Meha . . . He brought many workmen, captured by his strong arm from every foreign land, and he filled the estates of the gods with the children of Syria as bounty.[25]

The Great Temple, naturally enough, belonged to Ramesses, and its façade was designed to display the king in all his glory. Two colossal statues of Ramesses wearing the double crown of Upper and Lower Egypt sit on either side of the central doorway, their eyes angled to allow them to look down on the mortal visitors to the site. At over 65 feet (19.5 metres) high Ramesses dwarfs the figure of the god carved high above the doorway. Here Re-Herakhty stands, the goddess Maat by his left leg and the hieroglyphic sign for User by his right, so that the image of the god may be read as the name 'User-Maat-Re'. Nominally dedicated to Amen, Re-Herakhty and Ptah, the temple is effectively the temple of Ramesses II in the form of Re.

Between the seated colossi are featured the more important members of the royal family arranged in groups of three, one standing on each side of the colossus and one in front. In a revival of Amarna tradition it is the royal women, rather than the princes, who are so honoured and only two men, the eldest sons of the two principal wives, are included. From left to right, facing the temple, the triads are as follows: Princess Nebettawi, Princess Iset-Nofret II, Princess Bintanath; Dowager Queen Tuya, Prince Amenhirkhepshef, Queen Nefertari; Queen Nefertari, Prince Ramesses, Princess Baketmut; Princess Meritamen, Princess Nefertari II, Dowager Queen Tuya. A stela giving details of Ramesses' Hittite marriage was eventually carved at the southern end of the terrace fronting the façade, where there was a small sanctuary dedicated to Thoth. The northern end housed a chapel dedicated to the worship of the sun.

Beyond the façade the temple extended some 160 feet (48 metres) into the cliff. The great hall, bisected by two rows of four pillars in the form of Ramesses as the mummified Osiris, was decorated with scenes of the victorious king displaying his earthly triumphs before the gods. The northern part of the hall was dedicated to the northern deity Re-Herakhty. Here on the short walls we see the king leading defeated Hittites to Re and smiting Libyans before Re, while the battle of Kadesh is given pride of place on the long north wall. The opposite half of the hall was dedicated to the southern Amen-Re; on the short walls the king leads and smites Nubians before his god while the long wall is decorated with scenes of Syrian and Nubian campaigns. So far these are entirely conventional tableaux reflecting the role of the mortal pharaoh as defender of *maat*. Although the divine Ramesses does make an appearance on the western wall, it is clear that his figure is a late addition to the original scene.[26]

A doorway in the west wall of the great hall, once guarded by two hawk-headed sphinxes now housed in the British Museum, led to a second pillared hall. Here, and in the sanctuary beyond, we can detect a definite change in the nature of the images. The king has become divine, and so we now find Ramesses offering to himself, or performing rituals before the barque of his deified self. That this change in status occurred some time after the decoration of the temple had started is clear; in a vignette originally carved to show Ramesses offering to Amen and Mut a third deity – Ramesses identified with Khonsu – has been squeezed in between the royal couple, forcing Mut to stand to make way for her divine son. In the gloom of the sanctuary, beyond the second hall, four gods sit facing the barque shrine. Three of these four figures represent the gods of the powerful capitals of Egypt: Ptah of Memphis, Amen-Re of Thebes and Re-Herakhty of Heliopolis. Between Amen and Re sits Ramesses himself, the living deity of Pi-Ramesse.

As its modern name suggests, the Small Temple of Abu Simbel is built on a much smaller scale than its neighbour, extending only 80 feet back into the mountain. This temple was officially dedicated to Hathor of Ishbek (a 'ocal form of Hathor) who is strongly identified throughout with Queen Nefertari. Here the façade displays six colossal standing figures; two of Nefertari wearing the cow-horns and carrying the sistrum of Hathor, and four of Ramesses. The lesser figures of their children also appear. As befits a 'feminine' temple, the images on the internal walls are less overtly masculine than those of the Great Temple, and only on the scenes immediately to the left and the right of the entrance do we see Ramesses slaying the enemies of Egypt. Instead we are shown images of temple ritual, of Hathor the sacred cow and of Tawaret the hippopotamus goddess who protects women in labour. The columns in the first hall are topped with Hathor heads, while the niche at the back of the sanctuary contains the carved image of Hathor in the form of a cow, protecting Ramesses who stands beneath her head.

Year 30 saw an unexpected catastrophe – an earthquake – at Abu Simbel. The Smaller Temple suffered little damage but the Great Temple was badly affected. Inside the temple the pillars cracked and started to collapse, but the main damage was to the outside. Here the north door-jamb collapsed, the colossus to the north of the entrance lost an arm and the colossus to the south of the doorway lost its entire upper body. Restoration work started at once. The internal pillars were shored up, the door jamb was replaced and the missing arm restored. Little could be done about the collapsed colossus, however, and it remains disjointed to this day.

Worship at Abu Simbel survived the reign of Ramesses but eventually the cults were abandoned and the neglected temples were slowly but surely covered by a blanket of wind-blown sand. When Greek soldiers visited the Great Temple in the 6th century BC they left their graffiti at the new ground level, just under the knee of the southern colossus next to the entrance. By the time Johann Burckhardt rediscovered the site in 1813 the temple had been transformed into a massive mountain of sand. Recognizing the potential of his find Burckhardt referred the problem to an expert, and so in 1817 Giovanni Battista Belzoni went from organizing the transportation of the 'Younger Memnon' to excavating at Abu Simbel. Paying his workmen a penny per day, but promising them a share of the gold believed to be hidden within the temple, Belzoni stripped the temple of 30 feet (9 metres) of sand to reveal one of the most magnificent monuments of the Ramesside age. However, Abu Simbel was too far off the beaten track to attract many visitors. The evolution of Abu Simbel into one of the world's most popular tourist attractions is a relatively modern development.

When, in 1954, the decision was taken to build the Aswan High Dam, the monuments of Nubia came under unprecedented threat. The artificial lake planned to provide Egypt with a regulated supply of water would extend over 300 miles (500 kilometres) southwards along the Nile Valley from the Egyptian town of Aswan to the Dal Cataract in Sudan, and all monuments standing in its way – including the Abu Simbel temples and the temples of Beit el-Wali, Wadi es-Sebua, Derr and Gerf Hussein – would be irretrievably lost beneath the water. The problem was seen as an international one. An appeal was launched by UNESCO in 1960, and a series of touring exhibitions set off from Cairo to raise awareness of the crisis in Europe, Scandinavia and America. Even the international postal services became involved in the 'Nubian awareness' campaign, so that some three millennia after his death Ramesses smiled impassively from letters in countries as diverse as Pakistan, Nigeria and Guatemala.

The smaller, free-standing Nubian temples could be dismantled and moved with relative ease and so, in spite of grave doubts over the propriety of re-siting ancient monuments, this was done. While the Graeco-Roman temple of Philae was rebuilt on the neighbouring island of Agilkia, some monuments left Nubia altogether; the Metropolitan Museum of Art in New York, for example, received the Dendur Temple which is now reconstructed within the museum. Abu Simbel, massive and cut into the living rock, posed its own particular problems. Various solutions were proposed. Should the temples be covered by a protective dome and allowed to sink beneath the water? Should they be completely surrounded by a reinforced dam which would keep out the water? The solution eventually adopted was, in theory, the simplest one. If the water was to cover the monuments as they stood, the monuments must be moved clear of the water. At Abu Simbel this involved moving the temples plus sections of the original cliff face 215 feet (65 metres) above their original site to an artificially created environment. The practical difficulties, and the expense involved, would have been enough to make even Belzoni blanch.[27]

As work on the high dam had already started, and the water level was starting to rise, the first step was to build a coffer dam which would protect the vulnerable sandstone from contact with the water. With this temporary protection in place each temple was cut into giant blocks which were strengthened and then transported up the cliff face. Here they were reassembled inside two concrete domes which were subsequently covered by an artificial hill extending over and behind the monuments.

The operation took place between 1964 and 1968, and the temples were reopened on 22 September 1968. The rescue had involved some 1,700 workmen, a vast array of modern machinery and a total cost of 36 million US dollars.

Notes

1 This piece is illustrated and described in Freed, R. E. (1987), *Ramesses the Great; his life and world*, Memphis: 136.

2 Discussed, with the history of the development of the Egyptian temple, in Snape, S. R. (1996), *Egyptian Temples*, Princes Risborough: 12.

3 For an accessible guide to the monuments of Egypt, including those of Thebes, consult Seton-Williams, V. and Stocks, P. (1983), *Blue Guide: Egypt*, London and New York. See also Baines, J. and Malek, J. (1980), *Atlas of Ancient Egypt*, Oxford.

4 Newby, P. H. (1980), *Warrior Pharaohs: the rise and fall of the Egyptian Empire*, London: 164–5.

5 Talbot Kelly, R. (1902, revised 1912), *Egypt Painted and Described*, London: 95.

6 For a fascinating example of the Egyptologist working as a detective see Seele, K. C. (1940), *The Coregency of Ramses II with Seti I and the date of the great hypostyle hall at Karnak*, Chicago; this evidence is reviewed and revised in Murnane, W. J. (1975), 'The earlier reign of Ramesses II and his co-regency with Sety I', *Journal of Near Eastern Studies* 34:3: 153–90.

7 Ricke, H., Hughes, G. and Wente, E. F. (1967), *The Beit el-Wali Temple of Ramesses II*, Chicago: 3–5, 7–9.

8 Translation after Redford, D. B. (1971), 'The Earliest Years of Ramesses II, and the building of the Ramesside Court at Luxor', *Journal of Egyptian Archaeology* 57: 110–19. This article provides a useful discussion of the sequence of events during the early years of Ramesses' solo rule.

9 Translation after Redford, D. B. (1971), 'The Earliest Years of Ramesses II, and the building of the Ramesside Court at Luxor', *Journal of Egyptian Archaeology* 57: 110–19: 113.

10 Discussed in Kemp, B. J. (1989), *Ancient Egypt; anatomy of a civilization*, 192, 195.

11 The Abydos Dedication text. This text, and the building of the Seti temple, are discussed, with references, in Murnane, W. J. (1977), *Ancient Egyptian Co-Regencies*, Chicago: 73–6, 82–4. For a full translation of the text see Kitchen, K. A. (1996), *Ramesside Inscriptions Translated and Annotated 2: Ramesses II Royal Inscriptions*, Oxford: 162–74.

12 A suggestion made in Kitchen, K. A. (1982), *Pharaoh Triumphant*, Warminster: 45.

13 This area was the subject of ground-penetrating radar explorations conducted by David L. Grumman Jr, as part of a University of Pennsylvania mission in 1992, led by Steven Snape. The results of this work are as yet unpublished.

14 Quban Stela (Year 3) and Aksha Inscription; for a full translation of this text consult Kitchen, K. A. (1996), *Ramesside Inscriptions 2: Ramesses II Royal Inscriptions*, Oxford: 188–93.

15 These events are discussed with references in Kitchen, K. A. (1982), *Pharaoh Triumphant*, Warminster: 35, 119–20.

16 From a letter written by the visitor Pabasa; for a fuller translation of this letter see Menu, B. (1999), *Ramesses the Great; warrior and builder*, London: 77.

17 Papyrus Anastasi II 4–5. The geography of the city is discussed in detail in Uphill, E. P. (1984), *The Temples of Per Ramesses*, Warminster.

18 For a discussion of the king as god see Hornung, E. (1983), *Conceptions of God in Ancient Egypt: the one and the many*, London: 135–42. For a specific discussion of the deification of Ramesses consult Habachi, L. (1969), *Features of the Deification of Ramesses II*, Mainz.

19 The exhibition catalogue provides details of the restoration and transportation of the colossus. See Freed, R. E. (1987), *Ramesses the Great: his life and world*, Memphis.

20 Pliny, *Natural History*, Book 36:14.

21 For a detailed description of this piece, complete with photograph and bibliography, consult Desroches Noblecourt, C. (1985), *The Great Pharaoh Ramses II and His Time*, translated by E. Mialon, Montreal: exhibit 4.

22 The group statues of Ramesses and associated theories are discussed with references in Eaton-Krauss, M. (1991), 'Ramesses – Re who creates the gods', in Bleiberg, E. and Freed, R. (eds) *Fragments of a Shattered Visage: The Proceedings of the International Symposium of Ramesses the Great*, Memphis: 15–23.

23 It is possible that Tutankhamen, too, was worshipped at the Nubian temple of Faras. In contrast, the Asiatic temples, reflecting the more autonomous position of the eastern vassals, were generally dedicated to local gods.

24 Numerous works have been published on the temples of Abu Simbel; as a preliminary reference consult Porter, B. and Moss, R. (1951 reissued 1975) *Topographical Bibliography of Ancient Egyptian Hieroglyphic Texts, Reliefs and paintings 7: Nubia, the desert and Outside Egypt*, Oxford. For the Greater Temple see El-Achirie, H. and Jacquet, J. (1984), *Le Grand Temple d'Abou-Simbel*, Cairo. For the Smaller Temple see Desroches Noblecourt, C. and Kuentz, C. (1968), *Le Petit Temple d'Abou Simbel: 'Nofretari pour qui se leve le Dieu-Soleil'*, 2 Vols, Paris.

25 Kitchen, K. A. (1980), *Ramesside Inscriptions 3: Ramesses II, his contemporaries*, Oxford: 203–4.

26 For a discussion of the evolution of the decoration of the temple see Habachi, L. (1969), *Features of the Deification of Ramesses II*, Gluckstadt: 2–10.

27 The story of the international campaign to save the monuments of Nubia is told in Save-Söderbergh, T. (1987), *Temples and Tombs of Ancient Nubia: the international rescue campaign at Abu Simbel, Philae and other sites*, Paris and London.

5

Ramesses the Husband

Seti had marked Ramesses' co-regency – his effective coming of age – by presenting his teenage son with his own harem housing some of Egypt's most desirable women: 'female royal attendants who were like unto the great beauties of the palace'. Soon, in the memorable words of Kenneth Kitchen: '. . . the palace nurseries must fairly have resounded with the gurgles, yelps and whimpers of each year's crop of bouncing royal babies, taking no account of such as may have passed away in extreme infancy.'[1]

Polygyny, while not forbidden to commoners, was very much a royal pleasure. Few men could afford to maintain more than one family at a time and multiple marriages generally occurred in sequence, following death or divorce. It may be that, as in many societies, the lower status women included in a non-royal household, the servants, slaves and female dependants, were regarded as a legitimate target of the higher ranking males; unfortunately, this type of unofficial union is almost impossible to detect in the surviving textual record. No commoners, as far as we know, maintained an official harem and the king's houseful, or more accurately houses-full, of beautiful, sexually receptive women acted as a clear signal of his wealth and power and set him apart from other men.

The royal harems were not the dynastic equivalent of the Turkish seraglio: hot-houses full of nubile young women trained in the arts of love and guarded by impassive eunuchs. Nor were they the restrictive, shadowy prisons of imperial India, China and Japan, where upper-class females inhabited a twilight world hidden from any possible contact with men and where it was accepted by all that 'ghosts and women had best remain invisible'.[2] Although it undoubtedly served an important purpose in segregating the women chosen as sexual partners for pharaoh, the Egyptian harem also provided a secure home for the loose and unattached women of the court. Unmarried and widowed sisters, daughters and aunts, unwanted foreign brides and their retinues, and secondary wives with growing families of children could all be accommodated either temporarily or permanently in the extensive palaces which were dotted along the Nile. In this respect the Egyptian harem palaces may be compared to the convents of medieval Europe which housed large numbers of females, both those with a true religious vocation and those with no other place of refuge: orphans, illegitimate daughters of the nobility and clergy, disabled women, divorced women and widows plus their daughters.

The ladies of the royal harem spent their lives within the palace; at death, most were buried in the nearby harem graveyards with only a favoured few being honoured with tombs in the royal cemeteries. This was in many ways a comfortable and protected life. Nevertheless, particularly for those sent unwillingly to Egypt, life within the harem must have been a dull and somewhat lonely existence. There was no guarantee that the majority of the ladies would ever meet their king, let alone carry his child. Pharaoh, perpetually travelling up and down the Nile, would visit the harem as and when he wished. His favourites, and his consort, might travel with him, being accommodated in the women's quarters attached to all the royal palaces. The remainder, far too numerous to transport around the country, were left behind. Isolated from the day-to-day affairs of the court, the lower ranking ladies of the harem were expected to work for their keep. There was a constant demand for maids, hairdressers, cooks and washerwomen to service the higher ranking wives. The ladies of *Mer Wer*, a long-established harem palace situated on the edge of the Faiyum, ran a thriving textile industry.

Within the harem there were three broad categories of royal 'wife'. The degree of importance attached to the offspring of these various ladies can help us to rank the mothers. At the head of the pyramid stood the consort or principal queen, a titled lady of ritual importance whose son was destined to inherit the throne and whose children were considered to be part of the nuclear royal family. Next came the secondary wives or lesser queens whose numbers might include high-born Egyptian women, foreign brides of some prestige and favourites of the king; their children just might, given the appropriate circumstances, succeed their father. Finally came the numerous concubines of relatively humble birth whose main duty was to please the king and whose children were generally disregarded in terms of the succession. In addition, the harem palace housed the servants and attendants of the higher ranking ladies and the administrators, many of them male, who managed the day-to-day running of the estate.

Like any good Egyptian father, Seti made sure that his son acquired a suitable bride. Had not the 18th Dynasty scribe Any advised:

Take yourself a wife while you are young, so that she may give you a son. You should father him before you grow old and should live to see him become a man. Happy is he who fathers many children; he gains respect because of his progeny.[3]

The beautiful Nefertari was chosen as the wife of Prince Ramesses and as the mother of the future king of Egypt. Royal weddings were not the media events that they are today and the date of their union went unrecorded as did the births of their numerous offspring.[4] However, firm indirect evidence – a variety of scenes and texts preserved on the temple walls decorated early in Ramesses' reign – allows us a glimpse of the young queen and her growing family, confirming that Ramesses and Nefertari must have married and produced their first son before Seti's death.

Ramesses was the first member of his family to marry knowing that, barring accidents, his wife would become queen of Egypt. His father and his grandfather had both married before their royal destiny became clear; that their wives both had a proven ability to produce healthy male children was almost certainly an important factor in Horemheb's choice of Ramesses I as his successor. How then did Ramesses, or Seti on his behalf, set about choosing a future queen? Unfortunately we have no means of knowing.

Many of Egypt's queens were themselves of royal blood, being the daughter of the previous king and queen and therefore the half or full sister of their husband-brother. This was by no means essential, however; the old 'heiress princess' theory which stated that the right to rule was passed through the female line, compelling the crown prince to marry his heiress sister, is now discredited.[5] Incestuous marriages, a reflection of the divine brother–sister unions of Osiris and Isis, Seth and Nephthys, differentiated the royal family from the rest of humanity by emphasizing

Fig 5.1   Queen Tuya, her son-in-law Tia and daughter Tia

their right to emulate the gods. Such unions had several practical benefits. Sibling incest kept outsiders at arm's length from the throne, restricted the number of royal grandchildren, and ensured that a suitably trained princess rather than an uncouth commoner was entrusted with the most important role that an Egyptian lady could be asked to perform. Sibling marriage was, however, extremely rare if not unknown outside the immediate royal family and Ramesses I and Seti had both contracted the type of conventional unions that we would expect from Egypt's upper classes; they had married girls chosen from within their own social and economic circle, possibly from within their own extended family.[6]

Seti, himself married to Tuya, or Mut-Tuya, daughter of the Lieutenant of Chariotry Raia, had continued this tradition by marrying his daughter Tia to the confusingly named Tia, a high ranking civil servant and son of Amenwahsu, also a civil servant. Tia the husband later occupied two prominent Thebes-based positions, becoming 'Superintendent of the Treasury and Superintendent of the Cattle of the temple of Usermaatre Setepenre in the Estate of Amen [the Ramesseum]'. Tia, sister of Ramesses, played no formal role in her brother's reign although both she and her husband benefited from their royal connections. Tia followed the career path of many an upper-class Egyptian lady; she did not take paid employment outside the home but dedicated herself to religious causes, acting at various times as a divine singer of Hathor of the Syca-mores, of Re of Heliopolis and of Amen-Great-in-Victories. The couple, and their family and household, were eventually buried in the Sakkara necropolis. Their grand but somewhat shoddily built tomb, adjoining the tomb of Horemheb, included a colonnaded courtyard, a cult room, various chapels and even a pyramid.[7]

Tia had been born a commoner. The ephemeral Hentmire, a lady once firmly accepted as the much younger daughter of Seti and Tuya but now equally or even more likely to be their granddaughter, was born a princess.[8] This made a great deal of difference. Outside the royal family there were no constraints on marriage and we know of Egyptian-born women marrying both foreigners and slaves. Within the royal family, however, there was a tradition of hypergamy; a prince or even a king might marry a commoner but a daughter of the king did not marry beneath herself. She could not therefore marry a non-royal. Such a marriage would be considered degrading for the princess and, a more practical consideration, may well have led to problems over the succession as, in the absence of an obvious royal heir, an ambitious son-in-law might be tempted to claim the throne on behalf of his wife and children. The field of potential bridegrooms was therefore extremely limited for an Egyptian princess, a phenomenon which has been noted in other hypergamous cultures:

Since women of the highest group can only marry men of their own rank, women of high rank will either remain unmarried or the inequality must be addressed in some manner, as by the practice of polygyny, or by means of female infanticide . . .[9]

This perhaps explains why we know of few examples of commoner men bettering themselves by marrying into the royal family. Marriage with a princess was all but impossible, and so socially ambitious brothers and fathers schemed to introduce not themselves but their sisters and daughters into the royal family or, at a lower social level, to get them admitted to the royal harem. However, even at the highest levels it was not seemly to boast of a personal link with the royal family via a woman; Anen and Ay, brothers of Queen Tiy, failed to mention this most important relationship in their tombs.

Denied an Egyptian-commoner husband, Egypt's princesses were also forbidden to travel abroad and marry the foreign kings who might with some justification claim to be of equal status to pharaoh. The state propaganda which decreed all foreigners to be inferior effectively rendered such inter-state marriages inconceivable. The ban on non-Egyptian marriage was a long-established prohibition, made explicit by

Amenhotep III, who wrote to his brother-in-law, the King of Babylon, to explain that 'from time immemorial no daughter of the king of Egypt has been given in marriage to anyone'.[10] This left the Egyptian princesses in a difficult position, their only possible bridegrooms being their fathers, their brothers or their half-brothers. Princess Hentmire, daughter, sister or even niece of Ramesses, duly married her brother/father/uncle to become one of a series of secondary queens. She maintained a low profile throughout Ramesses' reign and, as far as we know, bore him no children. Predeceasing her husband, some time after Year 40 she was buried in the Valley of the Queens (QV75).[11] Like so many others her tomb was looted in antiquity, and her anthropoid sarcophagus was later reused by a 22nd Dynasty priest buried at Medinet Habu.

Status within the royal family was entirely dependent upon the relationship of the individual to the king. All official titles reflected this, so that where in modern English we might expect to find a queen, queen mother, prince and princess we find instead a 'King's Wife', 'King's Mother', 'King's Son' and 'King's Daughter'. These relationships could be compounded, allowing some lucky ladies to claim the multiple title of 'King's Daughter, King's Wife and King's Mother', and could be shared; the royal family often included many King's Children and more than one King's Wife, but rarely more than one living King's Mother.

Just as Ramesses was able to don the semi-divine mantle of pharaoh on the death of his father, so his principal wife, Nefertari, was able to gain status and ritual power at the moment of her husband's accession. At the same time the dowager queen, Tuya, immediately shed her queenly duties to assume the influential role of King's Mother. In Hatti there could only be one living queen and Pudukhepa would have been forced to wait for the death of her mother-in-law before she assumed the full queenship. In Egypt there was a place for both the queen and the queen mother. The queen's role seems to have been one of support and fertility; with the addition of a ritual element, the queen played the part of a conventional dynastic wife magnified on the public stage. The queen mother – usually past the age of fertility and invariably without a husband – was accorded a more political role, functioning as her son's advisor; under extreme circumstances she might even become regent, temporarily ruling on behalf of an infant king. Although the queen-consort played a prominent role on ceremonial and ritual occasions, it seems that she may well have achieved her maximum influence and power on the death of her husband. We know that Ramesses took some of the younger members of his family on his foreign campaigns; did he leave Queen Tuya behind to protect his interests?

The most obvious duty of the Egyptian queen was that of any wife: she was expected to provide her husband with at least one healthy son. If she failed the harem could usually be relied upon to produce a clutch of sons born to secondary wives, but this could lead to dynastic problems. How would the succession progress? Via the eldest son? Or the son born to the highest ranking or longest-serving secondary queen? Or the son born to the king's favourite? The presence of too many eager sons egged on by over-ambitious mothers was likely to complicate rather than simplify matters, and the unexpected succession of Hatchepsut, and the chaos at the end of the Amarna Age, served as an uncomfortable warning of what could happen when a series of queens failed to produce a legitimate male heir. Nefertari proved to be a fertile wife, providing Ramesses with as many as ten children, including his eldest son, Amenhirwenemef, his third-born son, Prehirwenemef, and Meritamen, one of his favourite daughters. None of these children, however, was destined to outlive their father.

The need for a queen went far beyond the requirement to produce an heir to the throne. It was accepted that the queen was an extension of the king, just as any wife could be seen as an extension of or substitute for her husband, so that on ritual occasions the queen became the personification of the female aspect of kingship. As such she became an essential component in the theology underpinning the Egyptian monarchy. To the king, as chief priest, fell the responsibility of offering to all the state gods. There were, however, a few rituals which required the participation of a woman. The God's Wife of Amen, and the God's Hand of Amen, were priestly titles borne by some of Egypt's most prominent New Kingdom ladies, including princesses, queens and dowager queens. Their ritual duties seem to have included the sexual stimulation of the great god himself, the 'god's hand' being a clear reference to the masturbation which enabled the lone creator god to reproduce. These roles seem oddly crude to modern ears; we are accustomed to separating the physical from the spiritual. To Egypt's farming community, nature's regular cycles, the rise and fall of the Nile, the fertility of the soil and the breeding of animals were of overwhelming importance and not a subject for false modesty.

Egypt's kings were obviously, aggressively male and only one king – Akhenaten – ever attempted to express both the feminine and masculine sides of his role by merging his appearance with that of his queen until it becomes impossible for modern observers to tell the two apart. It seems that this overtly masculine king was incapable of functioning correctly without his feminine counterpart. We therefore find the highly atypical female king Hatchepsut, in the absence of a wife, using her daughter Neferure to perform the actions normally allocated to the queen. Similarly, Queen Nefertiti, when conducting religious rituals normally reserved for the king, was accompanied by her eldest daughter, Meritaten, who was able to act as 'wife' to her mother.

Even though tradition could occasionally be stretched far enough to allow a woman to assume the male role, there was still a need for a queenly presence to make the royal action complete. Although the queen's role is almost invariably passive – she observes and supports her husband's actions without interfering with them – it is nevertheless essential. A king without the support of a queen would appear to be an offence against *maat*.

Queens, like kings, were undeniably born to human mothers and were, certainly up until the point of their husband's accession, fully mortal themselves. However, they slept with a semi-divine being, were often the daughter of a semi-divine being, and were expected to give birth to a being who would eventually become semi-divine. They could not fail to be affected by the cloud of divinity which surrounded them, becoming if not semi-, then at least slightly-divine in turn. The ceremonial regalia allotted to the New Kingdom queens – the double uraeus, vulture headdress, double feathers, sistrum and ankh – reflected this exalted position, being borrowed wholesale from various goddesses. The extent of the queen's divinity very much depended upon the perceived divinity of her king, with those monarchs who sought to promote their own deification allowing their wives to approach the roles of living goddesses. Thus we find Queen Tiy being worshipped at Sedeinga, her temple being the female aspect of Amenhotep III's Soleb temple, while at Amarna her daughter-in-law, Nefertiti, becomes a divine fertility symbol worshipped alongside Akhenaten and the Aten. Nefertari, with her temple at Abu Simbel, was following an established precedent.

The political duties of the queen varied depending on the needs of her time and the expectations of her husband. The queens of the New Kingdom had, on the whole, been a forceful group of ladies. The earliest queens, those of the late 17th and early 18th Dynasties, had helped their husbands to unify the country after the disruptions of the Second Intermediate Period. Tetisheri, Ahhotep and Ahmose-Nefertari had all become legends in their own lifetimes, with Ahmose-Nefertari surviving long after death as a deity worshipped by the tomb-builders of Deir el-Medina. Her cult became popular during Ramesses' reign, when statues of Ahmose-Nefertari were often manufactured with the face and dress of Nefertari.

Hatchepsut's (as far as we can tell) unchallenged assumption of power showed just how much political influence a determined queen/queen-mother could achieve; the fact that she managed to rule her country efficiently and peacefully for over twenty years is a strong indication that she must have had the backing of the male élite. The death of Hatchepsut, however, signalled a decline in the status of the queen. It would appear that her co-regent, Tuthmosis III, had had enough of strong women, and we know little of his wives and their immediate successors.

By the time of Amenhotep III strong queens were again in evidence. Queen Tiy was allowed to break many of the unwritten rules; she was included in diplomatic correspondence, depicted at the same scale as her husband, and even allowed to assume the guise of a sphinx to trample the enemies of Egypt. In Nubia, as we have already seen, she was eventually worshipped as a goddess. Tiy is the first queen to adopt the cow horns of Hathor, associating both herself and the queenship with this goddess at precisely the time that her husband was struggling to assert his own divine nature. Her daughter-in-law, Nefertiti, took this precedent to extremes; we find her engaging in a number of kingly and priestly roles which have led to speculation that she may even have ruled Egypt after her husband's death.[12] The tradition of strong-willed Amarna women continued with Ankhesenamen, the writer of the famous letter to Suppiluliumas, and Mutnodjmet, consort of Horemheb, who also appears in the guise of a sphinx.

The Ramesside women seem to have been more modest in their ambitions, with Queens Sitre and Mut-Tuya or Tuya remaining strictly conventional, rather shadowy consorts throughout their husbands' reigns. Sitre is rewarded for her reticence by her historical obscurity; her only monument is her tomb in the Valley of the Queens (QV38). Tuya, with her son's accession, enjoyed a late flourishing as the respected Mother of the King, a lady considered important enough to correspond with the Hittite court. Our best, most complete views of Tuya date to the period after her husband's death; there is a graceful standing statue of the queen housed in the Vatican Museum where Tuya appears with her daughter or granddaughter Hentmire, and a carved alabaster Canopic jar stopper in the form of her head, recovered from the Valley of the Queens and now housed in the collection of Luxor Museum.[13] These both show us the conventionally pretty, somewhat bland smiling face of an ageless Queen Tuya, her delicate features dominated by a long, heavy wig. Only her small square chin can be recognized as a family trait; the same chin can be seen on both Ramesses and his daughter Meritamen. Tuya died soon after Year 22 and was interred in an impressive tomb in the Valley of the Queens (QV80). Here she was stripped of the first part of her name to become plain Tuya for eternity; the loss of the prefix Mut- suggests that her death had ended an almost divine earthly status.

Like all good Egyptians, Ramesses loved his mother. Tuya's image was included on the façade of the Abu Simbel temple where she appears on the same scale as the other royal women and sons, standing beside the second and fourth colossi. She was featured heavily in the Ramesseum where she sat in colossal form beside her much larger son in the first courtyard, and appeared on the walls of the hypostyle hall where, along with Nefertari, she shook her sistrum. There was even a chapel dedicated to Tuya, where she was identified with Hathor, Mistress of the West. This temple is now entirely demolished and is represented only by a series of reused blocks found at Medinet Habu plus a doorpost incorporated within the dig house built by the Swiss excavator Edouard Naville.[14]

It would probably not be too cynical to suggest that Ramesses' promotion – or exploitation – of Tuya went further than simple filial love. Just as a woman gained status from her relationship to the king, so kings could gain increased legitimacy from their mothers. While it was by no means essential that the mother of the king should herself be of royal birth, it was accepted that a blue-blooded wife or mother could help to strengthen a dubious claim to the throne. Ramesses, born before his father became pharaoh, was denied a royal mother. Undaunted, he set about rewriting the story of his own miraculous birth to provide himself with a divine father. Now Ramesses was not only to be the son of Seti, he was to be the son of Amen himself. Queen Tuya was, of necessity, accorded a starring role in her son's revised nativity story.

Ramesses was only the third New Kingdom pharaoh to make an explicit claim of divine birth. King Hatchepsut had been the first to show her own mother, Queen Ahmose, coyly sitting on a bed to receive the ankh of life from Amen who, to preserve the queen's reputation, had considerably disguised himself as her absent husband. If the illustrations of this divine conception are modest and discreet, the accompanying text leaves nothing to the imagination:

She smiled at his majesty. He went to her immediately, his penis erect before her . . . She was filled with joy at the sight of his beauty. His love passed into his limbs. The place was flooded with the god's fragrance, and all his perfumes were from Punt.[15]

The royal baby is made in heaven on the potter's wheel of the ram-headed creator, Khnum, and born in Egypt some nine months later. The proud father, Amen, acknowledges his infant daughter, the gods rejoice and the people of Egypt celebrate the miraculous birth. The right of the infant to rule Egypt has been made explicit and is acknowledged by all.

Hatchepsut had good reason to devise this tale. As a woman her claim on the throne was tenuous and she consistently used every means within her power to justify her reign. Her story proved that, as the daughter of both Tuthmosis I and Amen, she was predestined to inherit her earthly father's throne. It is at first sight less obvious why Amenhotep III, the entirely legitimate heir of his father, Tuthmosis IV, should have felt the need to copy her cartoon story wholesale on the wall of the refurbished Luxor Temple. Amenhotep had the strongest of claims to the throne and enjoyed a long, peaceful and prosperous reign untroubled, as far as we can tell, by any rival. It therefore seems that his adoption of the myth was intended not to cast light upon his own royalty, but upon his own divinity.

These two birth stories would have been familiar to Ramesses as his workmen were involved in attempts to reverse the damage of the Amarna period at both Deir el-Bahari and Luxor. Rather than devise his own legend – and perhaps believing that a story which had so obviously 'worked' for two successful pharaohs would work for him too – he plagiarized his predecessors. The story of Ramesses' divine birth was told in the Ramesseum where it found an appropriate site in the chapel dedicated to his mother. Here were displayed all the now traditional images: the queen sat unchaperoned on a bed facing Amen who held the ankh in his right hand while stretching out with his left hand towards the queen. The now broken text which accompanied this scene made the proceedings specific: the queen is described as 'The Mother of the God, Mut . . . , the Mother of the King, Tuya . . .', and as for Amen, once again '. . . his scent was that of the land of the gods and his perfume was that of Punt . . .' Two scenes at Karnak were designed to reinforce this idea of divine birth: here we see the infant Ramesses suckled by a goddess and the pre-birth Ramesses moulded on the potter's wheel of Khnum, an image which is repeated in the Seti temple at Abydos.

Ramesses is using his legend to deliver two messages. The story confirms his predestined right to rule. More importantly, with a divine father, Ramesses himself must be recognized as at least semi-divine. *The Blessing of Ptah upon Ramesses II*,[16] a lengthy text dating to Year 35 and preserved at Abu Simbel and at Karnak, also includes details of the divine birth of the king. In this case however it is Ptah, rather than Amen, who is the heavenly father:

Words spoken by Ptah-Tatonen, he of the tall plumes and sharp horns, who begot the gods: I am your father, who begot you as a god to act as King of South and North Egypt on my seat. I decree for you the lands that I created, their rulers carry their revenue to you. They come to bring you their tribute, because of the greatness of [your renown] . . .[17]

The father-god may have changed, but the message is strengthened. Ramesses is the son of the gods; in this version Queen Tuya's role is minimized and Ramesses describes himself at one point as 'King of Upper and Lower Egypt, Usermaatre Setepenre, son of Re, who came forth of Tatonen [Ptah], born of Sekhmet the mighty, Ramesses II given life'.

Queen Nefertari is one of the most tantalizing figures from ancient

Egypt. Her name is tolerably well known to the modern world – particularly to those who have sailed on the Nile cruise ship *Nefertari* – and yet we know almost nothing about her. As their pre-royal lives were considered to be of little or no importance, few of Egypt's commoner queens provide us with details of their birth families while their families in turn traditionally made little or no reference to their illustrious in-laws. Nefertari's parentage therefore remains hidden, although the fact that she never claims to be a King's Daughter strongly suggests that she was not a member of the immediate royal family.

The discovery, within her tomb, of a curious glazed button or knob, possibly the head of a cane, decorated with the cartouche of King Ay has, however, become a matter of intense speculation. Was the knob included in her tomb because of a personal link to Ay, just as Tutankhamen had been buried with a lock of his grandmother's hair? Or was it merely included as a curiosity, or as part of a reused object? If the inclusion of Ay's cartouche within Nefertari's tomb was deliberate rather than accidental, can we hazard a guess that the queen was actually a member of his close family? A younger daughter of Ay would be the sister or half-sister of Queens Nefertiti and Mutnodjmet.[18] This suggestion seems to be supported by the otherwise curious discovery, in the temple of Min at the Middle Egyptian city of Akhmim (opposite modern Sohag), home town of Ay, of a colossal statue of Nefertari's daughter, Meritamen.

In theory it is entirely possible that Nefertari was the daughter of Ay. If we imagine that Nefertari was conceived at the very latest during the last year of Ay's reign she would have lived through the reigns of Horemheb (variously accorded a reign length of 12–32 years), Ramesses I (16 months) and Seti (10–16 years) and therefore must have been a minimum of twenty-four years of age when Ramesses came to the throne. Of course, the likelihood is that she would have been much older; a sister just slightly younger than Mutnodjmet would also have lived through the reigns of Akhenaten (17 years), Smenkhkare (2 years), Tutankhamen (9 years) and Ay (4 years) and would therefore be approaching sixty at the time of her marriage. Ramesses is unlikely to have contracted a marriage with such an elderly lady, no matter how impressive her pedigree, and it would perhaps be wise to widen the field of possible parents, and consider that Nefertari was possibly a lesser member of Ay's family, maybe a granddaughter, niece or great-niece.

Would Ramesses have married a lady so closely linked to the Amarna court which, having so grievously offended against *maat*, was soon to be obliterated from the Ramesside records of the Kings of Egypt? Probably. Kings did not avoid marriage with the daughters of their enemies – the brides in these diplomatic unions are perhaps to be seen as the ultimate hostages – and we have already seen Horemheb following a similar path by marrying Mutnodjmet, sister of Nefertiti. We should also remember that Ay's royal connections stretched back beyond the court of Akhenaten; as the brother of Queen Tiy he was also the brother-in-law of the great Ramesside role model Amenhotep III. As yet, the evidence cannot be considered conclusive and we can only state that Nefertari, like her mother-in-law before her, was almost certainly chosen from the restricted circle of Egypt's élite.

Fig 5.2   The goddess Isis holds the ankh to Nefertari's nostrils and so offers her eternal life

Nefertari's epithet 'Beloved of Mut' links the queen with the goddess-wife of Amen, and in so doing suggests that she may have been a southerner, although this is certainly not conclusive evidence; Tuya, or Mut-Tuya, believed to be a northerner, was also linked with Mut. Within the Abu Simbel temple Nefertari becomes the personification of the goddess Sothis. Like her mother-in-law before her, she was also associated with Hathor, the cow-headed solar deity who, in her most gentle form, embodied sexuality, love, music and drunkenness and who was believed to protect women in labour. Sexuality, music, drunkenness and childbirth could all, however, be considered dangerous activities and Hathor had her darker side, appearing as the unpredictable Daughter of Re and Eye of Re.[19] Effectively, Hathor's dual nature was the nature of all women – in a society where human biology was not fully understood the hidden workings of women's bodies, and in particular their ability to bring forth life, were regarded with a fair amount of fear.

Contemporary images show Nefertari to have been as conventionally beautiful, slender and graceful as all New Kingdom queens. Her epithets, orthodox phrases designed to stress the queen's fragile femininity, hailed Nefertari as 'Rich of praise' and 'Possessor of charm, sweetness and love'. Certainly many modern observers have been smitten by her charms:

It is not often that one can say of a female head in an Egyptian wall painting that it is beautiful; but in these [Abu Simbel] portraits of the Queen, many times repeated on the walls of the first Hall of the Temple of Hathor, there is, if not positive beauty according to our western notions, much sweetness and much grace.[20]

From the start of her husband's reign Nefertari is shown to be a dutiful wife, supporting Ramesses on all appropriate ceremonial occasions. She observes, with equal calm, as Ramesses offers incense before the barque of Amen, or wields a sword to despatch an enemy. It seems likely that she accompanied her husband on the long march to Kadesh, where Ramesses took care to ensure that the royal family were shielded from the dangers of battle; it would never do to have the Queen of Egypt captured by the enemy. Her two titles Mistress of the South and North, and Lady of the Two Lands, parallel her husband's titles and confirm her right to be consort. Occasionally Nefertari is minute, appearing at Karnak at a scale which renders her less than knee high to Ramesses. Often she appears slightly smaller than Ramesses and larger than commoners. As many of Ramesses' Theban statues were adopted from the unfinished statuary of Amenhotep III their proportions were, of course, predetermined. Several of our known representations of Nefertari may in fact be adapted from images of Queen Tiy. At the newly built Abu Simbel Nefertari appears both in miniature (twice) on the façade of the Great Temple and in colossal form on the façade of her own temple. Here she stands some 33 feet (10 metres) high, at the same magnificent scale as her husband.

Did Ramesses truly love Nefertari, as so many have claimed? Visiting the Abu Simbel temple at the end of the 19th century, Miss Amelia Edwards certainly believed so, and her views are worth quoting at length as they set the pattern for subsequent interpretations of the relationship between Ramesses and his consort:

On every pillar, in every act of worship pictured on the walls, even in the sanctuary, we find the names of Ramesses and Nefertari 'coupled and inseparable' . . . We see, at all events, that Ramesses and Nefertari desired to leave behind them an imperishable record of the affection which united them on earth, and which they hoped would unite them in Amenti. What more do we need to know? We see that the Queen was fair, that the King was in his prime. We divine the rest; and the poetry of the place at all events is ours. Even in these barren solitudes there is wafted to us a breath from the shores of old romance. We feel that Love once passed this way, and that the ground is still hallowed where he trod.[21]

If size of monuments can truly be equated with size of passion, if a series of statues and a beautifully decorated – and obviously expensive – temple can be viewed as tokens of affection, then Ramesses truly did love his queen. However, to interpret Nefertari's impressive collection of monuments simply as the physical manifestation of Ramesses' love would be a naive over-simplification. A revered, respected and occasionally worshipped wife brought nothing but glory to her husband and the monuments and images which Ramesses commissioned to honour his consort were monuments which were also designed to honour their generous builder. At Abu Simbel no one was left in any doubt as to who had endowed the temple: the façade proclaimed 'Ramesses II has made a temple, excavated in the mountain, of eternal workmanship . . . for the Chief Queen Nefertari Beloved of Mut . . . Nefertari . . . for whom the sun shines'. The temple dedicated to Nefertari and Hathor was the Ramesside equivalent of Queen Tiy's Sedeinga temple; in both cases the temples of the queens complemented and were a part of the more impressive temples dedicated to their kings and we should not be too surprised to find that it is Ramesses rather than Nefertari who appears on the inner wall of the sanctuary to offer to Hathor. Only in her tomb, a monument which excludes all mention of her earthly family, her husband and her children, is Nefertari honoured entirely for herself.

Nefertari was alive in Year 24, when the royal family travelled south to inaugurate the Abu Simbel temples. However, she may already have been suffering from the illness which was to kill her. The Abu Simbel stele of the Viceroy Hekanakht shows a seated Nefertari dressed in full queenly regalia and, on a separate register, Princess Meritamen accompanying her father as a queen to worship the gods of the temple.[22] Nefertari betrays no obvious sign of illness but then, in a country where even the dead were depicted as bursting with life, we should not expect her to. As Nefertari is absent from the jubilee celebrations of Year 30 may we tentatively suggest that her death occurred somewhere between Years 24 and 30?

Ramesses buried Nefertari in 'Ta Set Neferu' or 'The Place of Beauty' (occasionally translated as 'The Place of the Royal Children'), now known as the Valley of the Queens. This was a dry valley or wadi in the south-western part of the Theban necropolis which had first been used during the 18th Dynasty and which was now to become the principal burial ground of the Ramesside royal wives and children. Here Queen Sitre (QV38) and Queen Tuya (QV80) were already interred and here their burials were to be comprehensively looted during the disturbances which heralded the end of the New Kingdom. Traces of mummies are disappointingly rare in these ransacked royal graves. This is somewhat unexpected. The thieves who stripped the mummies of their gold and jewels did not court attention by lugging the bodies out of the tombs; they hacked the bandages apart in situ, sifting quickly through the human remains and discarding the valueless linen and bones as they searched. We should therefore expect to find some evidence of their work, some fragments of mummy, bandages and bones. However the only Ramesside human remains to be recovered from the Valley of the Queens come from the tomb of Nefertari herself. Dare we hope that the bodies of the queens and royal children were removed, like those of their kings, for storage in a yet to be discovered royal cache? Meanwhile, left with part of a mummified leg – variously described as a foot or a pair of knees – which may or may not have belonged to Nefertari, we have no means of determining her cause of death.[23]

The beautifully decorated tomb of Nefertari (QV66) was discovered in 1904 by an Italian archaeological mission from Turin Museum directed by Ernesto Schiaparelli. Unfortunately, it too had been emptied in antiquity, although a later biological survey did reveal the presence of several spiders, silverfish, rodent droppings and beetle cases![24] The systematic clearing of the tomb and its immediate area has, however, been rewarded with unexpected finds including resin-coated wooden *shabti* figures, the knob bearing the cartouche of King Ay which has already been discussed, and, poignantly, a pair of Nefertari's delicate woven sandals.

In plan the tomb was relatively simple, although it employed the 'bent-axis' which was to mark the more important Ramesside burials including that of the king himself. Beyond the entrance a stepped passage led to a small square antechamber and side chamber from which a stairway descended to a burial chamber furnished with four pillars and three small side rooms. It was the decoration of the tomb which was extraordinary. The poor quality of the limestone in this part of the necropolis had prevented the workmen from carving directly into the rock. Using a technique which was to become more and more common as the 19th and 20th Dynasties progressed, they had been forced to coat the tomb walls with a thick layer of plaster. This had first been carved in raised relief and then painted with some of the most remarkable scenes ever to be recovered from the dynastic age. Schiaparelli recognized that the tomb was in a highly fragile state with the plastered walls showing considerable deterioration, the result of an unhappy combination of local landslides, the low situation of the tomb and the formation of crystallized salt deposits. Essentially, salt crystals were forming on the surface of the rock, pushing the plaster off the walls and so destroying the beautiful paintings. To make matters worse, several areas of paintwork were experiencing their own specific deterioration caused by the decomposition of the paint or its binding medium.

After decades of debate, recording and experimentation by many experts, the Nefertari conservation project, a joint enterprise conducted between the Egyptian Antiquities Organisation and The Getty Conservation Institute, has been able to mount a remarkable rescue operation, restoring many of the paintings to their original glory while avoiding the use of modern paint. The scenes once again glow with colour and life and, somewhat contrary to the advice of the conservators, the tomb of Nefertari has once again been opened to the public.[25]

14. The Turin statue of Ramesses II.

15. Ramesses' rock temple of Abu Simbel as seen by David Roberts in 1838–9.

16. The god Re-Herakhty on the façade of the temple at Abu Simbel.

17. Resurrecting Ramesses – the Nubian rescue campaign.

18. Ramesses as a child before the god Hauron.

19. Ramesses the King; a Pi-Ramesse statue recovered from Tanis.

20. Meritamen, daughter and wife of Ramesses II.

21. The tomb of Nefertari in the Valley of the Queens. Nefertari is brought before the god Re-Herakhty.

22. The gods Osiris and Atum in the tomb of Nefertari.

23. The deceased Nefertari plays a game of senet in her tomb.

24. Nefertari is guided by the goddess Isis.

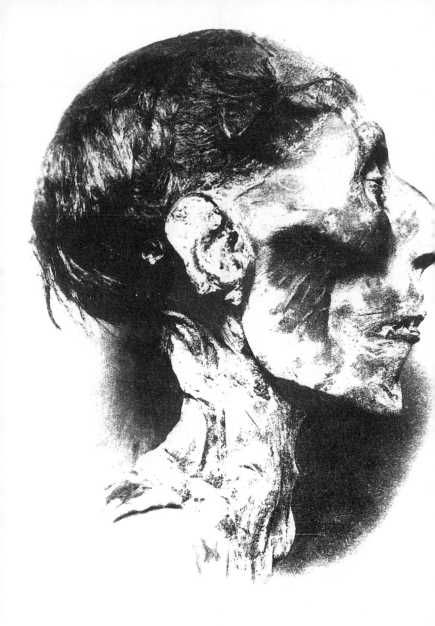

25. The mummified head of Ramesses II.

The artists who painted the tomb were not afraid to experiment with their medium. The introduction of shading – the darkening of folds of garments and skin, and the use of red to emphasize the contours of the face and arms – plus the use of a deep red for the lips brings a new life to the images. The carving in the tomb is of an extraordinarily high standard. Nevertheless, like so many Ramesside monuments there remain some signs of sloppy workmanship; paint-splashes, misplaced guide-lines, and un-retouched smudged edges all speak of rapid painting and it is obvious, and curious, that the ceiling was painted last, allowing blue drips to sully the paintwork beneath. The differences in the workmanship of the various gangs who painted the tomb are obvious to the modern eye.

The ceiling of the tomb is a dramatic dark blue night sky spangled with golden stars while the walls detail, in logical progression from antechamber to burial chamber, Nefertari's arduous progress from death as an embalmed mummy to perpetual life in the Kingdom of Osiris.[26] Chapters from the *Book of the Dead*, the essential spells which would guarantee Nefertari eternal life, are inscribed as an aid to the queen on her travels. In the antechamber we are shown the recently dead queen. Nefertari's mummified body lies on a bier protected by the divine mourners, Isis and Nephthys, who take the form of birds. Anubis, and the Four Sons of Horus, the divine beings most involved with the preservation of the body, are all present and Osiris himself appears to speak to the queen: 'I grant you eternity like Re, my father.' Here, too, in a separate scene we see Nefertari seated alone before her *senet* board; *senet* was a game enjoyed by the living but it was a game with strong religious undertones which would assist the deceased in the journey to the Afterlife. Within her tomb Nefertari is playing an invisible adversary and her victory – the victory of her goodness and purity – will help her to survive her forthcoming ordeals unscathed.

The entrance to the burial chamber is guarded by Maat, who opens her winged arms wide to protect the deceased. Within the chamber are representations of five of the twelve gateways to the Kingdom of Osiris, each guarded by three malevolent spirits. Nefertari must be able to name each of the gates, each of the gatekeepers and each of ten guards who squat, armed with large knives, in underworld caverns. Fortunately hieroglyphic inscriptions provide the correct answers. Finally, all ordeals successfully completed, the four columns surrounding the pink granite sarcophagus represent the resurrection of the queen. Here Horus appears as a priest to bring life to the deceased.

Nefertari's death left Ramesses without a wife and Egypt in need of a queen. This was a surprisingly rare event and there was little precedent for Ramesses to follow. Queens who survived the perils of childbirth tended to be hardy ladies who went on to outlive their kings; the institution of the harem may even have helped to prolong their lives by sparing them the ordeal of an annual pregnancy. Ramesses now turned to his harem to look for his new queen. It is generally accepted, but nowhere specifically stated, that Iset-Nofret, a secondary wife of long standing and mother of several of his favourite children, was promoted and left the seclusion of the harem to become Great King's Wife.

If we know little about Nefertari we know even less about Iset-Nofret, who is almost totally eclipsed by her glamorous predecessor and her charismatic children.[27] Iset-Nofret's origins are as determinedly obscure as those of Nefertari, although the fact that she too avoids the title of 'King's Daughter' implies that she was not of royal birth. Does the name of Iset-Nofret's eldest daughter, Bintanath or 'Daughter of [the Canaanite goddess] Anath', provide a clue to the new queen's origins? Egyptian babies were traditionally named by the mother at birth. Could the new royal mother have been of Canaanite extraction? The harem certainly included a number of foreign women, the spoils of Egypt's Asiatic empire, but there is no need to assume that Iset-Nofret was one of these. Anath was respected as a goddess in Ramesside Egypt and would have been considered an appropriate, perhaps pleasantly exotic, girl's name. None of Iset-Nofret's other children bore foreign names, although at least two of Ramesses' other children did: Meheranath or 'Child of Anath' and Astarteherwenemef or 'Astarte is on his right'.

The ages of their children indicate that Iset-Nofret and Nefertari were contemporaries, married to Ramesses at the same time and giving birth to his children in parallel. While Nefertari produced Ramesses' first-born son, Crown Prince Amenhirwenemef, Iset-Nofret delivered his second son, Ramesses, and his first daughter, Bintanath. Iset-Nofret eventually bore Ramesses at least four children: Prince Ramesses, Khaemwaset the scholarly priest, Merenptah the future pharaoh and Bintanath. It seems likely that Iset-Nofret II, a daughter of Ramesses and future queen of

Egypt, was also a daughter of Iset-Nofret I. Khaemwaset appears, with his half-brother Amenhirwenemef, on the wall of the Beit el-Wali temple built during the reign of Seti. He and his older brother must therefore have been born well before his father came to the throne.

Did their parallel positions lead to jealousy between the two wives, or to rivalry between their many children? Given the passage of time it is, of course, very difficult for us to tell. The only evidence that can be used in support of the jealousy theory takes the form of a black granite statue now housed in Turin Museum. Here we see a massive Ramesses accompanied by a miniature son and wife. The son is obviously Amenhirwenemef. The name of the queen has been deliberately erased, but it seems logical to deduce that she was the mother of the featured prince, i.e., Nefertari. There is no proof of when or by whom the attack on Nefertari's name was committed but if, as is generally assumed, this represents an attempt by the pharaoh Merenptah to erase the name of his stepmother, why would he allow her to retain her conspicuous position on more prominent monuments, including the Abu Simbel temple?[28]

The children of Iset-Nofret were singled out above all other harem children for their father's affection and at first sight it appears that Ramesses, Iset-Nofret, their daughter and sons made one tight, happy family group. Indeed, there is little observable difference between his treatment of his official and his less-official family. Bintanath is allowed to take precedence over her more royal but younger half-sisters, while sons by the two wives were eventually destined to share a tomb. There could only be one chief wife, however, and while Nefertari and her sons lived there seemed little hope that the sons of Iset-Nofret would succeed to the throne. Although the succession was nowhere explicitly stated, it was highly unlikely that Ramesses would reject the sons of his consort in favour of their half-brothers.

Their contrasting official positions would have ensured that for twenty-five years the two wives lived very different lives, with Nefertari very much in the public gaze and Iset-Nofret, lacking an official role, very much in the background. This, rather than petty jealousy, would explain why Iset-Nofret is conspicuously absent from the Abu Simbel temples although her daughters, who as princesses outrank their mother, are present. It is only after the death of Nefertari that Iset-Nofret is entitled to develop a high public profile, and even now she remains tantalizingly remote, with her more important images provided by her son, Khaemwaset. Surviving reliefs and statues of the new consort show an entirely conventional 19th Dynasty queen whose appearance, young, calm and bland, provides no clues to either her origins or her personality. Her beauty and charm are, as we might expect, without equal. She is:

. . . she who fills the colonnaded hall with the scent of her perfume; her fragrance is like that of Punt . . . her beauty pervades the Audience Chamber and her fragrance fills the colonnaded hall . . .[29]

Iset-Nofret appears as consort with Ramesses and their children on stelae erected by Khaemwaset at Aswan (Year 24–30) and in the temple of Horemheb at Gebel Silsila (Year 33–34). The Aswan stela shows Iset-Nofret, apparently alive, holding a floral sceptre and a papyrus or lotus. The fact that she holds an ankh sign, the symbol of life, in the Gebel Silsila stela while Bintanath holds a papyrus hints that Iset-Nofret might be dead by Year 34. However, so inconclusive is the evidence for Iset-Nofret's life, that it remains a distinct possibility that she had died considerably earlier than Year 34, possibly even predeceasing both Tuya and Nefertari. All that we can state with any degree of certainty is that she was definitely alive for the birth of Merenptah.[30] An early death would explain why Iset-Nofret had such a low profile throughout her husband's reign, but would force Ramesses to look elsewhere for a successor to Nefertari.

The most suitable wife for a king of Egypt was the daughter of a king of Egypt. Ramesses, a stickler for tradition, married four of his daughters, Bintanath, Meritamen, Nebettawi and the shadowy Hentmire. The first of these daughter-queens was Bintanath. The Abu Simbel temple includes a single, late-dating, image of Queen Bintanath carved on one of the pillars in the great hall, while the Aswan stela shows Queen Iset-Nofret and Queen Bintanath together with Princes Ramesses, Khaemwaset and Merenptah. Bintanath's promotion to queen may have occurred as early as Year 22; a reference to the new queen on a wine jar discovered in the tomb of Tuya would, if recovered *in situ*, place her promotion to no later than the death of her grandmother. We have already considered the Abu Simbel stela of Hekanakht which shows the still-living Nefertari

*Fig 5.3   Queens Iset-Nofret and Bintanath appear together on the Gebel Silsila
stela dedicated by Khaemwaset*

sitting by as her daughter Meritamen takes over her role as queen. Delving
back into recent dynastic history we find similar situations: Amenhotep
III promoted his eldest daughter Sitamen to the position of Great King's
Wife while Queen Tiy was still alive, later he also married his younger
daughters Henut-Taneb, Isis and Nebetah. There is also good circumstan-
tial evidence that Akhenaten married his three eldest daughters while
Nefertiti still lived.

Father–daughter incest is taboo in modern Western societies. It is
therefore tempting to interpret these father–daughter marriages as a form
of non-incestuous promotion; the father, realizing that his now mature
daughter has no chance of marriage outside the royal family, and expecting
to live for many years, contracts a symbolic marriage which will elevate
her to the highest position in the land. Marriage with the crown prince
would, of course, eventually achieve the same ends but, given the
unpredictability of death, who was to say which son would eventually
succeed to the throne? This interpretation would, however, be entirely
wrong. Bintanath is known to have borne at least one child who is clearly

labelled on the wall of her tomb. Similarly the three Amarna princesses each appear to have conceived a child with their father and indeed it seems highly likely that the middle princess, Meketaten, died in childbirth in her early teens.

Although the tradition of New Kingdom pharaohs marrying their young but sexually mature daughters is well established, the mechanisms of these marriages are, unfortunately, not at all clear. It is obvious that there is no simple substitution of the young daughter for the older mother or stepmother; we have seen Nefertari and Meritamen, and possibly Iset-Nofret and Bintanath, acting together. Nor do the new queens take immediate precedence over the older queen. Rather, they seem to act as deputy consorts, standing in for their mothers on ritual occasions whenever required. Is this merely a matter of convenience, designed to allow the new queen some glory and the old queen a well-earned rest? Or is it more significant? Are the fertile princesses expected to replace the mothers who, now past child-bearing age, are in turn expected to assume the vacant and highly valued older woman's role of queen mother? Queen Tiy certainly did not retire upon the promotion of her daughters; she retained her prominent position throughout her husband's reign and lived to be a dominant and vigorous presence at her son's court while her daughters, replaced by the new queen, Nefertiti, sank into obscurity following their father's death.

Iset-Nofret's tomb has yet to be discovered. For a long time it was assumed that she too would have been interred in the Valley of the Queens, probably in a tomb as grand as that prepared for Nefertari. As the two ladies appear to have married at the same time, it makes sense that work would have started simultaneously on the preparation of their tombs. Howard Carter's recovery of a 19th Dynasty ostracon 'map', however, suggests that she may instead have been buried in the Valley of the Kings. The map includes a tantalizing clue: 'from the tomb in preparation of Iset-Nofret to the tomb of Meri-Atum 200 cubits, from the end of the Water of the Sky to the tomb of Iset-Nofret 445 cubits'.[31] We know that a cubit measures approximately half a metre, but the location of the Water of the Sky is a mystery. Iset-Nofret was not, unfortunately, an uncommon name in the Ramesside royal family, and so there remains the unwelcome possibility that the map, when solved, will lead us to the tomb of an entirely different queen.

The excavation of the Memphite tomb of Horemheb has yielded *shabti* figures belonging to Princess (not yet Queen) Bintanath and in so doing has widened the field of potential graveyards. We know that Bintanath was eventually buried at Thebes. Was there a family link with the north that caused Iset-Nofret and her children, like Tia and Tia, to prefer interment in the Sakkara cemetery? A preference which, with their promotion to official royal family, was abandoned in favour of burial in the Theban necropolis. The unexpected link between Bintanath and Horemheb has provoked some speculation that the so-far parentless Iset-Nofret may actually have been a daughter of Horemheb and there-fore, by extension, a possible niece or step-niece of Nefertari. This would be chronologically possible but, given the current dearth of supporting evidence, must remain nothing more than an interesting possibility. It certainly prompts us to wonder why Nefertari, possible daughter of the relatively undistinguished Ay, should be given precedence over Iset-Nofret, daughter of the man who instigated the Ramesside dynasty.

Ramesses, twice widowered by Year 35 and with three of his daughters serving as queen, could not resist the daughter of the Hittite king. The bride was a young and beautiful maiden who, if any further encourage-ment was needed, came with the promise of a magnificent dowry: 'greater will be her dowry than that of the king of Babylon . . . this year, I will send my daughter, who will bring servants, cattle, sheep and horses'. The conspicuous arrival of such a dowry would serve as public affirmation of the Hittite king's vast disposable wealth. Ramesses, generally averse to allowing Hattusilis any good publicity, was willing and even eager to make an exception in this case. Negotiations were conducted slowly by letter, with each missive taking weeks to travel the 800 miles which separated the courts. At one point Ramesses, frustrated by the delays, wrote to query the absence of the promised dowry and, of course, his bride. Queen Pudukhepa, writing in the absence of her husband, was unimpressed by his plea of poverty and replied with a swift rebuke:

Now you, my brother, wrote to me as follows: 'My sister wrote to me "I will send you a daughter" yet you hold back from me unkindly, still. Why have you not given her to me?'

You should not distrust us, but believe us. I would have sent you the daughter by now, but . . . burnt is the palace. What was left over Urhi-Teshub gave to

the great gods. As Urhi–Teshub is there with you, ask him now whether this
is so or not . . .

My brother possesses nothing?! Really! If the son of the Sun-goddess or the
son of the Storm-god has nothing, only then do you also have nothing! That
you, my brother, should wish to enrich yourself from me . . . is neither friendly
nor honourable . . .[32]

With the dowry and the bride price agreed the deal was finally sealed
with the anointing of the bride's head with oil. The princess, accompanied
by her retinue, her dowry and her redoubtable mother, travelled to
southern Syria where she was received by the Egyptian authorities. A
long journey through Canaan and across Sinai followed. Fearing that
bad weather would delay the bridal party, Ramesses, safe in his Delta
palace, made an offering to Seth. A miracle was granted, the Levant
experienced an unprecedented spell of summer weather in winter, and
the princess and her entourage arrived safely in Egypt. Finally, in his new
capital Pi-Ramesse, pharaoh came face to face with his bride.

Ramesses was obviously pleased with what he saw. The Hittite princess
appeared 'beautiful in the heart of his majesty, and he loved her more
than anything'. She was given the Egyptian name of Maathorneferure
(the One who sees Horus, the Visible Splendour of Re) and was promoted
to the role of principal wife, an unusual honour for a foreign-born queen
and one which may have been given only at the insistence of her father.
The Hittites, like the Egyptians, believed that their daughters should come
second to none, and years before under similar circumstances Suppiluliumas had been forced to insist that his own daughter become principal
queen of Mitanni. Maathorneferure soon started to appear on royal monuments as a fully fledged Egyptian queen, although it seems that she never
actually served as such. Bintanath and her half-sisters, first Meritamen
and then Nebettawi, continued to fill this ritual role for their father.

In Egypt the royal marriage was celebrated in a lengthy inscription
which deviated somewhat from the truth, as revealed by the Hittite
correspondence. Ramesses, of course, had a certain reputation to maintain. He could never let his people forget that he had officially vanquished
the Hittites. The Hittite bride, daughter of a fallen enemy, was therefore,
to be seen as a superior form of tribute offered by a lesser king to his
master:

The Great King of Hatti wrote seeking to appease his Majesty year by year, but never would he listen to them. So that when they saw the land in this miserable state under the great powers of the Lord of the Two Lands, then the King of Hatti said to his soldiers and courtiers saying: 'Look! Our land is devastated . . . Let us strip ourselves of all our possessions, and with my oldest daughter in front of them, let us carry peace offerings to the King of Egypt so that he may give us peace and we may live. Then he caused his oldest daughter to be brought, the costly tribute before her consisting of gold, silver, ores, countless horses, cattle sheep and goats.[33]

This is the story that was displayed at Karnak, Elephantine, Amara and Abu Simbel. We can only imagine what the proud Queen Pudukhepa would make of this version of events!

Maathorneferure lived for a time at the palace of Pi-Ramesse, and we know that she also spent some time at *Mer-Wer*. Here, by fortunate accident, a scrap of papyrus discovered by Sir Flinders Petrie gives details of her laundry which included rolls of cloth '28 cubits 4 palms' long and '4 cubits' wide. She bore her husband at least one child, a daughter, much to the disappointment of her father who had been hoping for a grandson who might one day rule Egypt. Soon she faded into obscurity. Although foreign women did occasionally disappear in the royal harem – Kadeshman-Enlil of Babylon, whose sister was housed in the harem of Amenhotep III, had been driven to write to pharaoh demanding to know her whereabouts – it seems likely that Maathorneferure died young.

This tragedy did not lessen the friendship between the two courts. The Hittite Crown Prince Hishmi-Sharruma enjoyed a lengthy visit to Pi-Ramesse, and Ramesses even felt inspired to extend an invitation to Hattusilis and Pudukhepa. Hattusilis, initially unenthusiastic, eventually agreed to travel to Egypt, but the visit had to be postponed when the Hittite king contracted a painful 'burning of the feet'. Some ten years after the first marriage Hattusilis agreed to a second daughter marrying Ramesses. He even agreed to the provision of a second large dowry. We know nothing of the negotiations for this marriage, but once again the Egyptian sculptors set to work to record the momentous event:

The Great Ruler of Hatti, sent the rich and massive spoils of Hatti . . . to the King of South and North Egypt, Usermaatre Setepenre, Son of Re Ramesses

II, and likewise many droves of horses, many herds of cattle, many flocks of
goats, and many droves of game, before his other daughter whom he sent to
the King of South and North Egypt on what was the second such occasion.[34]

The name of this second Hittite bride went unrecorded, and her fate is
unknown.

Notes

1 Kitchen, K. A. (1982), *Pharaoh Triumphant*, Warminster, 39.

2 Heian Period Japanese lady quoted in Dickemann, M. (1981), 'Paternal confidences and dowry competition: a biocultural analysis of purdah', in Alexander, R. D. and Tinfele, D. (eds) *Natural Selection and Social Behaviour; recent research and new theory*, New York: 417–38.

3 From the 'New Kingdom Instructions of Any'. For a full translation of this text, with commentary, consult Lichtheim, M. (1976), *Ancient Egyptian Literature 2: The New Kingdom*, Los Angeles: 135–46.

4 The publicity which had attended the marriage of Amenhotep III and his commoner bride Tiy was highly unusual. Marriages were considered to be of little concern to either state or temple, and are rarely recorded. There was no equivalent of our wedding ceremony and for most couples their cohabitation confirmed their union. It was only when an unusual marriage occurred, for example the marriage of Ramesses and the Hittite princess, that the details were publicized.

5 Discussed in Robins, G. (1983), 'A Critical Examination of the Theory that the Right to the Throne of Ancient Egypt passed Through the Female Line in the 18th Dynasty', *Göttinger Miszellen* 62: 67–77. It seems that this theory was developed, perhaps inadvertently, as a means of justifying the sibling incest which many early Egyptologists found hard to accept.

6 For a discussion of the Ramesside family see Kitchen, K. A. and Gaballa, G. A. (1968), 'Ramesside Varia', *Chronique d'Egypte* 43: 251–70.

7 The tomb was excavated by Geoffrey T. Martin on behalf of the Egypt Exploration Society; see Martin, G. T. (1997), *The Tomb of Tia and Tia; a royal monument of the Ramesside period in the Memphite necropolis*, London.

8 See Sourouzian, H. (1983), 'Henout-mi-Re, fille de Rameses II et grande épouse de roi', *Annales du Service des Antiquités d'Egypte* 69: 365–71.

9 Rivers 1921; quoted in Dickemann, M. (1979), 'Female Infanticide, Reproductive Strategies and Social Stratification; a preliminary model', in Chagnon, N. A. and Irons, W. (eds) *Evolutionary Biology and Human Social Behaviour: an anthropological perspective*, North Scituate, Mass. Dickemann, writing about the Rajputs of India, notes that (p. 330) 'the pyramidal nature of hierarchical societies meant that the higher the status of the subcaste, the fewer options for its daughters; the operation of hypergamy in a pyramidal structure guarantees competition for a resource which is always scarce in relation to demand'.

10 Amarna Letter EA 4: for a full translation of this and all other Amarna letters consult Moran, W. L. (1992), *The Amarna Letters*, Baltimore and London. It seems that Tutankhamen's widow Ankhesenamen, in selecting a foreign royal bridegroom in preference to an Egyptian commoner as discussed in Chapter 2, was making a very difficult choice which went against centuries of tradition. Not until the 21st Dynasty was an Egyptian princess to be sent abroad as the bride of the Israelite King Solomon.

11 Leblanc, C. (1988), 'L'Identification de la tombe de Honout-mi-Re fille de Ramses II et Grande Epouse royal', *Bulletin de l'Institut Français d'Archéologie Orientale* 88: 131–46.

12 The fate of 'King' Nefertiti is discussed with references in Tyldesley, J. A. (1998), *Nefertiti: Egypt's sun queen*, London: 139–66.

13 See also Desroches Noblecourt, C. (1991), 'Abou Simbel, Ramses, et les dames de la couronne', in E. Bleiberg and R. Freed (eds) *Fragments of a Shattered Visage: the Proceedings of the International Symposium of Ramesses the Great*, Memphis: 127–66: 129.

14 For a summary with references of the monuments of Queen Tuya and the divine birth of Ramesses, consult Habachi, L. (1969), 'La Reine Touy, femme de Sethi I, et ses proches parents inconnus', *Revue d'Egyptologie* 21: 27–47.

15 The story of Hatchepsut's divine birth, with references, is discussed in Tyldesley, J. A. (1996), *Hatchepsut; the female pharaoh*, London, 102–6. For the publication of the scenes consult Naville, E. (1896), *The Temple of Deir el-Baharai Part 2*, London.

16 This text is also known as the 'Dialogue of Ptah and Ramesses II', and 'The Decree of Ptah for Ramesses II'. For a fully referenced discussion of the text consult Goelet, O. Jr (1991), 'The Blessing of Ptah', in E. Bleiberg and R. Freed (eds) *Fragments of a Shattered Visage: the Proceedings of the International Symposium of Ramesses the Great*, Memphis: 28–37.

17 Kitchen, K. A. (1996), *Ramesside Inscriptions Translated and Annotated 2: Ramesses II, Royal Inscriptions*, Oxford: 99–110.

18 Discussed in Hari, R. (1979), 'Mout-Nofretari épouse de Ramses II: une descendent de l'héritique Ai?', *Aegyptus* 59, 3–7; Bianchi, R. S. (1992), *In the Tomb of Nefertari*, Santa Monica: 43–5.

19 For a review of Hathor and her cults, with a useful bibliography, consult Roberts, A. (1995), *Hathor Rising; the serpent power of Ancient Egypt*, Totnes.

20 Edwards, A. B. (1877 revised 1888), *A Thousand Miles up the Nile*, London: 297.

21 Edwards, A. B. (1877 revised 1888), *A Thousand Miles up the Nile*, London: 296–7.

22 The suggestion that Nefertari was already ill at the celebration of the opening of the temple is made in Kitchen, K. A. (1982), *Pharaoh Triumphant*, Warminster: 100.

23 See Schiaparelli, E. (1924), *Relazione sui lavori della Missione Archeologica Italiana in Egitto I: esplorazione della 'Valle della Reigne'*, Turin: 55.

24 Biological Investigations conducted by Hideo Arai, reported in Corzo, M. A. ed. (1987), *Wall Paintings of the Tomb of Nefertari: scientific studies for their conservation*, Cairo: 54–7.

25 For details of the history of the conservation of the tomb, consult Corzo, M. A. and Afshar, M. eds. (1993), *Art and Eternity; the Nefertari wall paintings conservation project 1986–92*, Getty Conservation Institute. It is to be hoped that the moisture and bacteria introduced to the tomb by the daily influx of 150 visitors will not cause further, irredeemable, decay.

26 Discussed in detail by Mahasti Afshar, 'Iconography of the Nefertari Wall Paintings', in Corzo, M. A. and Afshar, M. eds. (1993), *Art and Eternity; the Nefertari wall paintings conservation project 1986–92*, Getty Conservation Institute: 31–41.

27 The best summary of the evidence for Iset-Nofret's life is given by Leblanc, C. (1993), 'Isis-Nofret, Grande Epouse de Ramses II, la reine, sa famille', *Bulletin de l'Institut Français d'Archéologie Orientale* 93: 313–33.

28 Discussed in Jansen, J. J. (1963), 'La Reine Nefertari et la succession de Rameses II par Merenptah', *Chronique d'Egypte* 38: 75: 30–36.

29 For a full translation of this text consult Kitchen, K. A. (1996), *Ramesside Inscriptions Translated and Annotated 2: Ramesses II, Royal Inscriptions*, Oxford: 557.

30 The suggestion that Iset-Nofret may have died before Nefertari is proposed in Christophe, L. A. (1965), 'Les temples d'Abou Simbel et la famille de Rameses II', *Bulletin de l'Institut d'Egypte* 38: 118. This is discussed further in Sourouzian, H. (1989), *Les Monuments de Merenptah*, Mainz: 2–7.

31 Thomas, E. (1977), Cairo Ostracon J.72460, SAOC 39: 209–16.

32 Translation after Kitchen, K. A. (1982), *Pharaoh Triumphant*, Warminster: 84.

33 Quoted and discussed in Gardiner, A. (1961), *Egypt of the Pharaohs*, Oxford: 265. See also Kitchen, K. A. (1996), *Ramesside Inscriptions Translated and Annotated 2: Ramesses II, Royal Inscriptions*, Oxford: 86–96.

34 Kitchen, K. A. (1996), *Ramesside Inscriptions Translated and Annotated 2: Ramesses II, Royal Inscriptions*, Oxford: 110–12.

6

Ramesses the Father

Ramesses was inordinately proud of his ability to father children. Never one to hide his light under a bushel he wanted everyone to be aware of his impressive fertility, a fertility that he saw as an important aspect of his role as pharaoh and which was linked at a very basic level to the fertility and survival of Egypt and the Nile. And so we see his sons and daughters, named and divided by sex, processing in two single files along the walls of their father's temples in Egypt and Nubia where they represent the living proof of Ramesses' supreme fitness to rule.[1] Other New Kingdom monarchs, most notably Akhenaten, had featured the nuclear royal family (king, consort and their female offspring) on their monuments but Ramesses is the first to allow us the opportunity to count scores of children, both male and female, far more than could realistically be attributed to the relatively small circle of principal consorts and secondary queens.[2]

We have already seen that nothing was ever left to chance on the walls of Egypt's temples where both size and position were matters of immense importance and where the carving or erasure of an image or name could affect the progress of history itself. No sensible dynastic artist would have contemplated depicting the royal children in completely random fashion. The list of the princes and princesses must therefore have been sorted into some kind of order, an order which is unfortunately nowhere made explicit. The most obvious ranking, that used in almost all pharaonic art, would be that of status which would in turn equate to closeness to the crown. Considering the list of princes we might reasonably expect to find the list headed by the sons of Nefertari ranked in order of birth followed by the sons of Iset-Nofret in birth order, then a chronological progression through the sons of the secondary wives and the lesser harem women, with those children considered too remote from the succession perhaps excluded from the list. The same ranking might be expected for the daughters of the king.

This is not, however, what we find. The children of Nefertari and Iset-Nofret, mixed in what we must presume to be order of birth, head the list of princes with Amenhirwenemef son of Nefertari being recorded as the highest-ranking son followed by Ramesses son of Iset-Nofret and then Prehirwenemef, second son of Nefertari. The list of daughters shows the same mixing with Bintanath, a daughter of Iset-Nofret rather than Nefertari, at the top of the list followed by Baketmut, an ephemeral daughter of Nefertari. This is less of a surprise; we have already seen that Bintanath takes precedence over her royal half-sisters, becoming queen-consort before either Meritamen or Nebettawi. The sons and daughters ranked lower down the lists are presumably born to the less-important anonymous women of the harem, and have little or no realistic chance of succeeding to the throne.

Should we then assume that the temple lists show the royal children in simple birth order? This, if true, would indicate that only Nefertari and Iset-Nofret bore Ramesses' children during the early years following his inheritance of the 'great beauties of the palace'. The first four sons and the first seven daughters have all been attributed to these two ladies, while Nefertari and Iset-Nofret between them produce at least seven of the first thirteen sons. Although perfectly possible, this seems somewhat unlikely. More realistic is the assumption that there has indeed been a ranking, with the older offspring born to the ladies of the harem demoted in favour of the children born to Nefertari and Iset-Nofret. The children born to these two queens are mingled, an indication that they were regarded as being of roughly equal status.

A multitude of children born to many different mothers is not unknown in history, but it still invokes a sense of wonder in modern observers:

His [Ramesses'] family . . . amounted to no less than 170 children, of whom 111 were princes. This may have been a small family for a great king three thousand years ago. It was but the other day, comparatively speaking, that Lepsius saw and talked with old Hasan, Kashef of Der . . . and he, like a patriarch of old, had in his day been the husband of sixty-four wives, and the father of something like 200 children.[3]

Some early Egyptologists, impressed by what they saw, miscounted, attributing to Ramesses anything up to an incredible 400 children.

Terence Gray was even inspired to do some mathematics. He came up with some astonishing results:

How literally such a man may have been the 'Father of His People' can best be realised by considering this large number of children and his long life; for taking them at 400, 200 males and 200 females, allowing for the males 20 children each, and for the females 5, we get 4,000 and 1,000, in all 5,000 grandchildren. Allowing for these 2,500 males and 2,500 females, 10 children each for the males, and 2 for the females of this second – and so shorter – generation, we get 25,000 and 5,000, in all 30,000 great grandchildren ... Moreover, in a lifetime of a century there might well yet be another generation in being, so that, added together, there would be nothing outrageous in Ramesses having up to or well over thirty-five thousand descendants of himself living in Egypt ...[4]

Gray's figures are, of course, a vast over-exaggeration. Most experts would today agree that Ramesses fathered between 85 and 100 children, a maximum of 45–6 sons and 40–55 daughters rather than the 170 that appear in error in many older texts, and the 400 used in Gray's calculation quoted above.

If we attempt to follow Gray's reasoning, and to calculate the number of Ramesses' living descendants at the time of his death, we need to reduce this figure even further. Infant and maternal mortality during pregnancy and childbirth were common enough tragedies as the lack of medical skills and the ever-present dangers of disease and infection made labour a particularly hazardous ordeal for both mother and child. It is difficult to be precise over rates of infant mortality as there was no official register of births and deaths at this time, while the custom of denying very young babies the normal burial rites distorts the statistical evidence preserved in the dynastic graveyards. Sir Flinders Petrie discovered in his 1889 excavation of the Middle Kingdom town of Kahun, for example, that it was customary to bury infants under the floors of the houses, possibly in the hope that their spirits would enable the mother to become pregnant again. Figures based on research into the élite of pre-industrial European societies, while not providing a perfect parallel, suggest that we should not expect more than two-thirds of Ramesses' children to have survived to the age of fifteen.[5] We might therefore expect that, out of a maximum one hundred children fathered by Ramesses, only thirty sons and thirty-six daughters would reach the age of sexual maturity.

Yet more reduction is necessary. It is possible that the majority of Ramesses' higher-ranking daughters remained unwed, unable to find suitable husbands. A select few, of course, married Ramesses himself; although apparently consummated, these marriages produced surprisingly few children and we know of only one daughter-queen bearing a child by her father. The fate of the lesser daughters is not known, but we must assume that of these who did marry some might prove infertile (or married to infertile husbands) while others might die during pregnancy and childbirth. The estimate of each son fathering twenty surviving children should similarly be adjusted to allow for infertility, gaps between pregnancies during breast-feeding, parental and child deaths and brother–sister marriages which should not be double counted. Only those princes favoured with the delights of a private harem could hope to emulate Ramesses and father scores of children. The pleasures of the harem were, however, reserved for those in the direct line of succession, a mere four or five of his sons.

History teaches that fathering a vast number of offspring by no means guarantees the foundation of a long-lived dynasty, and parallels may be drawn with the English royal families of King Henry VIII (six wives, only three surviving legitimate children, no grandchildren) or Queen Anne (one husband, eighteen pregnancies, no surviving children). Ramesses, unusually long-lived, was eventually succeeded by his 13th son having seen many of his children predecease him.

Although Ramesses did not follow his father in appointing a co-regent, it was always made clear who, at any given time, was the designated heir to the throne. The higher-born sons, the potential heirs, were educated to serve their father as soldiers, priests and scribes, the perfect training for those who might one day become king and a useful means of obtaining high-quality staff. The lives of the lesser sons and daughters are to a large extent lost to us. What little evidence we do have suggests that the sons at least lived relatively normal lives, far removed from the glamour and luxury of pharaoh's court. The younger sons occasionally emerge from contemporary documents and texts, and so we know that Prince Simontu (son number 23) served as administrator of the royal vineyard at Memphis and made a practical if unexciting match marrying Iryet, the daughter of a Syrian sailor. Less is known about the hunch-backed Prince Ramesses-

Meriamen-Nebweben (son number 46) who died suddenly in his thirties while living at the harem palace of *Mer-Wer*. His unexpected death had left the royal family searching for a suitable coffin. Eventually they discovered an old two-coffin set which had been engraved for his great-grandfather Ramesses while still Vizier but discarded as unsuitable when the Vizier was promoted to prince. Ramesses-Meriamen-Nebweben was buried in the outermost of these second-hand coffins, its inscriptions suitably but not very thoroughly altered, close to *Mer-Wer*. The discovery of his remains in their palimpsest coffin was to cause Egyptologists intense confusion, particularly when the inner coffin of the Vizier Paramessu was subsequently discovered, empty but adapted for use by Ramesses-Meriamen-Nebweben, at the bottom of a shaft at Medinet Habu, Thebes.[6]

The children of Nefertari, those closest to the throne, are tolerably well known. Nefertari gave birth to Ramesses' first-born son, Prince Amenhirwenemef, 'Amen is at his right hand', during her husband's co-regency. At the time of his father's succession Amenhirwenemef inherited Ramesses' old title, becoming the official Senior King's Son or Crown Prince. Henceforth he was to be known as Amenhirkhepeshef, 'Amen is his strong arm', an unexplained change of name which caused early Egyptologists to double count him when totalling the list of royal sons. Like his father before him Amenhirkhepeshef proved to be a brave soldier, rising to the rank of General-in-Chief. By Year 20, however, he had disappeared from his father's monuments. Suggestions that, as the first born son of Ramesses, Amenhirkhepeshef may have been killed by the last and most dramatic of the biblical plagues of Egypt, have yet to be proved:

And it came to pass that at midnight the Lord smote all the firstborn in the land of Egypt, from the firstborn of Pharaoh that sat on his throne unto the firstborn of the captive that was in the dungeon; and all the firstborn of cattle. And Pharaoh rose up in the night, he, and all his servants, and all the Egyptians; and there was a great cry in Egypt; for there was not a house where there was not one dead.[7]

The next in line to the throne should have been his full brother, Ramesses' third son, Prehirwenemef. He too had been a brave soldier, a teenage veteran of the battle of Kadesh rewarded for his efforts by the titles 'First Brave of the Army' and later 'First Charioteer of His Majesty'. Prehirwenemef, however, was already dead, as were Sety (9th son) and Merire the Elder (11th son). Only two living sons of Nefertari remained: Meriatum (16th son), and his enigmatic younger brother Sethirkhepeshef. At first sight it seems that Ramesses passed over Meriatum, appointing Sethirkhepeshef heir apparent and priest of his father's official cult. We find the newly promoted Crown Prince writing to the Hittite court at the time of the signing of the historic peace treaty (Year 21), while the rejected Meriatum eventually becomes High Priest of Re at Heliopolis, an important position which he filled competently but without conspicuous distinction for some twenty years.

However, there is a problem with this interpretation. Sethirkhepeshef, whose existence is proved both by the Hittite correspondence and by his appearance on several monuments, is not included among the first twenty-five of Ramesses' sons preserved on the temple walls. It is of course possible that Sethirkhepeshef was a much younger son, a particular favourite of his father able to leap-frog over his older, higher-born brothers to become Crown Prince. Such blatant favouritism would, however, appear to be a recipe for dynastic disaster; Ramesses, an astute politician, would surely have realized that an unjust promotion would incense the true heirs to the throne, many of whom as army officers might be expected to have military support in any planned coup. It seems far more likely that Sethirkhepeshef did feature amongst the earlier sons, albeit under a different name. Seth, patron god of the Ramesside family, was the Delta equivalent of the southern god Amen. Could Amen-hir-Khepeshef and Seth-hir-Khepeshef be one and the same person, using different styles of the same name at different times and in different parts of the country?[28] A similar double name seems to have been borne by Ramesses' eighth son, who is known both as Amen-em-Wia and Seth-em-Wia. This would, of course, mean that Amenhirkhepeshef had not died, but had continued as Crown Prince Sethirkhepeshef until his death which occurred some time between Years 25 and 40.

Whoever Sethirkhepeshef was, his death marked the passing of the royal succession from the children of Nefertari to the children of Iset-Nofret. There was no question of the succession passing from Crown Prince to son of deceased Crown Prince as it would in modern Britain;

the death of the heir apparent effectively eliminated his sons from the succession race. Nor did the succession pass from Sethhirkhepeshef to his still-living full brother Meriatum. If we are correct in the assumption that Amenhirkhepeshef and Sethirkhepeshef are the same person, we can in fact see that the succession passed from the oldest son to the second oldest son as shown on the temple walls, irrespective of the mother. Did Ramesses always intend that the sons of Iset-Nofret would rank as equals alongside their half-brothers in the succession?

Of all Nefertari's daughters, Meritamen, 'Beloved of Amen' (4th daughter) is the most famous. By Year 24, as we have already seen, she has become a queen consort, deputizing for her elderly and possibly sick mother. Unfortunately, we know very little of her private life beyond the fact that, dying during her father's reign, she was buried in a tomb alongside that prepared for her mother in the Valley of the Queens (QV 68). Meritamen has, however, survived for us in statue form. A beautiful but broken coloured limestone image of an anonymous queen-princess, recovered from the vicinity of the Ramesseum in 1896 and subsequently housed in Cairo Museum, was for a long time known simply as the 'white queen'. Almost one hundred years later the fortunate discovery of a named colossus in the ruins of the temple of Akhmim, a figure which bears a striking resemblance to the 'white queen', made the identity of the latter clear. She was Meritamen 'with the splendid face, magnificent in the place, the beloved of the Lord of the Two Lands, she who stands by her master like Sothis is beside Orion . . .'[9] The Ramesseum figure shows us a graceful, pale and calm Meritamen with a young, rounded face, slightly prominent eyes, a square chin and slightly smiling full lips. She is dressed in a tight-fitting white robe, with two rosettes covering her nipples, and on her head she wears the *modius*, a flat crown of uraeii and sun discs. Her wide collar includes the hieroglyphic sign for *nefer*, or beauty. In her left hand she holds the *menit* beads which indicate that she is a priestess of Hathor; we may guess that in her now-vanished right hand she once held a sistrum.

Nebettawi, 'Lady of the Two Lands' (5th daughter) also became her father's consort, possibly as successor to the dead Meritamen. In the fullness of time she too was buried in the Valley of the Queens (QV 60).[10] Her burial was looted in antiquity and her tomb reused as a chapel during the Christian era. Princess Henoutawi (7th daughter) appears on the façade of the Small Abu Simbel temple and so may be classed amongst the daughters of Nefertari, although it seems that she may already have been dead when her image was carved. A statue of unknown provenance, now housed in Berlin Museum, has been attributed to this lady, although the identification is by no means certain. We know nothing of Henou-tawi's life beyond the fact that she was eventually buried in the Valley of the Queens (QV73).[11] Princess Nefertari II (3rd daughter), whose given name and whose presence on the façade of the Great Abu Simbel temple combine to confirm her status as a further daughter of Nefertari, is again a complete mystery to us as is her full sister Baketmut (2nd daughter). Baketmut's tomb has never been discovered and it is presumed that she died young.

Iset-Nofret's children seem to have been hardier and longer-lived than their ill-fated half-siblings. Her first-born son, Ramesses (2nd son), grew up to become a respected general and served a long and fruitless apprenticeship as Crown Prince following the death of Amen/Sethirk-hepeshef. We know that during his father's Year 30 Prince Ramesses served as judge in the trial of a Theban treasury official and his wife accused of stealing from the royal stores. This was no petty pilfering, but fraud on a truly impressive scale; the couple had apparently transferred to their own warehouse, among other things, several fully equipped chariots, 30 bulls, 5 jugs of wine, over 400 pairs of sandals and a vast amount of precious metal and linen. The case grew complicated when the accused swore his innocence and declared his intention of making a personal appeal to pharaoh! Unfortunately the outcome of the case has not been preserved.

Prince Ramesses died in Year 52/53 and was succeeded as heir apparent by his full brother the *Sem*-Priest of Ptah, Khaemwaset (4th son). He, already elderly, died soon after in Year 55. Finally Merenptah (13th son; not unlucky in this case) became the fourth Crown Prince of his father's reign. Initially responsible for the administration of the Delta as far south as Memphis, Merenptah slowly grew in importance until, for the final twelve years or so of his father's reign, he effectively ruled Egypt.

As the oldest daughter Bintanath heads the long line of Ramesside princesses. She plays a prominent role in her father's reign and we find her image standing with that of the colossal Ramesses at Karnak, at Wadi es-Sebua and at Pi-Ramesse. We have already seen Bintanath become

Fig 6.1   Bintanath and her daughter, presumed to be the child of Ramesses, from the wall of Bintanath's tomb

King's Wife, bearing her father the anonymous daughter who appears twice on the walls of the impressive tomb in the Valley of the Queens where she is identified merely as the 'King's bodily daughter' (QV71). The septuagenarian Bintanath was one of the few royal children to outlive her father, dying during the reign of her brother Merenptah. The 'Royal Daughter, Royal Sister, Great Royal Wife Bintanath' appears on a statue of Merenptah in front of the Luxor pylon; for some this is clear proof that Bintanath married her brother after her father's death. However, given her age, and the fact that she was effectively Merenptah's widowed stepmother, this seems unlikely. Parallels with Nefertari II daughter of Nefertari, Iset-Nofret II daughter of Iset-Nofret, and the much earlier junior Amarna princesses Meritaten-the-Younger and Ankhesenpaaten-the-Younger (assumed to be the daughters of Meritaten and Ankhesen-paaten by their father Akhenaten) suggest that this new Bintanath 'wife of Merenptah' may in fact be Bintanath II, the hitherto anonymous daughter of Bintanath and Ramesses.[12]

Iset-Nofret II (6th daughter) survived her father to become the consort of her full brother Merenptah.[13] Given that both were elderly at the death of their father, and that Iset-Nofret II is likely to have been slightly older than her brother, it would appear that theirs was a well-established marriage made during Ramesses' lifetime. The chance preservation of a private letter written by her devoted servants Pentaweret and Pawekhed allows us a peek into the private life of Iset-Nofret II during her father's reign:

Greetings! A message to say that I say to the gods and goddesses of Pi-Ramesse 'May you [Iset-Nofret] be healthy, prosperous and alive! May you enjoy the favour of the god Ptah . . . We are alive today, but cannot speak for tomorrow . . . May Ptah have us brought back in safety so that we may see you . . . we are very, very, concerned about you . . .'[14]

Khaemwaset, 'Rising in Thebes', fourth son of Ramesses and second son of Iset-Nofret, is, with the exception of Merenptah, the best documented and most famous of Ramesses' many sons.[15] He was highly regarded as a scholar and antiquarian during his lifetime; his reputation survived and grew for centuries beyond his death, transforming Khaemwaset into a semi-mythological sage, a magical, mystical figure who became the inspiration of many a curious tale.

Our first glimpse of Khaemwaset is provided by the Beit el-Wali temple. Here, as a small boy some five or six years old, he has accompanied his father and his slightly older half-brother Amenhirwenemef to fight in the glorious Nubian campaign. Ramesses, like Seti before him, believed in exposing his young sons to the thrills and excitement of battle and Khaemwaset was to play an active part in several Asiatic campaigns before Ramesses, perhaps realizing that his son was not suited to the life of a professional soldier, appointed him to the position of *Sem*-Priest of Ptah, a priest concerned with rituals associated with mortuary cults and funerals. Khaemwaset now became deputy to Huy, High Priest of Ptah at Memphis, while his full brothers, Ramesses and Merenptah, became professional soldiers.

His new position suited the scholarly Khaemwaset down to the ground. Ptah of Memphis, creator god and patron of craftsmen, has been described as 'an intellectual deity because his particular kind of theology was abstract

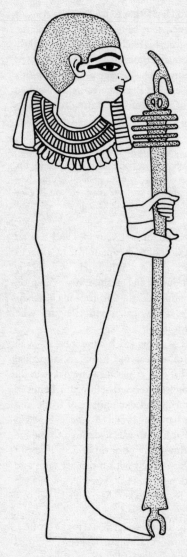

Fig 6.2   Ptah, patron god of Memphis

and cerebral'.[16] Intellectual Ptah may have been, rich he certainly was. He was the owner of a magnificent temple equal if not superior to the temple of Amen at Karnak, and a firm favourite of Ramesses who did much to promote his cult both in Egypt and Nubia. The role of *Sem*-Priest of Ptah was one with well-established royal connections; Tuthmosis, eldest son and heir presumptive of Amenhotep III, had occupied this important position over a century earlier, assuming particular responsibility for the burial of the Apis bulls. Now Khaemwaset was set to follow in his footsteps.

In Year 16, soon after Khaemwaset had taken up his position, the Apis bull, a living god, died. The Apis, identified by the markings of his coat, lived the life of a god-king at Memphis. He had his own palace, his own servants and access to a harem full of attractive cows. In death, tradition dictated that the Apis be given a suitably regal funeral with burial in the nearby sacred bull cemetery. Now Khaemwaset observed with interest as the dead god was embalmed and interred in a tomb topped by a decorated chapel. Some fourteen years later, when the next Apis died, Khaemwaset was in charge of the funeral arrangements. Breaking with tradition, he interred the second bull alongside the first, allowing the two to share both burial chamber and chapel. This was to become the only Apis burial to be recovered intact; some three thousand years later Auguste Mariette discovered the ill-preserved remains of the two bulls in their massive wooden sacrophagi. Accompanying the bulls was gold jewellery bearing the names of Ramesses and Khaemwaset.

Khaemwaset, still not satisfied with the new arrangement, was contemplating a radical new departure. Henceforth, the Apis bulls were to be buried together in a special cemetery, an underground gallery or corridor known today as the Serapeum. Here successive bulls would be interred in a series of side rooms opening off the main gallery, the side rooms being sealed after each burial for protection. Over time the gallery could be extended, and further side rooms excavated, as and when needed. Above ground the individual chapels would be replaced by one splendid Temple of Apis. Here the embalmed bull would rest in the hours before burial, and here the cult of the Apis could be celebrated with all due ceremony. Khaemwaset, with true Ramesside modesty, recorded his plans in a lengthy inscription carved at the entrance to the Serapeum:

... the Osiris, the *Sem*-Priest and King's Son Khaemwaset, he says: 'I am a valiant heir, a vigilant champion, excelling in wisdom in the opinion of Thoth ... Never has the like been done, set down in writing in the Great Festival Court before this temple ... I have endowed for him [Apis] the sacred offerings; regular daily offerings, feasts whose days come on appointed dates and calendar feasts throughout the year ... I have built for him a great stone shrine before his temple, in which to repose in spending the day when preparing for burial. I have made for him a great offering-table opposite his great shrine, of fine Tura limestone ... It will indeed seem to you a benefaction when by contrast you look upon what the ancestors have done, in poor and ignorant works ... Remember my name ... I am the *Sem*-Priest, Khaemwaset.'[17]

The first Apis bull was interred in Khaemwaset's new gallery in Year 55. So successful was this development, known today as the Lesser Vaults, that the gallery continued to house the Apis burials for over a thousand years. Eventually, in 612 BC, King Psammeticus I ordered the building of the Greater Vaults. It is these, rather than the earlier vaults of Khaemwaset, that are today open to the public.

Memphis, a flourishing city since the dawn of the dynastic age, was surrounded by the decaying remains of Egypt's glorious past. Sakkara and Giza, the ancient royal burial grounds, were nearby. Here stood the pyramids, the imposing tombs of the earliest rulers, already over a thousand years old. Stripped of their bodies and their riches, crumbling and covered in wind-blown sand, they now served as sad monuments to the long-dead kings of a bygone age. The pyramids were already attracting tourists, and a steady stream of Ramesside visitors made their way into the desert to marvel at the wonders of an almost mythical ancient world. Like many a modern sightseer, the 19th Dynasty day-trippers felt the need to leave their mark. Thus a lengthy graffito dating to the reign of Ramesses details a visit to the Sakkara complex of Djoser:

Year 47, 2nd month of winter, day 25 [January 1232 BC], the Treasury-Scribe Hednakht, son of Tjenro and Tewosret, came to take a stroll and enjoy himself in the west of Memphis, along with his brother Panakht . . . He said: 'O all you gods of the West of Memphis . . . and glorified dead . . . grant a full lifetime in serving your good pleasure, a goodly burial after a happy old age, like yourself . . .'[18]

Khaemwaset, dismayed by the air of neglect, decided to spruce up these monuments. In so doing he earned his modern title of 'the world's first Egyptologist'. In fact, as we have already seen, the renewal of the relics of the past was an accepted means of restoring *maat* to chaos, one which Ramesses had already exploited to his own advantage at Abydos. Khaemwaset would have had little difficulty in interesting his father in his plans, and permission for the work was soon granted. Khaemwaset himself acted as supervisor as his workmen tidied, restored, and appended huge permanent labels to the monuments; each label carved into pyramid, tomb or temple bore the name of the original owner, the name of Ramesses II as patron of the conservation scheme and, of course, the name of Khaemwaset as chief restorer.

Egyptology was, however fascinating, only a hobby. Khaemwaset's real work, that of a priest and administrator, grew in complexity and responsibility as his father's reign progressed until eventually he became High Priest of Ptah, succeeding Huy, Pahemneter and Didia. By now Khaemwaset's own family was well established. His eldest son, named

Ramesses after his illustrious grandfather, was a civil servant who was to spend almost five years as heir apparent before his father's death caused the succession to fall on his uncle Merenptah. His younger son, Hori, dedicated himself to the service of Ptah, eventually becoming High Priest in turn, following Prehotep who had followed Khaemwaset. A daughter Iset-Nofret III was named after her grandmother and her aunt.

His position as *Sem*-Priest ensured that Khaemwaset played an important part in the organization of his father's jubilee celebrations or *sed*-festivals. The *heb-sed*, an ancient ritual particularly associated with the deity Ptah-Tatonen, was originally a public ceremony of rebirth designed to reaffirm and re-enforce the ageing king's powers after each successive thirty years of rule. By the New Kingdom it was accepted that the *sed*-festival would be celebrated after the first thirty years and then every three or four years thereafter. Very few kings enjoyed thirty years on the throne; in the 18th Dynasty only Tuthmosis III and Amenhotep III, the great Ramesside role models, had been able to celebrate more than one *sed*-festival. These two, coming to the throne young, were eventually able to enjoy three *heb-seds*.[19] Needless to say, Ramesses broke their record, celebrating legitimate jubilees in his regnal years 30, 33/34, 36/37, 40, 42/3, 45/46, 48/49, 51/52, 54/5, 57/8, 60/61, 63/64 and 66/67. As the king grew older, and in greater need of rejuvenation, his jubilees became almost annual events.

After his first two jubilees we see a definite change in Ramesses' style of kingship. The frenetic race to build now seems to be over, there are to be no more battles, and Ramesses appears content to develop more cerebral pursuits. In particular, like Amenhotep III before him, he now turns his attention to the development of his own divinity.

Amenhotep III had paid great attention to the presentation of his own jubilees, searching through the palace archives to discover an ancient order of service and rewriting his pageant accordingly. The *heb-sed* of Amenhotep III was celebrated not, as custom dictated at Memphis, but at the newly built Malkata Palace on the west bank at Thebes where the presence of a large artificial lake allowed the king to introduce a water procession into the ritual. Ramesses, too, changed the traditional venue; his jubilee would be proclaimed by Khaemwaset at Memphis but re-enacted in the magnificent columned Halls of Jubilee at Pi-Ramesse where the festivities, including a re-enactment of his coronation and a ceremonial race designed to test his fitness to rule, could last for up to two months. Meanwhile, as Ramesses celebrated at Pi-Ramesse, and supplementary celebrations were under way in the regional temples, Khaemwaset was recovering from a lengthy journey undertaken to carry the good news from Memphis to Aswan.

The *heb-sed* was particularly associated with the annual flooding of the Nile, the source of Egypt's fertility. As the floodwaters renewed the tired land, so the tired king would in turn be renewed by his ceremony. By happy coincidence, Ramesses' first jubilee was associated with a particularly high Nile flood, confirmation indeed that the gods were pleased with their king. Khaemwaset established stelae celebrating the royal jubilees at Aswan and at Gebel Silsila, sites particularly associated with the Nile and its gods, and it is here that we see his mother make two of her rare appearances as consort. The same pattern was repeated for the next four jubilees. By Year 45, however, Khaemwaset had tired of his continual travelling and from now on his deputies were entrusted with the task of proclaiming and spreading the good news.

Having dedicated much of his life to the cult of Apis and the development of the Serapeum, Khaemwaset not unreasonably decided that he would prefer to be interred at Memphis rather than Thebes. The precise location of his tomb is, however, something of an archaeological puzzle. When in 1852 Mariette used explosives to clear the debris which blocked the Serapeum he found the burial of Khaemwaset – the ill-preserved body of a mummified man wearing a golden mask lying in half a gilded coffin – in the centre of the Lesser Vaults, hidden beneath piles of debris from a collapsed ceiling.[20] It seemed either that Khaemwaset had chosen to be buried amongst his beloved Apis bulls, or that he had been reburied here after building works had disturbed his original tomb. However, so destructive was Mariette's method of excavation by explosion that the possibility of Khaemwaset's body being blown into the gallery from another tomb cannot be totally discounted. The recent discovery of the nearby remains of a limestone structure apparently built by Khaemwaset in an archaic style but subsequently dismantled, reassembled and then ruined simply adds to the confusion.[21]

The dead Khaemwaset was quickly transformed into the magician, Setne Khaemwaset, Setne being a corruption of his most frequently used title *Sem*-Priest or *Setem*-Priest. Setne Khaemwaset is the hero of a cycle of fantastic adventures told and retold over the centuries. Today, just two papyri preserve part of these tales of the supernatural for modern readers to enjoy. Setne 1 is written on a torn Ptolemaic papyrus now housed in Cairo Museum (No 30646) while Setne 2 survives on a Roman papyrus in the collections of the British Museum (No 604).[22]

In Setne 1 we learn how Setne Khaemwaset uses his powers to steal the magical *Book of Thoth* from its guardian, the dead priest Naneferkaptah. Naneferkaptah, who himself perished along with his wife and child in an attempt to steal the book, warns Setne that his prize will bring him nothing but harm. Our hero, of course, will not listen to this good advice. The two play a game of *senet* and the game ends with Setne in possession of the book and Naneferkaptah vowing to make him return it. Ramesses, when told of the theft, advises his son to give back the book without delay, but Setne is blind to reason and settles down to read.

From this moment onwards everything that can go wrong does. Setne is ensnared by the beautiful but evil priestess Tabubu who demands that he kill his children before she will allow him to make love to her. So besotted is the prince that he allows the dastardly deed to be done, and Tabubu and Setne drink together as the bodies of his innocent children are eaten by the neighbourhood dogs and cats. Then Setne said to Tabubu:

'Now let us do what I long to do. Everything that you have asked of me, I have done for you.' Tabubu said to him, 'Come now to this storehouse.' Setne went to the storehouse and lay down on a bed of ivory and ebony. His dream was about to come true. Tabubu lay down next to Setne and he put out his hand to touch her. Opening her mouth wide, Tabubu let out a great scream. Setne awoke in a state of great heat, his penis was in a [unknown word], and he was naked.

Ramesses happens to be riding by, but Setne is too embarrassed to speak to his father because of his lack of clothes. Pharaoh, seeing his son, stops and advises him to return to Memphis where he will find his children still alive. Setne, coming to his senses, returns the *Book of Thoth* to its guardian and, perhaps undeservedly, his story has a happy ending.

Setne 2 is the tale of Setne's beloved son, Si-Osiri. Si-Osiri is a greater magician than his father and he is able to take Setne into the land of the dead. Here Setne sees the good enjoying the pleasures of eternal life while the bad endure perpetual punishment; some are tortured with food and drink suspended permanently out of reach, while others are condemned to constantly plait ropes which are immediately chewed open by donkeys. Si-Osiri, however, turns out not to be the son of Setne at all; he is the legendary sorcerer Horus-son-of-Paneshe from an earlier age, come back to defend Egypt in a magical contest. The story ends in best pantomime tradition with the fake son vanishing in a puff of smoke and a real son being born to Khaemwaset and his wife.

If the more important Ramesside women were accorded the privilege of individual tombs in the Valley of the Queens, the women of lesser importance were buried in the harem cemeteries and Khaemwaset was interred close to the Apis bulls at Sakkara, where were their brothers buried? By the end of his reign Ramesses had lost many of his higher-ranking sons: Amenhirkhepeshef, Prehirwenemef, Sety, Merire the Elder and Ramesses, to name but a few, had all predeceased their father, and if we include the lesser sons of the harem, and the sons of the royal sons, there must have been many more royal deaths. Processions to the Theban necropolis must have been a depressingly regular occurrence, with the never-ending sequence of funerals serving as a harrowing reminder of his own mortality for the increasingly frail and ageing king.

For a long time the lost tombs of the royal princes remained one of the teasing questions of Ramesside studies. Then, in 1989, the rediscovery of tomb KV 5 provided a spectacular and unexpected answer. KV 5 had not always been lost. One of thirteen tombs known in the 18th century but since vanished, it had been included on some of the earliest sketch maps of the Theban necropolis, and its blocked chambers had been minimally explored and mapped by the British traveller and explorer James Burton in 1825. Burton had been struck by the unusual nature of the tomb, which was:

. . . all in a state of ruin. On the ceiling alone which has in general fallen in vast masses are to be seen some small remains here and there of colouring. The substance of the rock between the small chambers and the large ones above cannot be more than eighteen inches. Being full of mud and earth the descent from the pillared room to those underneath is not perceptible. The catacomb must have been excavated very low in the valley or the valley much raised by the accumulation of earth stones and rubbish brought down by the rains . . . It is possible that there is some passage leading from below the centre of the pillared chamber into that where the sarcophagus stood . . .[23]

Later, the tomb doorway, clearly labelled with the cartouche of Ramesses II, had been recorded by Lepsius in 1850 and cleared in 1902. Since then the doorway had vanished, buried beneath tons of debris tipped down from Howard Carter's higher-level excavations. When it was realized that a proposed road-widening scheme might destroy KV5, the Theban Mapping Project, a team led by American Egyptologist Kent Weeks and dedicated to producing a complete and accurate plan of the royal necropolis, set out to rescue and record the tomb before it was lost for ever.[24]

The tomb, located via a combination of the old maps and geophysical survey techniques, was found to be completely blocked by a mass of compacted rubble which had been carried into the tomb by floodwater. Burton's exploratory channel, cut through this solid debris over a century earlier, was still in place. Unfortunately the tomb entrance had been contaminated by a leaking sewage pipe, but once this insanitary problem had been cleared up it was possible to crawl cautiously down Burton's tunnel and so gain some impression of the plan of the foremost chambers. The painstaking, meticulous work of clearing the blocked chambers and passages could then begin. Work progressed at a rate of less than two cubic metres per day, but slowly and surely the unprecedented size of the royal tomb was revealed. First came anterooms and an extensive sixteen-pillared hall. Then, in 1995, a long corridor some two metres wide was discovered beyond the hall. Opening off this corridor were doorways, ten on each side, while the lowest two doorways in turn led to more corridors with further small side chambers. Eventually the tomb proved to contain over 150 passageways and chambers, moving its excavator to compare it to 'an octopus, with a body surrounded by tentacles'.[25] It was effectively a catacomb, a usurped 18th Dynasty tomb greatly enlarged to house the burials of the sons and perhaps some of the daughters of Ramesses, similar in intent if not in precise plan to the Serapeum built by Khaemwaset to house the burials of the Apis bulls.

Already in the antechamber, on the north and west walls, there had been signs that the tomb might have held more than one burial. Here was Amenhirkhepeshef being presented by his father to the goddesses Hathor and Sokar, and here too standing before the god Nefertum was his half-brother 'the King's Principal Son of His Body, the Generalissimo Ramesses, justified'. Later evidence emerged to suggest that both Meriatum and Sety had been buried here. Work on the tomb is still in progress, and further discoveries are eagerly awaited. So far no intact burials have been discovered and there has been little substantial funeral debris: thousands of potsherds, faience *shabti* figures, beads, amulets, fragments of Canopic jars, of wooden coffins and of granite sarcophagi have been recovered but no intact sarcophagi, mummies or mummy cases, suggesting that much of the tomb may have been unused. Those burials which were made in KV 5 were thoroughly looted in antiquity, leaving little or no remains. However the recovery of some displaced human skeletal material (three skulls and a fragile complete skeleton) from a pit in one of the chambers, and tantalizing hints that the painted plaster floors may conceal further layers beneath the known corridors, offer hope that yet more human remains will be found within the tomb. The Turin 'Strike Papyrus', a legal document detailing thefts in the royal necropolis during the reign of Ramesses III, specifically mentions nefarious activities in the vicinity of KV 5:

Now Usherhat and Pawere have stripped stones from above the tomb of Osiris King Usermaatre Setepenre, the Great God . . . And Kenena son of Ruta did it in the same manner above the tomb of the royal children of King Osiris Usermaatre Setepenre, the Great God . . .[26]

We are not told what became of Kenena son of Ruta, nor of his ill-gotten gains. The penalty for tomb robbery was impalement on a wooden stake.

Notes

1 But see Gomaa, F. (1973), *Chaemwese; Sohn Ramses' II und Hoherpriester von Memphis*, Wiesbaden: 9: 'The purpose of the representations on the temple walls was not that Ramesses wanted to boast about the large numbers of his children, but rather to recommend his children to the mercy of the gods . . .'

2 The lists were originally inscribed, and now survive at varying levels of preservation, at the Ramesseum, Luxor, Karnak, Pi-Ramesse, Abydos, Abu Simbel, Derr, Wadi es-Sebua and Gerf Hussein. For a full summary of all these lists consult Kitchen, K. A. (1996), *Ramesside Inscriptions Translated and Annotated 2: Ramesses II, Royal Inscriptions*, Oxford: 559–63, 597–603.

3 Edwards, A. E. (1888 revised edition), *A Thousand Miles up the Nile*, London: 267. One is left with the sneaking suspicion that while Ramesses is actually telling the truth, old Hasan, Kashef of Der, is exaggerating both the number of his wives and the number of their offspring.

4 Gray, T. (1923), *'And In The Tomb Were Found' . . . Plays and portraits of Old Egypt*, Cambridge.

5 Figures taken from Boone, J. L. (1986), *Parental Investment and Elite Family Structure in Pre-industrial States: a case study of late Medieval–early modern Portuguese genealogies*, American Anthropologist 88:4: 859–78.

6 See Brunton, G. (1943), 'The Inner Sarcophagus of Prince Ramessu from Medinet Habu', *Annales du Service des Antiquités de l'Egypt* 43: 133–48.

7 Exodus 12: 29–30.

8 Discussed in Bierbrier, M. (1991), 'Elements of Stability and Instability in Ramesside Egypt: the succession to the throne', in E. Bleiberg and R. Freed (eds) *Fragments of a Shattered Visage: the Proceedings of the International Symposium of Ramesses the Great*, Memphis: 9–14.

9 Translation from Desroches Noblecourt, C. (1985), *The Great Pharaoh Ramses II and His Time*, translated by E. Mialon, Montreal.

10 Leblanc, C. (1985), 'Les Tombes no 58 (anonyme) et no 60 [Nebet-Taouy] de la Vallée des Reines – achèvement des dégagements et conclusions', *Annales du Service des Antiquités de l'Egypte* 70: 51–68.

11 Leblanc, C. (1986), '*Henout-Taouy* et la tombe no 73 de la Vallee des reines', *Bulletin de l'Institut Français d'Archéologie Orientale* 86: 203–26.

12 This possibility is suggested in Desroches Noblecourt, C. (1991), 'Abou Simbel, Ramses, et les dames de la couronne', in Bleiberg and R. Freed

(eds) *Fragments of a Shattered Visage: the Proceedings of the International Symposium of Ramesses the Great*, Memphis: 127–48.

13 But see Cruz-Uribe, E. (1977), 'On the wife of Merenptah', *Göttinger Miszellen* 24: 23–9. The proliferation of Iset-Nofrets within the royal family can be extremely confusing for modern observers.

14 Translation adapted from Kitchen, K. A. (1982), *Pharaoh Triumphant*, Warminster: 111.

15 For a summary of the life of Khaemwaset, including a useful catalogue of his monuments, consult Gomaa, F. (1973), *Chaemwese; Söhn Ramses' II und Höherpriester von Memphis*, Wiesbaden.

16 James, T. G. H. (1991), 'Ramesses II: appearance and reality', in E. Bleiberg and R. Freed (eds) *Fragments of a Shattered Visage: the Proceedings of the International Symposium of Ramesses the Great*, Memphis: 38–49: 41.

17 For a full translation of this text consult Kitchen, K. A. (1996), *Ramesside Inscriptions Translated and Annotated 2: Ramesses II, Royal Inscriptions*, Oxford: 569–70.

18 The full graffito is quoted in Kitchen, K. A. (1982), *Pharaoh Triumphant*, Warminster: 148.

19 Ever idiosyncratic, Akhenaten had celebrated his first *sed*-festival after a mere three years on the throne; possibly this celebration coincided with his own thirtieth birthday.

20 Mariette, A. (1882), *Le Serapeum de Memphis I*, Paris: 145.

21 Discovered by a Japanese expedition from Waseda University directed by Izumi Takamiya and Sakuji Yoshimura.

22 The Setne stories are told in full in Lichtheim, M. (1980), *Ancient Egyptian Literature 3: the Late Period*, Los Angeles: 125–151.

23 James Burton, unpublished diaries, MSS 25613–75: British Library.

24 The tale of the rediscovery and clearance of the tomb is told in Weeks, K. (1998), *The Lost Tomb: the greatest discovery at the Valley of the Kings since Tutankhamun*, London. The translations of the wall inscriptions are given on pages 100–1.

25 Kent Weeks, quoted by Lemonick, *Time* 29 May 1995: 52.

26 Edgerton, W. F. (1951), 'The strike in Ramesses III's twenty-ninth year', *Journal of Near Eastern Studies* 10: 137–45.

7

Ramesses the Mortal

The first half of Ramesses' reign had been a time of non-stop action and adventure. Battles were fought and won, temples were built and dedicated and both cities and children were raised as Ramesses proved to everyone that he was indeed the greatest of the pharaohs. The second half of his reign – the period after the celebration of his second jubilee – was a time for consolidation and contemplation. His major achievements stood complete or nearly so, there was continuing peace in the near east, and Ramesses was at last able to relax and enjoy his developing divinity, secure in the knowledge that he had already achieved more than any other king of Egypt.

Ramesses was not, however, ready to retire from the world stage and he retained his interest in Levantine affairs. A solitary stela recovered in 1994 from Kesweh, some 16 miles (25 kilometres) to the south of Damascus, and dated to the summer of his Year 56, hints at unusual Egyptian activity in this area at this time.[1] Unfortunately we have no idea why the stela was erected. The text merely gives the date, the king's titulary and a brief summary of the king's good relationship with Amen and Seth, while its original context is unknown. When recovered in 1994 the stela was being used to roof a Roman tomb.

It would be nice to imagine the widowered Ramesses waiting eagerly in Pi-Ramesse while a third Hittite bride, perhaps a daughter of the new king, Tudkhalia IV, started the long journey towards Egypt. However, Damascus, far off the direct route, would be an unlikely resting point for a Hittite princess.[2] More realistic, but infinitely less romantic, is Professor Kitchen's suggestion that the stela may have been erected to commemorate the arrival of Egyptian troops sent to lend support to Tudkhalia who felt himself threatened by the growing might of Assyria.

Slowly but surely the inconveniences and indignities of old age were starting to take their toll. Ramesses had once been proud of his physical fitness but now his body was starting to betray him. His teeth, riddled with cavities, hurt more often than not, while arthritis and bad circulation caused him to stoop and made it difficult to walk without the aid of a cane. His official portraits, of course, show none of this deterioration; to his people Ramesses would remain as hale and hearty as he had ever been and only his closest associates were allowed to see the crumbling behind the regal façade. Ramesses refused to be daunted by old age. He clung on to his power, never appointing an official co-regent, but slowly, as time slipped by, he allowed Prince Merenptah to take over the running of his country. By the end of Ramesses' reign Merenptah, himself an elderly gentleman in his late sixties, was ruling Egypt.

Ramesses, nominally head of the civil service, the army and the priesthood, had throughout his reign delegated much of his responsibility to others. For preference he passed his work on to his most loyal subjects, his sons, sensibly ensuring that they held the highest-ranking military positions and thereby preventing non-family members from gaining undue influence over the army. Not even Ramesses, however, could hope to father enough children to fill every official position in Egypt. He, like all pharaohs before him, was forced to rely on a small coterie of educated élite who ensured the efficient running of the country. The positions of Egypt's highest officials were generally passed from father to son, or from uncle to nephew; at Abydos, for example, the High Priest Wennofer belonged to a family which was to serve Osiris for six successive generations stretching from the 18th to the 20th Dynasties.[3] Marriages between the various high-ranking families ensured that Ramesses was surrounded by those with an inherited tradition of high-level service to the crown. It seems that almost everyone in high office was related to everyone else, so that in our brief survey of Ramesses' more important officials we find the same names occurring over and over again.

Some of Ramesses' chosen aides were his contemporaries, the privileged sons of Seti's ministers who had been educated with a view to their future alongside Ramesses in the school attached to the royal harem. As the fathers grew old their sons gradually took over their roles and, having married, fathered the sons who in time would become their own replacements.

We have already met the forceful Asha-Hebsed who played an important part in the building of the Abu Simbel temples. Asha-Hebsed had started his career as Commandant of Troops under Seti before becoming first Royal Foreign Envoy and then King's Cup-Bearer to Ramesses, the latter being an honorary title which implied far more than simple domestic service. Asha-Hebsed was very proud of his connection with the royal family. Indeed, it may even be that he changed his name to flatter his master: '[Ramesses] Asha-Hebsed' literally means '[Ramesses] Rich in Jubilees'; his name therefore represents a pious wish that the king might live for many years. Another boyhood friend was Ameneminet, a well-connected youth who served as personal companion to Prince Ramesses before becoming Royal Charioteer and Superintendent of Horses on the death of Seti. In the reshuffle which followed the enquiry into the Kadesh debacle Ameneminet was promoted to Royal Foreign Envoy.

Iuny, the elderly 'Royal Son of Kush' or Viceroy of Nubia, had been inherited from Seti's administration. It was under his guidance that building works started at Amara West and Aksha, and on his orders that the first blocks of the Abu Simbel temples were cut. Here, on the Abu Simbel cliff, Iuny commemorated his work with a rock-cut scene showing himself standing before his King. After ten years Iuny retired to be replaced by the Viceroy Hekanakht whose own Abu Simbel rock-cut stela shows the now famous scene of Queen Meritamen and Ramesses at the inauguration of the temples in Year 24. In Year 25 Hekanakht was followed by Viceroy Paser (a cousin of Ramesses' friend Ameneminet, not to be confused with the Theban Vizier of the same name) to whom fell the responsibility of restoring the Great Temple following the disastrous Abu Simbel earthquake. Paser was succeeded by Huy, the elderly diplomat who had, to great public acclaim, escorted the Hittite bride to her wedding at Pi-Ramesse. Finally, in Year 38, came the Viceroy Setau who retained his position until at least Year 63 and who was responsible for all Ramesses' later Nubian temples. Setau was a graduate of the royal school, and he already had an impressive record of royal service which he detailed in a lengthy autobiographical inscription carved, like those of his predecessors, at Wadi es-Sebua:[4]

I was one whom his Lord caused to be instructed . . . as a ward of the palace. I grew up in the royal abode when I was a youth . . . When I was a youth I was appointed to be Chief Scribe of the Vizier; I assessed the entire land with a great scroll, a task which I was able to perform . . . His majesty promoted me to be High Steward of Amen. I served as Superintendent of the Treasury and Festival Leader of Amen ... My Lord again recognized my worth ... I was appointed Viceroy of Nubia ... I directed serfs in thousands and tens of thousands, and Nubians in hundreds of thousands ... I rebuilt entirely the temples of the lords of the land of Kush that had fallen into ruin ...

Setau set out to make his mark on Nubia. Unfortunately, he was handicapped by inferior raw materials and an untrained workforce, many of whom were snatched from the Libyan oases. The buildings which he supervised, although at first sight magnificent, were by no means well built while even his own great stela was full of spelling mistakes.

Back in Egypt Ramesses' chief administrators, his two deputies, were the Northern (Memphite) and Southern (Theban) Viziers. Paser, son of the old High Priest of Amen Nebneteru, had been appointed Southern Vizier by Seti. A man of outstanding abilities, he was to prove a loyal servant to both Seti and Ramesses, becoming one of the most influential and long-lived non-royals of his time. As Vizier, Paser's duties were many and varied: he was at once chief justice, treasurer, administrator and tax collector and he liaised with the royal court on an almost daily basis, spending much of his working life at Pi-Ramesse rather than Thebes. Paser was directly responsible for the workmen at Deir el-Medina who, during his lengthy tenure, laboured on the tombs of Seti, Ramesses and their wives and children. It is a testament to Paser's efficiency, and of course to the long lives of his two masters, that both royal tombs were ready when needed. In Year 1 Paser's father Nebneteru had been succeeded as High Priest of Amen by Nebwennef who in turn died during Year 12. The next High Priest, Wennofer, was the father of Ramesses' boyhood friend Ameneminet who was himself promoted at this time to become Chief of Works of the Royal Monuments with special responsibility for the Ramesseum. Eventually, on Wennofer's death in Year 27, Paser became High Priest of Amen, a position he was to hold until his death in approximately Year 38.

Deir el-Medina was a purpose-built village, a New Kingdom housing estate specifically designed to provide a home for the artisans who laboured in the royal tombs in the nearby Valleys of the Kings and Queens.[5] The village survived from the beginning of the 18th Dynasty to the end of the 20th, seeing almost 500 years of continuous occupation with only a minor interruption during the Amarna era, and enjoying unprecedented prosperity during Ramesses' reign. This was an idyllic time for professional tomb builders as there were many royal tombs to be built and sufficient resources to pay for them. Ramesses was able to increase the rations which served as wages while decreasing the working hours of his workforce, a highly popular move much appreciated by his villagers. After Ramesses' death, however, royal resources gradually dwindled while corruption and theft in the necropolis became a way of life. Eventually, the village was abandoned at the end of the 20th Dynasty. Left behind in the village were enough ostraca (inscribed pottery and stone sherds), papyri and other archaeological evidence to allow us to reconstruct the lives of the Deir el-Medina workers with a surprising degree of accuracy.

The majority of Egypt's peasants lived in villages or hamlets set back from the cultivated land which fringed the Nile. They earned their living by working the fertile fields and lived in clusters of mud-brick houses which grew organically; as extra rooms were needed, extra rooms were simply built on to the existing walls. These dwellings, sturdy enough when well maintained, have with time and encroaching damp crumbled back to the earth from which they came. While some in the Nile Delta have been left as raised mounds, the vast majority have been flattened and built over or spread on the fields as fertilizer. Today, few domestic sites survive to bear witness to the day-to-day life of their dynastic inhabitants.

At Deir el-Medina, things were very different. Of necessity the village was situated in the desert close to the royal necropolis but some distance away from the Nile and the cultivated land. This meant that the villagers were to a large extent isolated from contact with the outside world. They led an insular, slightly claustrophobic existence, their lives revolving around the ongoing work in the royal necropolis. This was seen as a good thing and the top-secret nature of the work in the Valleys encouraged the officials who ran Deir el-Medina to reinforce this isolation in every way possible. However, the remote location had one major drawback. There were no wells and no streams near Deir el-Medina, and so every drop of water had to be carried in by donkey for storage at the official water stations which acted as the village wells. This was no mean feat when we consider that at its peak the village was home to some

Fig 7.1   The Deir el-Medina workman Pashedu drinks in the shade of a palm tree: an image from the walls of his tomb

120 families, maybe up to 1200 people plus their livestock. Provisions, too, had to be imported, and food made its way into the village as rations paid at the end of each month by the Vizier. Grain was the chief component of the ration; the standard monthly wage included four sacks of emmer wheat which would be used to bake bread, and one and a half sacks of barley which would make good Egyptian beer. Other foodstuffs and commodities would be paid as and when available, and the basic diet could be supplemented by barter, by home-grown produce and, for those who had some free time, by river fish.

During the regime of the efficient Paser there was little problem with supplies. Paser was concerned enough to take a personal interest in the feeding of his men:

The Mayor of Western Thebes, Ramose, greets the Chief Workmen and the whole gang . . . Look, the Governor and Vizier Paser has sent to me saying 'Let the dues be brought for the workmen of the Royal Tomb, namely vegetables, fish, firewood, jars of beer, food and milk. Do not let a scrap of it remain outstanding . . . Do not let me find that you have held anything that is due back as balance. Be careful over this . . .'[6]

Paser's successor, Khay, evidently experienced a few logistical problems, prompting his workmen to write polite but determined letters requesting their missing rations and the supplies that would allow them to continue with their work: '. . . Let a despatch be sent to the High Steward of Thebes, to the High Priest of Amen, to the 2nd Prophet of Amen, to the Mayor of Thebes, and to the controllers in charge of the treasury, to request of them all that we need . . .'[7]

Deir el-Medina was built on well-organized military lines with not an inch of space wasted. The entire village was surrounded by a thick mud-brick wall and for a long time there was only one official gateway, an arrangement which allowed the Vizier to retain a tight control over those who entered and left such a sensitive site. Originally, the northern entrance led directly on to the main street which bisected the village and which was lined on each side with a long row of terraced housing. These houses had no gardens or courtyards, they opened straight on to the street and backed on to the surrounding village wall. Later extensions to the village, built to the west during the late 18th Dynasty, and to the south during Seti's reign, made it necessary to provide further access roads and a new entrance, but this expansion too was well regulated, and Deir el-Medina never saw the higgledy-piggledy growth found at other Egyptian villages both ancient and modern.

Outside the village wall were the tombs and chapels which the villagers built for their own use. Within the wall the foremen and the scribes were allotted the largest homes. Their fellow villagers were packed into long, dark, narrow houses which seem impossibly small by modern Western standards, measuring approximately 49 by 16 feet (15 by 5 metres), given that some families raised eight or nine children. The houses were all built to a similar plan. The doorway led to a porch and then to a front chamber or reception room, home to a curious cupboard-like structure whose purpose is as yet unexplained but which has been variously identified as a box-bed or a birth bower used by the women of the family while in labour. Beyond this was a second reception room, the main living room lit by clerestory windows. A staircase led down to the cellar while a doorway led to a storage room or bedroom. Finally came the kitchen whose roof, presumably for safety purposes, was partially open to the sky. The flat roof of the main house was accessed via a stairway, and served as a much-needed extra room.

One resident of Deir el-Medina enjoyed an unusually high standard of living. The scribe Ramose, protégé of the Vizier Paser, was rich enough to have left us an unprecedented series of stelae, tombs (three!) and chapels, each bearing his name and many also bearing the name of his patron, Paser. Paser and Ramose in turn are occasionally named in the tombs of their workmen; surely a sign of mutual respect and affection between the bureaucrats and their subordinates. Great wealth does not always bring great happiness, however, and Ramose and his wife Mutem-wia had one constant sorrow. They were childless and Ramose had no son to succeed him as scribe. After years of hope and of fruitless offerings to Hathor, Min and Tawaret, the couple took the practical option and adopted a boy named Kenhirkhepeshef son of Panakht.[8] Eventually Kenhirkhepeshef took his place as scribe of the royal tomb. However Kenhirkhepeshef did not share his adopted father's honest and upright nature. The new scribe was disliked by his subordinates and, after being discovered diverting workmen to work on his own projects, was severely reprimanded by the Vizier Khay.

In spite of, or perhaps because of, his aggressive business methods, Kenhirkhepeshef, too, grew rich. In his old age, he was wealthy enough to attract the attention of a young bride, Naunakhte. She, all too soon a wealthy, childless widow, remarried and had eight children including a son whom she named after her late first husband. Many years later Naunakhte was unhappy and her will, sworn before a court tribunal, was the talk of Deir el-Medina!

I am a free woman of Egypt. I have raised eight children, and have provided them with everything suitable to their station in life. But now I am grown old and behold, my children don't look after me any more. I will therefore give my goods to the ones who have taken care of me. I will not give anything to the ones who have neglected me.[9]

The men who worked in the royal tombs were known as the 'Servants in the Place of Truth'. Their work was hard and often dangerous but it was both well paid and highly regarded. A vast gulf separated the noble labours of the quarrymen of Deir el-Medina from the ignominious labours forced on the poor unfortunates who toiled in pharaoh's mines and quarries, and places in the Deir el-Medina work gangs were eagerly sought after and jealously guarded. In the royal necropolis, as in all other aspects of Egyptian life, we find fathers training their sons and grandsons to follow in the family footsteps.

Every ten days the workmen left the village to walk along the mountain path to 'their' tomb. They would spend the next eight days lodging in temporary huts close to their workplace, returning home for the ninth and tenth days which served as the weekend. Food and drink for the working week had to be carried from home, and we have several desperate notes from workmen pleading with their nearest and dearest to send them additional rations. Some workmen didn't bother to turn up for work. Absenteeism was rife at all times, and an amazing variety of excuses were logged as valid reasons for missing a shift. Fortunately, the record of absences has survived, and we can see that these included absence due to illness, scorpion bite or a hangover, the celebration of a personal or state religious festival and even the indisposition of female relations. Poor Harmose – understandably absent from work during Year 40 as on the 1st month of winter day 15 he was being mummified by his friend

Amenemwia – had died in the village. By curious coincidence a letter detailing his simple funeral arrangements has been preserved to confirm the accuracy of the attendance records kept by the tomb scribe:

... This man died in the house of Horemheb who sent word to me saying 'Harmose is dead!' I went with Mahuhy and we saw that this was so. And we made arrangements for him, we had the undertaker fetched, saying 'Take care of him really well, we are looking after him.'[10]

Those workmen who did turn up for work were divided into two teams or gangs of about thirty men and these two gangs, under the direction of a foreman and his deputies, worked the left- and right-hand sides of the tomb. The names of some of these workmen have been preserved for us, and we know that the left side of Ramesses' tomb was worked by Qaha, his son Anhur-khaw and their gang, while the right side was the work of Neferhotep senior, Nebnufer and Neferhotep junior and their men. There was always a scribe present; his duties included keeping track of both workers and supplies and handing out the metal tools which, as valuable royal property, were distributed at the start of each shift and collected in again when work was over. Security guards completed the teams; they were considered necessary to ensure the secrecy of the enterprise.

Ramesses had picked the site for his tomb at the start of his reign. KV7 was to lie at the entrance to the Valley of the Kings, on the opposite side of the modern tourist road to KV5, the tomb of the royal sons. KV8, the site eventually chosen for Merenptah's tomb, was close by. An ostracon recovered from the Ramesseum tells us that work on KV7 started the 13th day of the 2nd month of winter, Year 2, when a silver tool was used to make the first ritual cut in the rock.[11] All ceremonies over, the hard work could begin. The labourers started to dig through the rock, roughing out the initial passageway using copper or bronze chisels, hammers and picks and removing the debris in woven baskets. The waste stone was dumped a discreet distance away from the tomb entrance.

As they progressed down into the mountain, their work lit by scores of lamps, the labourers were immediately followed by the more skilled workmen: the architect, plasterers, draughtsman, sculptors and painters who would give the rooms and passageways their final form. The rough-cut walls were checked with plumb-lines and made as straight and as square as possible. A coating of plaster was used to remedy any defects in the wall surface, and then outlines for the sculptors were laid down in red ink, with any corrections or amendments being made in black. Finally the sculptors carved the images and the painters brought the scenes to life using a palette of glowing colours: principally black, red, blue, yellow, green and white. It must have been both inconvenient and messy to have the stonecutters working at the same time as the painters, but this was a necessary inconvenience. Death could strike at any time, and the tomb had to be ready for use with only seventy days' notice. In KV7 work went at a fast pace. The decoration of the first passageway gives Ramesses' name as Usermaatre without the Setepenre which was added by the end of Year 2.

KV7 was not, with hindsight, a good choice of site. The surrounding rock proved to be of inferior quality, while its position low down in the valley made the tomb vulnerable to thieves and highly susceptible to flooding. The Valley of the Kings, normally a very dry environment, occasionally experiences ferocious cloudbursts when rainwater rushes downwards, pouring over the cliffs so that the lower-level tombs, including KV5 and KV7, are effectively situated beneath temporary waterfalls. The effect of this flooding, bad enough in antiquity, has become more severe in modern times due to the development of roadways to service the tourist industry, and the removal of the dry stone barriers erected by the tomb builders. We have already seen the devastating effect of these floods on the tomb of the royal sons. The waters, which have on at least a dozen separate occasions swirled into Ramesses' tomb, have wreaked havoc, tearing the beautifully carved and painted illustrations off the walls, making the ceilings unstable and filling the passages with a hard compacted mass of debris similar to that encountered in KV5. Further damage has been inflicted by the swelling and subsequent contraction of the moisture-laden shale underneath the tomb, which in turn causes the overlying limestone to crack and distort.

Unlike KV5, KV7 was never 'lost'. It remained at least partially open from the end of the dynastic age onwards and many early expeditions showed an initial interest in clearing the compacted rubbish, only to be discouraged by the practical difficulties and, of course, by the fact that

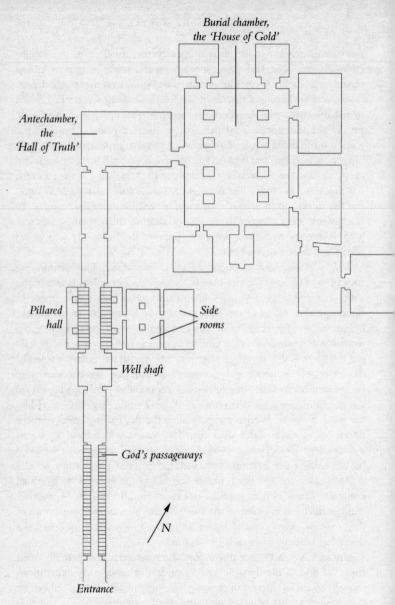

Burial chamber,
the 'House of Gold'

Antechamber,
the
'Hall of Truth'

Pillared
hall

Side
rooms

Well shaft

God's passageways

N

Entrance

Fig 7.2   KV7: the tomb of Ramesses II

they were unlikely to make a major (or valuable) find in an open tomb. Both Salt and Lepsius excavated in the tomb but until recently the only detailed clearance recorded is that of the British archaeologist Harry Burton, conducted during his 1913/14 season when he was working on behalf of his American patron, Theodore Davis. Noting that the tomb was 'practically full of debris, stones etc. carried in by water', and pulling down dangerous areas of ceiling as he worked, Burton was able to crawl as far as the burial chamber:

. . . The sarcophagus chamber is in a very bad state. All the eight columns have fallen and brought down much of the roof with them. My predecessor, whoever he was, dug three trenches but apparently found no sign of the sarcophagus.[12]

Unfortunately, in March 1914, soon after Burton stopped his work, the west bank suffered another torrential downpour and the tomb of Ramesses was further damaged. Howard Carter was later to do some survey work in the tomb, but the general consensus of opinion amongst Egyptologists was that KV7 was beyond redemption. It is only now, with the painstaking work of a French team led by Christian Leblanc, that the tomb is starting to receive the attention that it deserves. Clearance of the tomb is now well under way but as yet their work is incomplete and so unpublished.

Ramesses' tomb, although not as long or as deep as the tomb of Seti, is nevertheless extremely impressive. It has been calculated that KV7 is more than 8,800 square feet (820 square metres) in area with the burial chamber alone measuring some 1,950 square feet (181 square metres).[13] Ramesses made little effort to hide the entrance to his tomb, displaying an unwarranted trust in the honesty and efficiency of the necropolis guards, and only a wooden door, bolted and sealed but not plastered over, was to protect the king and all his earthly possessions. The stone lintel above the entrance displayed the golden yellow sun of daytime, the solar disc of Re, positioned between the goddesses Isis and Nephthys, principal players in the legend of Osiris. The opposing reveals of the doorway showed Maat kneeling above the lily and papyrus plants which symbolize Upper and Lower Egypt. Within the tomb the sun's disc would be painted red; here it has become the darker sun of evening and of night.

If the Egyptian temple may be read as a symbolic map of the cosmos at the time of creation, the tomb must be seen as a plan of the journey to eternal life of the deceased. At a more practical level, the tomb was the permanent home of the king's body, and as such it had to provide sufficient storage space for all his goods and chattels. Although it was certain that Ramesses would achieve immortality, his precise route was not known. The ancient traditions taught that a dead king might sail for ever in the solar boat of Re, or might dwell in the Field of Reeds with Osiris. By the 19th Dynasty theologians were starting to argue that these two beliefs might be combined so that at night – the time when the sun dropped below the horizon to sail through the Netherworld, illuminating the deceased – Re might be equated with Osiris, King of the Dead. Ramesses might therefore expect to spend his eternity in the solar boat of Re, being reborn every morning to bring light to the sky, setting every evening to spend the twelve hours of night at one with Osiris-Re.

Ramesses' tomb reflects this theological dichotomy, and we find the night-time sun disc of Re appearing alongside the mysteries and rituals of the Osirian afterlife. Re takes precedence in the foremost part of the tomb while the back, symbolically the western part, is the region of Osiris, Lord of the West. Immediately within the entrance to KV7 a sequence of passageways and stairs known as the 'God's Passageways of Re' leads downwards to a square well-shaft. The God's Passageways are intended to trace the nocturnal journey of Re, and are appropriately decorated first with scenes from the *Litany of Re*, a solar funerary text in praise of the sun god, and then with the *Amduat*, or *The Book of what is in the Netherworld*, an Osirian survival manual which, if followed to the letter, would ensure that Ramesses reached his heaven with few problems. The well, which may perhaps be read as the symbolic representation of the tomb of Osiris, served a practical purpose in deterring unwanted visitors from progressing towards the burial chamber.

Beyond the well comes a pillared hall and side rooms, the 'Chariot Hall' or the 'Hall of Repulsing Rebels', which is decorated with the Osiris shrine – opposed images of the god – and with scenes from the *Book of Gates*. This hall marks the turning point in the tomb; from here onwards preference is given to the mortuary rituals of Osiris. A staircase descends to the lower passageways, decorated with scenes of the 'Opening of the Mouth' ceremony, which lead in turn to a large antechamber known as the 'Hall of Truth'. Here are scenes from the *Book of the Dead*, never before included in a royal tomb. An unexpected right-angled turn creates the bent-axis plan already seen in the tomb of Nefertari. This may be a deliberate reference to the 18th Dynasty bent-angled royal tombs, or simply a practical means of avoiding a difficult area of shale. Finally comes the vaulted, pillared burial chamber, the 'House of Gold', which is decorated with scenes from the *Book of Gates*, the *Amduat* and the *Book of the Divine Cow*. There are four storage rooms and four side rooms ('the Resting-Places of the Gods') leading off the burial chamber, and it is possible that there may be a further descending passageway similar to that found in the tomb of Seti.[14]

Ramesses, like his father before him, died and was embalmed in the north; examination of his mummy has revealed marine rather than riverine sand within his bandages, a clear indication that he was not mummified on the banks of the Nile. No official document preserves the details of his passing, but it seems that he died of old age during August 1213 BC in his 67th regnal year.[15] Quickly, before putrefaction could set in, Ramesses was sent to the embalming house. Here he was to spend seventy days as his body was prepared for eternal life. Meanwhile Egypt plunged into mourning and messengers sped post-haste to Thebes where the great tomb, empty for so many years, was finally to be made ready to receive its master.

Ramesses would have been collecting his funerary equipment throughout his reign, perhaps storing it for security at the nearby Ramesseum. Now the time had come to pack the tomb with all the objects that a dead king might need in the Afterlife. These would include food, drink, clothing, furniture, chariots, jewellery and miniature human figures or *shabtis* who could come alive by magic and perform any task required of the deceased. We have only to think of the magnificent funerary equipment supplied for Tutankhamen's modest burial to imagine the treasures which would have been provided for Ramesses the Great. Unfortunately very little of this equipment has survived. We have two wooden *shabti* figures (now in Brooklyn Museum and the British Museum) and a rare cast bronze *shabti* (Berlin Museum) which has been hammered flat and snapped in two. The recent French excavations in KV7 have recovered a beautiful stone *shabti*, fragments of the Canopic chest (the chest which held the mummified entrails of the king) and pieces of calcite inscribed on two faces with the *Book of Gates*. The latter, still bearing traces of pigment, surely represent the remains of Ramesses' anthropoid stone coffin or sarcophagus, which must have been similar in design to the beautiful stone coffin provided for his father. No trace of any exterior stone sarcophagus has been recovered from either KV7 or KV17 and, given the impressive size of the Seti coffin, it is perhaps unlikely that one was provided. Either the anthropoid coffin stood as the sole covering, or a wooden sarcophagus (or sarcophagi) was provided. Ramesses' anthropoid stone coffin now stood empty in the middle of the burial chamber where it rested on a massive limestone support or funerary bed guarded by two wild cats.

At Pi-Ramesse, in the house of embalming, Ramesses was stripped of his finery and cleaned with a solution of natron and Nile water in a ritual act intended to symbolize the rebirth of the dead.[16] Before his purified corpse could be embalmed it was necessary to remove the soft tissue that would otherwise decay and cause his body to rot. First came the extraction of the brain. Equipped with a small chisel, a hook, a long-handled spoon and a jug of water the undertakers were able to drag and flush cranial matter out of the skull via the nose. Next, using a ritual stone knife, a cut was made in Ramesses' left side and the contents of his abdomen, apart from his kidneys, were removed and stored. A cut through the diaphragm made it possible to remove the lungs. The organs taken from the chest and abdomen would later be cleaned, anointed, coated in hot resin, wrapped in finest linen and stored in four Canopic jars within his tomb. Unfortunately, Ramesses' heart was accidentally extracted with his lungs. It was essential that the heart be left in place as it would be required to testify before the court of Osiris, and so the undertakers took up their golden thread and sewed the missing organ on the right rather than the left side of the king's chest. As the king's skin would shrink during drying, his finger- and toe-nails were tied in place with twine. His body was then washed, packed with temporary stuffing and placed on a sloping board where it was covered with powdered natron and left for forty days.

Then Ramesses' body, now far lighter in weight and somewhat darker in colour, was transferred to the house of purification. Here it was emptied of its temporary stuffing and once again washed and dried before being repacked with resin-soaked linen. Peppercorns were placed up the dead king's nostrils and, before the abdominal slit was closed, his body was massaged with softening oils. The wrapping of the mummy was a lengthy business. Ramesses, lying on his back on a wooden trestle, was first covered with a shroud. Then the bandaging started with the wrapping of each toe and finger, progressing to each hand and foot, each arm and leg. Ramesses' arms were bound and crossed left over right on his chest in a reversal of the traditional right-over-left royal pose. The bandagers then worked their way down the body from the head to the feet. As each body part was wrapped, spells were spoken and jewellery and protective amulets were incorporated within the bandages. Finally the king was dressed in one or more shrouds knotted at the head and the feet. Ramesses was now ready to make his final journey south.

Fig 7.3   Ammit, the heart-eating monster who, in Osirian legend, waited to destroy those deemed unworthy of the Afterlife

Ramesses set sail for Thebes accompanied by his son and heir Merenptah. Well over half a century had passed since the young Ramesses had travelled south with Seti's mummy and there were few now alive who remembered the rituals of royal death. We are lacking a specific record of Ramesses' funeral but it seems that it would have progressed, albeit on a far grander scale, along similar lines to a commoner Theban funeral:

A goodly burial arrives in peace, your seventy days having been fulfilled in the place of embalming. You are placed on the bier . . . and are drawn by bulls without blemish, the road being sprinkled with milk, until you reach the door of your tomb. The children of your children . . . weep with loving hearts. Your mouth is opened by the lector priest and your purification is performed by the *Sem*-priest. Horus adjusts your mouth and opens your eyes and ears, your flesh and bones being perfect in all that appertains to you. Spells and glorifications are recited for you ... You enter into the land given by the king, into the sepulchre of the west.[17]

Arriving at Thebes some time in late October, Ramesses' body was dragged on a wooden sledge first to the Ramesseum and then on to the Valley of the Kings. His impressive cortège included the two Viziers, priests, statesmen, family members, friends, professional mourners and two actresses dressed as the goddesses Isis and Nephthys. At the door of the tomb the procession halted to be greeted by the *muu*-dancers (ritual dancers) and by a priest wearing the jackal-headed mask of Anubis. Here Merenptah, acting as his father's *Sem*-Priest, would perform the all-important 'Opening of the Mouth' ceremony. By touching the eyes, nose, mouth and ears of the mummy with a series of ritual implements including a knife, an adze and the foreleg of an ox sacrificed for the funeral feast, Merenptah could both ensure that Ramesses would be re-animated in the Netherworld and confirm his own right to rule Egypt.

The funeral feast was held in the entrance to the tomb. By now Ramesses rested in his nest of coffins. None of these have survived, but comparison with the burial of Tutankhamen suggests that Ramesses would have been provided with a solid gold funerary mask and a series of golden coffins, at least one of which would also have been of solid gold. The funeral meal finished, Ramesses was carefully dragged down to the burial chamber where he was placed in his magnificent stone coffin. As the mourners and workmen left, the tomb was swept clean. Finally the lights were extinguished and the great door closed and bolted. At sunrise on the following day Ramesses would experience his first rebirth and start his perpetual journey in the solar barque of Re. Meanwhile his physical body was to rest in its tomb for less than 200 years.

Notes

1 For a preliminary publication of this stela see Taraqji, A. F. (1999), 'Nouvelles découvertes sur les relations avec l'Egypte à tel Sakka et à Keswe, dans la region de Damas', *Bulletin de la Societé Française d'Egyptologie* 144: 40–4; for a commentary on the publication see Yoyotte, J. (1999), 'La stèle de Ramses II à Keswe et sa signification historique', *ibid* 44–58.

2 Discussed in Kitchen, K. A. (1999 in press), 'Note on a stela of Ramesses II from near Damascus', *Göttinger Miszellen*. I am grateful to Professor Kitchen for drawing this stela to my attention.

3 The family of Wennofer is discussed in Gaballa, G. A. (1979), 'Monuments of Prominent Men of Memphis, Abydos and Thebes', in Ruffle, J. *et al.* (eds) *Glimpses of Ancient Egypt: studies in honour of H. W. Fairman*, Warminster: 42–50: 46.

4 For the stela of Setau see Kitchen, K. A. (1975), 'The great biographical stela of Setau, Viceroy of Nubia', *Orientalia Lovaniensia Periodica* 6: 295–302; Wente, F. F. (1985), 'A new look at the Viceroy Setau's Autobiographical Inscription', *Mélanges Gemal Eddin Mokhtar 2*, Cairo: 347–59. The translation given here is adapted from Kitchen, K. A. (1982), *Pharaoh Triumphant*, Warminster: 136–8.

5 For a summary of life at Deir el-Medina, and full bibliography of earlier works see Valbelle, D. (1985), *Les Ouvriers de la Tombe: Deir el-Medineh à l'époque Ramesside*, Cairo.

6 Letter written by the Mayor of Western Thebes to the workmen and their foremen, translation adapted from Kitchen, K. A. (1982), *Pharaoh Triumphant*, Warminster: 125.

7 Letter of Anhur-khaw. This translation adapted from Kitchen, K. A. (1982), *Pharaoh Triumphant*, Warminster: 196.

8 This story is told in Bierbrier, M. (1982), *The Tomb-Builders of the Pharaohs*, London: 32.

9 Discussed in Tyldesley, J. A. (1994), *Daughters of Isis*, London: 42.

10 Kitchen, K. A. (1982), *Pharaoh Triumphant*, Warminster: 205.

11 Leblanc, C. (1999), 'La "Demeure d'Eternité" de Ramses II', in Barbotin, C. and Leblanc, C. (eds) *Les Monuments d'Eternité de Rameses II*, Paris: 49–57: 50.

12 H. Burton, unpublished excavation journal, Metropolitan Museum of Art, New York.

13 Figures given by Reeves, N. and Wilkinson, R. H. (1996), *The Complete Valley of the Kings*, London: 140–3: 142.

14 John Romer mentions finding a 'void' lying off the burial chamber which he was unfortunately unable to excavate further: Romer, J. (1981), *Valley of the Kings*, London: 75.

15 See Peden, A. J. (1994), 'A note on the accession date of Merenptah', *Göttinger Miszellen* 140: 6.

16 Ramesses' body was to be stripped of its bandages in antiquity and re-wrapped. This summary of events in the embalming house of Pi-Ramesse is therefore based on our current understanding of 19th Dynasty mummification. For further details consult Ikram, S. and Dodson, A. (1998), *The Mummy in Ancient Egypt*, London.

17 Text from a stela in TT 110; for a full translation see Davies and Gardiner (1915), *The Tomb of Amenemhat*, London: 56.

8

Decline and Decay:
The Last Ramesses

Merenptah, although already an elderly man approaching his seventh
decade, was by no means content to rest on his father's laurels. He too
wanted to prove himself a model king, a mighty warrior and a monumental
builder, and he was not prepared to make concessions towards his
advanced years. As we might expect, portraits of Merenptah as pharaoh
show a young and vigorous man, handsome in spite of his somewhat
prominent ears and narrow eyes. He bears more than a passing resemblance
to his perpetually youthful father, a resemblance which is enhanced by
Merenptah's habit of usurping not only the statuary of Amenhotep III
but of the great Ramesses himself.

Egypt was in grave need of a warrior pharaoh. Merenptah had gained
his throne at a time of growing international insecurity, an insecurity
which was worsened by the death of the Mediterranean world's longest-
reigning monarch in recent memory. Following the signing of the historic
Hittite peace treaty, Egypt and the Near East had enjoyed over forty
years of prosperous tranquillity. This treaty remained in operation and
Egypt and Hatti were still on the friendliest of terms, with Merenptah
on one occasion supplying the famine-struck Hittites with much-needed
grain. The Hittites, however, could no longer be regarded as powerful
allies. They were struggling to survive in the face of an unhappy mixture
of natural disasters and territorial disputes. In this they were not alone. A
combination of circumstances, including the weakness of the Mycenaean
economy, famine in Greece and Anatolia and possibly an outbreak of
plague along the Aegean coast, had prompted disturbances and population
shifts which, having commenced in the Aegean, were now beginning
to unsettle the entire eastern Mediterranean. Nomadic groups were
starting to band together, targeting the prosperous city states. As once-

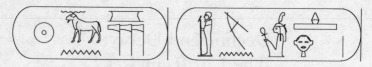

Fig 8.1   The cartouches of King Merenptah

mighty states buckled and weakened under the strain of these aggressive migrating hordes, lesser states and tribes found themselves released from the domination of their overlords and free to act as they wished. International law and order were slowly starting to crack, and once again the Mediterranean was plagued with bands of pirates.

Some time between Years 1 and 5 Merenptah mobilized his army and marched eastwards. We are given few details of his campaign, but it would appear that the new pharaoh had found it necessary to reassert his authority in the southern Levant which had typically reacted to the change of monarch with a minor revolt. After a brief stay in Canaan and south Syria, and some fighting at Ashkelon, Gezer and Yenoam, the victorious Egyptian army returned home in triumph. The eastern empire was, for the time being, secure.[1] Merenptah had been trained as a soldier by his father, but he was now an old man, albeit an active old man who did not hesitate to travel between Pi-Ramesse and Thebes and even further south. Whether he fought in person for his country, or whether he was content to mastermind the battle-plan, leaving the actual fighting to his middle-aged son Prince Seti-Merenptah, is not made clear. However Merenptah, as pharaoh, was certainly to be credited with Egypt's victories.

A more serious challenge to Merenptah's authority came from the west. The Libyans, a diverse band of nomads who had threatened trouble at the start of Ramesses' reign, were now firmly allied with the 'Sea Peoples': a confederation of sea-borne itinerants and pirates including not only the Sherden people who had menaced Ramesses but various groups recorded as the Shekelesh, Luka, Teresh and Ekwesh. Planning the unthinkable, an invasion of Egypt with a view to permanent settlement in the fertile Nile Delta, the Libyans sent messengers southwards in an attempt to encourage a Nubian rebellion which would create an effective diversion and stretch Merenptah's military resources to breaking point. Fortunately, in Year 5, with not a moment to lose, Merenptah's somewhat inefficient intelligence service learned of the Libyan plans. The danger was very near; the invaders had already reached the outskirts of the Delta. The Egyptian army, inspired by the god Ptah, marched westwards and won a hard-fought six-hour battle, slaughtering over 6,000 of the enemy and taking thousands more captive. Meanwhile the Nubians did indeed revolt, but they did so too late to help their allies. Encouraged by the western victory Merenptah's troops marched southwards and emphatically crushed the Nubian rebellion.

The details of the glorious Libyan campaign were recorded in poetry and prose on the back of a stela which Merenptah had appropriated from the mortuary temple of Amenhotep III and re-erected in his own mortuary temple. A copy of the text was also displayed at Karnak. The bold style of the piece, and the message that it conveys, is highly reminiscent of Ramesses' far more lengthy Kadesh inscriptions:

Year 5, 3rd month of summer, day 3. Under the Majesty of *Horus*: Mighty Bull, rejoicing in Maat; *King of Upper and Lower Egypt*: Baenre-Meramen, Son of Re; Merenptah, Content with Maat . . . an account of his victories in all lands, to let all the lands know and let the glory of his deeds be seen . . . Their [Libyan] archers abandoned their bows and the hearts of their runners grew faint as they fled. They loosened their water-skins and threw them down and their packs were untied and thrown away. The vile chief, the Libyan enemy, fled in the dark of night, alone, with no plume on his head and his feet unshod. His wives were carried away from him, his food supplies were stolen and he had no drinking water to sustain him . . . Great joy has arisen in Egypt. Shouts go up from her towns. They speak of the Libyan victories of Merenptah, Content with Maat. How beloved is he, the victorious king.[2]

This stela is known today as the Poetical Stela or the Israel Stela because it makes a passing reference to the Israelites – 'Israel is desolated and has no seed' – amongst the lengthy list of Egypt's vanquished, thereby confirming that, whatever the nature of the biblical Exodus, the Hebrews were a genuine socio-political entity dwelling in Palestine before Year 5 of Merenptah's reign.

Ramesses had built and restored at all the important, and many of the unimportant, sites of Egypt, leaving his son little scope to display his own architectural skills. Undaunted, the new king simply followed his father's example by adding his own name and texts to the monuments of his predecessors.[3] Under Merenptah Pi-Ramesse retained its position as Egypt's capital city, but Memphis was now allowed to regain some of her former importance and it was here that the new king built himself a grand ceremonial palace close to the Ptah temple. This palace, which was designed to include a throne-room, ten bedrooms, some eight or nine bathrooms and a lavatory but no harem quarters or storage facilities, seems to have functioned as a private retreat for the king during the celebration of the Memphite festivals.[4] It is now totally destroyed. Further south Merenptah built, completed and usurped monuments at Hermopolis, el-Sirirya, Dendera, Abydos and Gebel Silsila.

Merenptah never seemed a likely candidate for a long reign; the ten years which he eventually enjoyed were an unexpected bonus in one so old. It was therefore seen as vital that work commence at once on his tomb and mortuary temple. The temple, situated on the west bank between the mortuary temples of his father and Amenhotep III, was a grand building, although far smaller in scale than the neighbouring Ramesseum. In order to speed up the construction, and to reduce costs, it was built principally from blocks taken from the partially collapsed Amenhotep III temple. His temple was intended to be Merenptah's principal monument; unfortunately, it too was completely destroyed in antiquity.

Merenptah's tomb (KV8) was a simplified straight-axis version of the tombs prepared for his father and his grandfather. Its most innovative features were the entrance, which was now designed to form an imposing and very obvious façade, and a small side chapel opening off the side chamber attached to the first pillared hall which was dedicated to Ramesses II. Here Merenptah was buried in c. 1204 BC. His mummified body was laid to rest cocooned in a series of concentric coffins and a nest of four huge sarcophagi; three rectangular boxes of red granite and an innermost anthropoid sarcophagus of white calcite. The third of these sarcophagi was to be removed from the tomb during the 21st Dynasty when it would be used for the burial of King Psusennes I at Tanis. Meanwhile Merenptah's mummy, stripped of its precious amulets, badly damaged and evicted from its own tomb, was to be rewrapped and reinterred by the necropolis priests. Merenptah was eventually discovered by Victor Loret lying with other members of the royal family in the tomb of

Amenhotep II (KV 35). He was taken to Cairo where he was unwrapped by G. Elliot Smith on 8 July 1907:

The body is that of an old man and is 1 metre 714 millimetres in height. Merenptah was almost completely bald, only a narrow fringe of white hair (now cut so close as to be seen only with difficulty) remaining on the temples and occiput. A few short (about 2 mill.) black hairs were found on the upper lip and scattered, closely clipped hairs on the cheeks and chin. The general aspect of the face recalls that of Ramesses II, but the form of the cranium and the measurements of the face much more nearly agree with those of his father, Seti the Great.[5]

Merenptah, like Ramesses before him, showed the classic debilities of Egyptian old age. His teeth were in a terrible condition with many of the molars missing, and he too had suffered from arthritis and arteriosclerosis. Further indignities had been inflicted in the embalming house, where his testicles had been misplaced, the ensuing wound being unconvincingly mended with resin. Finally tomb robbers had pulled off his right arm, hacked open his abdomen, snapped off the tip of his penis and damaged his right shoulder with an axe.

The death of a long-lived king was often a time of fraught uncertainty as conservative Egypt struggled to come to terms with the ending of an era and the start of a new regime. Merenptah had been so closely associated with Ramesses during his final years that the transfer of power had passed smoothly from father to son and Merenptah's reign in many ways became a continuation of what had gone before. However, the new king's advanced years were obvious to all and it seems that, from the moment of Ramesses' death, there was jostling for position amongst Merenptah's sons, brothers and nephews. The unusually high number of surviving children and grandchildren of Ramesses, and in particular the survival of sons born to deceased princes older than Merenptah, now proved to be a hindrance rather than a help in sorting out the succession. Merenptah, aware of the dangers of dynastic uncertainty, had already nominated his heir. Crown Prince Seti-Merenptah, son of Merenptah and his sister-queen Iset-Nofret II, bore the titles of 'Heir of the Two Lands, Generalissimo and Senior Prince'. Although, like his father before him, Seti-Merenptah was never officially proclaimed co-regent, it should have been obvious to all that he would follow his father on the throne. However, Merenptah was most unexpectedly succeeded by a man of mystery, Amenmesse.

Amenmesse's exact position within the royal family is nowhere explained. His paternity goes unrecorded but he is most likely to have been the son of either Merenptah or Ramesses II; the chances of a non-royal outsider snatching the throne from under the noses of a host of genuine royal males would have been very slim. His mother, Takhat, is equally mysterious. In the unfinished Theban tomb which she intended to share with her son (KV 10) she claims neither to be a King's Daughter nor a King's Wife, and is simply recorded as a King's Mother. However, it must remain an outside possibility that she was one of the younger and more insignificant daughters of Ramesses II. Amenmesse's consort, the Great Royal Wife Beketwerel, was also destined to share his tomb and she, too, for similar reasons, appears to have been of non-royal birth.

The precise sequence of events following the death of Merenptah remains unclear, but the most reasonable assumption is that the old king died unexpectedly while Seti-Merenptah was for some reason absent from court. To imagine Seti-Merenptah as present at his father's death, yet somehow overlooked as heir, would perhaps be stretching the imagination too far. However, if the Crown Prince was indeed absent from his father's sick-bed, we must further deduce that he must have been some considerable distance away, possibly even outside the borders of Egypt, as the traditional seventy-day embalming period would have allowed him ten weeks in which to return home and bury his father. Was he sick and so unable to attend the funeral? Did no one tell him of the death until it was too late for him to return home? Somehow Amenmesse, in the absence of the true heir and presumably with the support of at least some of the more prominent members of the court, seized his chance to bury the old king and in so doing had himself proclaimed pharaoh. He was rewarded for his bold actions by a brief, undistinguished reign which was possibly restricted to the south of the country and which ended with his death during his Year 4.

Amenmesse was succeeded by Seti II, whom most historians have identified with the displaced Seti-Merenptah. Not surprisingly, the new king, having piously buried his predecessor and so asserted his right to rule, immediately set about erasing all trace of the usurper from the records of Egypt, leaving modern Egyptologists with a tangled legacy of superimposed cartouches. The middle-aged Seti II enjoyed a reign of some six years during which he too accomplished very little. His titles are strongly militaristic, indicating his interest in the ideal of pharaoh as warrior, but we have no evidence that he fought any major battles. His principal monuments were his unfinished tomb (KV15), his mortuary temple and a small triple shrine at Karnak.

It is unlikely that Amenmesse would have been able to succeed in his spectacular coup had Egypt not been suffering the first effects of what was to be a long-term bureaucratic crisis. Already, towards the end of Ramesses' reign, we have seen the first hints of economic insecurity; the gradual tailing off of Ramesses' building programme and the frequent use of recycled building materials and shoddy construction techniques all point to a slow but steady decline in standards. Little had changed within Egypt's borders, but the instability in the eastern Mediterranean, which had grown worse since the time of Merenptah, was starting to interrupt the royal cash flow. A strong, long-lived king may have been able to unite his country, protect his borders and reimpose bureaucratic order. This, however, was not to be. Crown Prince Seti-Merenptah, son of Seti II and his consort Queen Twosret, had already died and the throne passed instead to a young man of disputed parentage. Ramesses-Siptah is variously described as a son of Ramesses II, Merenptah, Amenmesse or, most likely, Seti II, born either to a queen named Tia or to a secondary wife of Syrian origin named Sutailja.

King Ramesses-Siptah, a minor, ruled Egypt under the joint guardianship of his forceful stepmother Twosret and the mysterious 'Chancellor of the Whole Land', Bey, 'He Who Established the King on his Father's Throne'. Bey's unusual name indicates that he too might have been of Asiatic extraction, possibly again a Syrian. His precise role at Siptah's court is unknown, but he obviously held a position of great power and his unprecedented titles specifically suggest that he had been instrumental in ensuring that Siptah inherited his throne. This in turn implies that Siptah's succession had been by no means automatic or unchallenged. Bey had himself depicted standing behind Siptah's throne, he was mentioned in the foundation deposits of Siptah's mortuary temple and was even allowed to build his own tomb close to that of his young master in the Valley of the Kings (KV13). He was clearly a force to be reckoned with. He vanished, however, during Siptah's Year 4, leaving Queen Twosret as the sole power behind the throne. By Year 3 the young king had changed his name to Merenptah-Siptah. He died without issue some three years later. Siptah's mummy, recovered from the royal cache in the tomb of Amenhotep II (KV35), shows that the young king had a distorted left foot and an atrophied lower leg, possibly the result of cerebral palsy. This deformity is not shown in any of his portraits where he appears as a physically perfect, stereotypical monarch.

Siptah had proved too weak to deal effectively with the Libyan tribes who were now blatantly flouting Egyptian authority by crossing the western border to settle in the Nile Delta. This influx of unwanted foreigners was by no means Siptah's only, or even his major, problem. Papyrus Salt 124, a copy of a legal document dated to the end of the 19th Dynasty, highlights an unacceptable level of lawlessness on the Theban west bank, with looting, robbery and casual theft now everyday occurrences.[6] Deir el-Medina, an isolated and claustrophobic environment, was entirely dependent upon the government funding which provided the villagers with their food and provisions. The villagers therefore act as a litmus test of state stability; any failure to pay the rations is greeted with immediate dissent, strike action, and an increase in theft from the richly endowed royal graves and mortuary temples. Now we learn how the Chief Workman Peneb, an all-round bad-guy who is variously accused of bullying, seducing women and plotting murder, had been caught stealing from the tomb of Seti II:

. . . And when the burial of all the kings was made I reported Peneb's theft of the things of King Seti Merenptah . . . and he took away the covering of his chariot . . . and he stole the incense of the ennead of gods of the necropolis and he divided it between himself and his fellows . . . and he took away his wines and sat on the sarcophagus of pharaoh although he was buried . . . and he hacked up the ground which is sealed in the place which is hidden. And yet he swore the oath saying 'I did not upset a stone in the neighbourhood of the Place of Pharaoh.'

Siptah's childless death left Twosret free to inherit his throne. Assuming full kingly regalia she became the first female king to rule Egypt since Hatchepsut some 250 years earlier. Twosret and Hatchepsut shared strikingly similar personal circumstances. Both were royal ladies, ex-queens, with no living son. Both were expected to rule Egypt on a temporary basis on behalf of their young stepsons. Both were influenced by charismatic men: Hatchepsut by Senenmut, Twosret by Bey. There was, however, an important difference. Hatchepsut had come to the throne at a time of peace and prosperity. Her rule had no obvious justification beyond those which she herself suggested, but it proved to be a successful one and she reigned for over twenty-two years. Twosret, in contrast, ruled at a time of civil disturbance and escalating political crisis. These circumstances are reminiscent of events surrounding the accession of Sobeknofru, the Middle Kingdom female pharaoh who ruled Egypt as the last king of the 12th Dynasty. Sobeknofru, totally acceptable to her people, is generally interpreted as a courageous woman struggling against all the odds to preserve her dynastic line. Twosret's reign is often less favourably regarded, and many have seen her as a power-crazed woman contributing to, rather than attempting to avert, the growing unrest within Egypt. She herself provides no explanation of her assumption of power.

Twosret enjoyed a mere two years of solo rule over a strife-torn Egypt. Her main monuments were to be her tomb and a mortuary temple that was to stand to the south of the Ramesseum, but which was never completed. It is in her tomb in the Valley of the Kings (KV14) that we can follow her personal history. Started at the end of the reign of Seti II, the tomb was designed to be a relatively modest structure ideally suited to a 'King's Great Wife'. With Twosret's assumption of regal power, however, her tomb was extended to become a burial place fit for a king. Curiously, one scene in her tomb shows Twosret standing behind Siptah in a conventional wifely pose. Siptah's name has, however, been erased from the tomb and replaced by that of Seti II. Did Twosret marry her young stepson in order to consolidate her hold on the throne? And did she later delete his image, preferring to be associated for eternity with her first and more glamorous husband Seti? Her reign marks the end of the 19th Dynasty and the end of the direct line of Ramesses' descendants. Twosret's tomb was usurped soon after her death and her body has never been positively identified, although there is a mummy attributed to her now housed in Cairo Museum.

After a brief hiatus the unknown Setnakht came to the throne as the mysterious founder of Dynasty 20. It seems likely that the new king was connected with the preceding regime. Setnakht himself, however, makes no effort to justify his rule by linking himself to the successful Ramesside kings, a surprising omission as earlier New Kingdom monarchs did not hesitate to claim a fictitious relationship with their more successful predecessors; Tutankhamen, for example, had claimed to be the son of the glamorous Amenhotep III, although it is more likely that he was actually the son of the discredited Akhenaten. Setnakht simply tells us, on a stele carved at Elephantine, that he came to the throne via a divine oracle, and that in so doing he brought *maat* to a land in chaos. All that we can say for certain is that Setnakht was the father of Ramesses III and the husband of Queen Tiy-Merenese. Setnakht reigned for a mere two years leaving no substantial monuments apart from two tombs in the Valley of the Kings. The first tomb (KV 11) had to be abandoned when it inadvertently cut into the tomb of Amenmesse (KV 10), and so Setnakht usurped the tomb of Twosret where he attempted to erase both her name and image from its walls.

Ramesses III was a determined monarch who set out to model his reign on the reign of Ramesses II without ever claiming direct descent from his great role model.[7] Already, less than fifty years after his death, Ramesses II had become a legendary heroic pharaoh, his reign a golden period of peace and prosperity which must have seemed particularly attractive to those living during more uncertain times. The new monarch, *King of Upper and Lower Egypt*, Usermaatre Meriamen, *Son of Re*, Ramesses III, Ruler of Heliopolis, not only borrowed his hero's name and titles, he named his own numerous children after the children of Ramesses II. Wherever possible he replicated the deeds of the great Ramesses. Egypt's shrinking empire meant that he lacked the resources to be a great builder, and was forced to confine his monuments to within Egypt's borders, but his mortuary temple, sited on the Theban west bank at Medinet Habu, was a splendid complement to the nearby Ramesseum.

Medinet Habu was graced with imposing pylons, elegant columned courts, a royal palace and lines of royal children whose names were curiously left unrecorded even though space had been left for their labels. One surprising feature was a gatehouse built in the style of a *migdol* or Syrian fortress complete with crenellated towers. Today, Medinet Habu represents the most complete of the west bank mortuary temples. As we

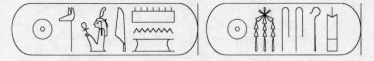

Fig 8.2   The cartouches of Ramesses III

might expect, Ramesses used his temple walls to display scenes of royal triumph.[8] Here we find stereotypical – and probably false – images of victory in Nubia and anachronistic scenes showing the storming of the Syrian town of Tunip and assaults on Hittite strongholds copied wholesale from the Ramesseum. Ramesses III had no need to usurp his hero's battle scenes. He too had been called upon to fight for his country, although, unlike Ramesses II, he had been asked to defend rather than expand Egypt's borders.

Ramesses had become king at a dangerous and unsettled time. The Sea Peoples who had threatened Merenptah were once again active and once again in league with the assorted tribes who made up the highly mobile Tjehenu or Libyans. Ramesses mustered his troops and set to work to repel the invaders who were threatening the stability of the Nile Delta. Three mighty battles followed.

In Year 5 Ramesses fought successfully against three representative Libyan tribes: the Libu, the Meshwesh and the Seped. The official reason given for this campaign is the need to suppress a rebellion sparked off by the imposition of a new Tjehenu chief chosen by the Egyptians against the wishes of the tribes people. In fact, it seems that Ramesses had found it necessary to drive back the Libyans who, from the reign of Siptah onwards, had been settling in the western Delta. Once again there were copious quantities of Libyan blood spilt, as Ramesses 'destroyed them and slew them at one stroke. I overthrew them, felled them in their own blood and turned them into heaps of corpses'.[9]

Three years later came a far greater threat. The Aegean-based Sea Peoples had already wrought havoc in the eastern Mediterranean, bringing about the collapse of the Hittite empire and the annihilation of, among others, Tarsus and Ugarit. Now firmly ensconced in Syria, the Sea Peoples had started to move southwards by land and boat with the declared intention of invading and not merely robbing but settling in

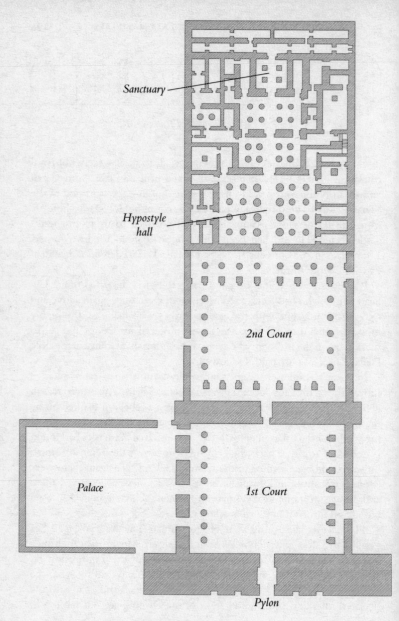

Fig 8.3   Medinet Habu: the mortuary temple of Ramesses III which was
modelled on the nearby Ramesseum

the Nile Delta. Ramesses was confronted with a two-pronged attack. He responded with fierce land fighting in Canaan and a naval battle fought off the Delta coast. This sea battle is graphically depicted on the walls of Medinet Habu, where we see the Sea People in boats with distinctive duck-shaped prows and sterns. The accompanying text brings the scene to life:

Year 8 . . . The king is a heroic lord, one far-reaching of arm who removes breath from the foreign lands with the heat of his body; one of great splendour who rages when he sees the battle line like Sekhmet raging at the time of her fury . . . The rebels who do not know Egypt consistently faint when they hear of his strength; they come in praise with their limbs trembling at the mere mention of him . . . The foreign lands made a plot in their countries, dislodged and scattered by battle were the lands all at one time, and no land could stand before their arms . . . But the heart of this god, the Lord of Gods, was prepared and ready to ensnare them like birds . . . I caused the river mouth to be prepared like a strong wall with warships, galleys and skiffs. They were completely equipped both fore and aft with brave fighters carrying their weapons and infantry of all the pick of Egypt, being like roaring lions upon the mountains. The chariotry had competent fighters . . . their horses quivered in all their limbs ready to crush the foreign lands under their hoofs . . .[10]

Finally, in Year 11, came further conflict on the western border. Libyan settlers had already infiltrated the Delta to the west of the Canopic branch of the Nile. Now they were prepared to use force to secure the entire Delta. They had underestimated the strength of pharaoh's army:

The Libu and the Meshwesh were settled in Egypt and has seized the towns of the Western Tract from Memphis to Keroben, and had reached the Great River [the Canopic branch of the Nile] on every side . . . Behold I destroyed them, slain at one stroke . . . overthrown in their blood and made into heaps. I made them turn back from trampling upon the boundary of Egypt. I took of those whom my sword spared many captives, pinioned like birds before my horses, their women and their children in tens of thousands and their cattle in number like hundreds of thousands.[11]

The stark brutality of the Egyptian revenge may be seen on the walls at Medinet Habu, where piles of Meshwesh hands and penises attest to the

Fig 8.4   Ramesses III: pharaoh triumphant

wholesale slaughter of the defeated enemy. The message was clear. Ramesses would not deal leniently with such a blatant challenge to his authority. Those Libyans who escaped death and capture were evicted from the Delta and sent westwards. Meanwhile the Sea Peoples had retreated to settle on the Levantine coast, with the Peleset tribe eventually giving their name to Palestine. This was not ideal from the Egyptian viewpoint, but Ramesses could do little about it. His empire was already starting to collapse around him.

The wars of the first eleven years now gave way to a period of peace and stability. Superficially everything appeared to be going well. The Harris Papyrus, a lengthy and heavily biased account of Ramesses' rule compiled during the reign of his son, Ramesses IV, tells us that there were impressive building works at Pi-Ramesse and at Tell el-Yahudiya, a successful trading mission to the mysterious land of Punt, and the resumption of expeditions to the copper and turquoise mines. Beneath the surface, however, Egypt's economy was starting to collapse. Three military campaigns in seven years had cost Egypt dear at a time when tribute from the eastern vassal states was dwindling and international trade routes were gradually closing. The harvests were generally poor and the resulting inflation caused grain prices to rise. Meanwhile there were pressing internal problems. The priesthood of Amen was once again gaining power in the south, their ascent aided by the slow but sure collapse of the state bureaucracy. Incompetence and inefficiency were now the norm, and delays in the payment of the monthly rations led to strikes in the Theban necropolis and sporadic thefts from the royal monuments, including an attempted break-in at the tombs of Ramesses II (KV 7) and his sons (KV 5). Even the royal palace was not safe from intrigue:

The great enemy Paibekkamen sometime Chief of the Chamber. He was brought in because he had been plotting with Tiy and the women of the harem. He had made common cause with them. He had proceeded to carry their words outside to their mothers and their brothers who were there saying 'Arouse the people and incite hostility so as to make rebellion against their lord.' And they set him in the presence of the great officials of the Court of Examination. They examined his crimes and found him guilty. And his crimes took hold of him, and the officials who examined him caused his punishment to befall him . . . Wives of the men of the harem gateway, who had colluded with the men who plotted these matters, were placed before the officials of the Court of Examination. They found them guilty, and caused their punishment to befall them. They were six women . . .[12]

This extract is taken from a papyrus, now housed in Turin Museum, which is merely one of several official documents detailing a harem conspiracy aimed at the assassination of Ramesses III and his replacement with one of his lesser sons, Pentawere, son of the secondary wife Tiy. The plot involved six wives and some thirty-one male conspirators, and further complications arose when five of the trial judges were also arrested, accused of collusion and of gross misconduct with the women of the harem. The punishments meted out to the guilty were, as we might expect, severe; conspiracy within the royal household was seen as the ultimate betrayal. Tiy's fate is uncertain, her son Pentawere was left to 'die of his own accord'. Many were executed, others were mutilated by amputation of the nose and ears.

We do not know whether, after thirty-two years on the throne, Ramesses was indeed murdered. If he was, the plot failed in its ultimate aim to divert the succession away from the intended heir as the conspirators were caught and punished while the late Ramesses was followed on the throne by his son, Ramesses IV. The mummified body of Ramesses III shows no obvious wound, but the hardened 20th Dynasty linen which still sticks to his limbs makes it difficult to be certain of this. Poison, often considered a woman's weapon, need not, of course, leave any tell-tale signs. Ramesses' head, freed from its linen mask by Maspero on 1 June 1886, revealed such a grim aspect that it has since served as the model for a number of mummy-based horror films. His tomb (KV 11), popularly known as 'The Harper's Tomb' or 'Bruce's Tomb' after the Scottish explorer James Bruce, was one of the first to be explored and the findings published by Western travellers.

Ramesses III was followed by his son, Ramesses IV, another Ramesses II 'wannabe', and then by a further six called Ramesses, a jumbled mixture of fathers, sons, uncles and nephews all descended from Ramesses III and all attempting to emulate the great Ramesses II. Their reigns, increasingly plagued by an unstoppable cycle of drought in north-east Africa, low Nile levels, poor harvests, inflation, famine, civil unrest, official corruption and tomb robbery, heralded the end of the New Kingdom.[13] Diodorus Siculus thought that he knew where the blame lay:

The Kings who succeeded to the throne for seven generations were confirmed sluggards devoted only to indulgence and luxury. Consequently in the priestly record no costly building of theirs nor any deed worthy of historical note is handed down in relation to them.[14]

Diodorus was to a certain extent correct; inter-family feuding between the various branches of the royal family did little to restore confidence in a monarchy whose effectiveness, measured by their ability to preserve *maat*, was open to serious doubt. None of the Ramesses were, however, obviously weak kings. They appeared to do all the right things; they built, they mined and they even launched the occasional warning raid on the Libyans, but they were lacking the resources and maybe the personal drive to make their work effective. Slowly and surely, as reign gave way to reign, the kings of Egypt became powerless, their sphere of influence largely confined to the north of the country where they ruled first from Pi-Ramesse and then from Tanis, the new capital built largely from the remains of Pi-Ramesse. The eastern empire had long been lost and, although the Theban necropolis was still in use as the royal graveyard and the west bank remained the acknowledged site for the associated mortuary temples, the south was now effectively controlled by the High Priest of Amen whose position was by now considered hereditary. Corruption was everywhere, and no one was above suspicion.

During Year 16 of Ramesses IX came a wave of robberies at Thebes. So concerned was the king that a team of government inspectors was sent to report on the condition of the west-bank tombs. These inspectors, led by Paser, Mayor of eastern Thebes, examined both royal and private graves from the 11th to the 18th Dynasties. Most unexpectedly, and probably falsely, they discovered that the royal burials were still substantially intact although many of the private burials had been desecrated and their contents lost. Who could be responsible for such a heinous offence? All the evidence pointed towards Paweraa, Mayor of western Thebes, the man with direct responsibility for necropolis security. However it proved impossible to implicate Paweraa in the thefts, and the virtuous Paser disappeared soon after filing his report, leaving Paweraa free to continue in his life of crime.

Ramesses XI, last of the Ramesses, reigned for twenty-seven years. The early part of his reign (Year 8 or 9) saw virtual civil war at Thebes as the High Priest of Amen, the state-appointed Amenhotep, was deposed by an unnamed rival. He later regained his position with the backing of the king and his henchman the Viceroy of Nubia, Panehsy, who led his Nubian troops northwards to fight on the streets of Thebes. The peace which followed the restoration of Amenhotep was a very tentative affair. By Year 19 the powerful Panehsy had fallen out of favour with Ramesses. No reason is given for his fall from grace but it seems likely that he had in some way overstepped his authority. The 'General of the Pharaoh'

Piankh was now sent south to lead a military campaign against Panehsy who was eventually driven back into Nubia.

This extraordinary sequence of events coincided with the 'Year of the Hyenas', a period of famine at Thebes when yet more robbers were brought to trial accused of stealing from the royal temples and tombs. By now there was a new and very powerful High Priest of Amen, Herihor, a man who in addition to his priestly duties, had been given some of the titles belonging to the disgraced Panehsy so that he bore the heavy responsibility of being General, Viceroy of Nubia and Southern Vizier. Effectively, Panehsy continued to control Nubia while Herihor ruled southern Egypt. Although Ramesses was still nominally king of the entire land, Herihor now assumed the cartouches and titulary of a reigning monarch. A badly damaged text inscribed in the Temple of Khonsu at Karnak makes it clear that, like so many kings before him, Herihor has been elevated above other men by the divine oracle:

The High Priest of Amen-Re, King of the Gods, the King's Son of Kush and Overseer of the Granaries, [Herihor] . . . and the god recoiled . . . your city? . . . 'May you grant those years which you shall give me.' And the god agreed emphatically . . .[15]

In the north Smendes now ruled from Tanis, theoretically junior to Ramesses XI. With the death of Ramesses XI in approximately 1070 BC the New Kingdom finally came to an ignominious end. Egypt was now irrevocably split in two. Smendes, founder of the Third Intermediate Period 21st Dynasty, continued to rule the north while the High Priests of Amen, the descendants of Herihor – first his son-in-law Piankh and then his grandson Pinodjem I – controlled the south.

By now many of the great royal burials, including the tombs of Seti I and Ramesses II, had been looted and irretrievably damaged. The first serious outbreak of thefts had occurred during the reign of Ramesses IX; a group of papyri dating to his regnal Years 16–20 detail the crimes and trials of the accused. Later during the reign of Ramesses XI, at the time when the High Priest of Amen, Amenhotep, was forced out of office, the mortuary temples of Ramesses II and Ramesses III had been vandalized and several of their valuable fittings stolen. Few could have been surprised that the robbers turned out to be the temple priests:

They said to him: 'Tell of the gold that you stripped from the House of Gold of King Usermaatre Setepenre, and tell us the names of your companions . . .'

He said: 'I went to the door-jambs of the House of Gold along with my companions. We brought away two deben of gold from them, which we divided up amongst ourselves . . . Now, some days later, I went with them again and we brought out the portable shrine which is taken up to the sanctuary. We collected the gold that was on it, and melted it down . . .'[16]

It is clear that the royal tombs, too, were under attack at this time, although the official records remain for the large part discreetly silent on so sensitive a matter.[17] Indeed, so insecure had the royal necropolis become that Ramesses XI abandoned his own almost complete tomb in the Valley of the Kings (KV4), possibly making emergency plans to be buried in the north.[18] This did little to boost morale in the necropolis workforce who were now out of a job and faced with the prospect of abandoning the village that had housed their families for many generations. As we might expect, the crime rate rose alarmingly as the villagers sought to capitalize on their local knowledge. The necropolis officials were not blind to the problem but they appeared powerless, or reluctant, to act.

For centuries necropolis officials had carried out periodic inspections of the royal tombs, making good any damage to either mummies or grave goods, filling the corridors with stone chips and blocking off the breached doorways. By the end of the 20th Dynasty, however, the royal burials were in such a disgraceful condition that more drastic action was needed. Gathering together the remains of the violated pharaohs, the Priests of Amen transferred the royal mummies to a series of temporary workshops. Medinet Habu, now the administrative headquarters of the royal cemetery, housed one such workshop as did the tombs of Seti I and Ramesses XI. Here the priests set about repairing the mummies using modern bandages to conceal the damage caused by the robbers. This was by no means a simple act of piety. The rebandaging of the mummies provided the ideal opportunity to strip the exposed corpses of any remaining valuables, and the impoverished government laid claim to all objects salvaged in this way, together with all goods recovered from the tombs. Indeed, it seems likely that several of the mummies had been substantially intact before they came to the notice of the government officials. Tomb robbery was now a highly profitable, officially sanctioned recycling business.

The rewrapped mummies were placed in wooden coffins denuded of all gold leaf. Both bodies and coffins were labelled and then groups of mummies were stored in convenient well-guarded chambers dotted about the necropolis. Now stripped of all valuables, these caches were of little interest to the robbers who still preyed on the tombs of the nobles. It was not until the tourist boom of the 19th century that the mummies themselves were to be seen as valuable items. From time to time these groups were inspected and moved, until eventually there was a major collection of royal mummies housed in the family tomb of the High Priest Pinodjem II at Deir el-Bahari (DB 320). Behind its tiny entrance this tomb had been enlarged so that it became a massive storage depot. Here were housed the remains of some of Egypt's greatest pharaohs including Ahmose, Tuthmosis I–III, Ramesses I, Seti I and Ramesses II plus the Pinodjem family burials, which were left in place.

This, although the most spectacular, was by no means the only cache of dynastic mummies that has come to light. Two other non-royal Deir el-Bahari caches were discovered in 1858 and 1891, while a second royal cache was established in the tomb of Amenhotep II (KV 35); here were stored, among others, Tuthmosis IV, Amenhotep III, Seti II, Siptah and Ramesses IV–VI.

Local legend holds that in 1871 Ahmed el-Rassul, an inhabitant of nearby Gurna village, was searching for a lost goat when he stumbled across the concealed entrance to the Pinodjem vault. Ahmed, a professional tomb robber, naturally failed to inform the authorities of his amazing discovery. Slowly, over the next ten years, a series of objects from the Pinodjem burials was released on to the antiquities market as the el-Rassul family took full advantage of their good fortune. It became obvious to the authorities that a new tomb had been discovered, but where and by whom?

After an intensive investigation, on 6 July 1881 Mohammed el-Rassul, brother of the intrepid Ahmed, was 'persuaded' to lead a party of officials along the steep mountain path which led to the hidden tomb. Emile Brugsch, assistant to the director of the Antiquities Service, was the first of the party to be lowered down the shaft. Passing through a tiny doorway, he shuffled into a low corridor almost blocked by an enormous coffin, the first of many. Soon this corridor turned to the right, and here it was possible for him to stand upright. Descending a short flight of steps Brugsch found himself in the store-room. Here, by the flickering light of his candle, he saw an amazing sight. The chamber was packed with an unimaginable collection of coffins, their golden surfaces softly gleaming in the light of his candle.

Brugsch, overcome by emotion, rushed from the tomb. Some time later, fully recovered, he made his way past the New Kingdom mummies to discover the burials of the Pinodjem family which lay in the further chamber. In the face of such unexpected richness – now an obvious target for all local tomb robbers – he panicked and made what with hindsight has to be classed as a remarkably bad decision. The entire cache was to be cleared at once and the mummies were to travel by boat to the Bulaq Museum in Cairo. Three hundred workmen were rounded up and set to work. The mummies were taken from their cool, dark tomb, winched up the narrow shaft and laid out in rows in the hot summer sun. Here they baked as they awaited their temporary wrappings. Soon each pharaoh was wrapped in protective matting and sewn into sailcloth. Within a mere two days the lost kings of Egypt were on their way northwards, to Cairo.

Ramesses II had been recovered lying in a 19th Dynasty anthropoid, wooden coffin. Although experts are agreed on stylistic grounds that this is unlikely to be his original coffin – it is more likely to be the one prepared for his grandfather Ramesses I – the labels scribbled on both coffin and bandages make it clear that this is indeed Ramesses the Great. The body within the bandages is, as we might expect, that of a man approaching ninety years of age and therefore there seems no reason to doubt this identification. From his labels we can trace the journey of Ramesses' corpse as, under the authority of Herihor (Year 25 Ramesses XI), it was taken from the violated KV7 to the tomb of Seti I (KV17) where it was 'restored', stripped of any valuables and rebandaged. Some sixty years later, during the reign of the 21st Dynasty King Siamen, Ramesses was included in a group of mummies despatched to the Deir el-Bahari storage tomb of Queen Ahmose-Inhapi. After forty years came a further move to the Pinodjem family tomb.[19] Here Ramesses was to rest for almost three thousand years.

Following his hurried public unwrapping at the hands of Maspero (described in Chapter 1), Ramesses was stored in the Bulaq Museum. When the collection was moved to Giza he naturally moved too, and in 1902 he again moved to the current Cairo Museum situated on Tahrir Square. Here in 1907 Pierre Loti stood and marvelled before Ramesses the Great, listening to the stories of the museum guards:

One day, suddenly, with an abrupt gesture, in the presence of his guards who let out a howl of fear, he raised the arm which is still in the air and which he does not wish to lower.[20]

Ramesses remained in the mummy room of Cairo Museum (Room 52) until the 1930s when the royal mummies were first withdrawn from display and then transferred to the mausoleum of Saad Zaghlul. This proved to be a temporary move, and the mummies soon returned to Room 52. The mummy room was closed to the general public in 1980 on the orders of President Sadat who felt that his country's long-dead kings should be allowed to rest in the more appropriate surroundings of a purpose-built mausoleum. This mausoleum was never to be built, and today the royal mummies, including Ramesses II, are once again on display in Cairo Museum.

Egypt's pharaohs have generally been treated with great and appropriate respect, a respect which has unfortunately prevented them being regarded as objects suitable for conservation. Ramesses has spent much of the past century lying in the bottom half of a wooden coffin housed in a glass display case, a far from ideal environment for so fragile a specimen. With no means of controlling temperature, humidity or light, and no systematic monitoring of his body, Ramesses deteriorated. His skin cracked and was invaded both by bacteria and by over a hundred species of fungi. Loti tells us that some time prior to 1907 the king was given a mercury bath in order to kill a severe infestation. Later he was studied in detail by Elliot Smith, while in the late 1960s he was included in a project, sponsored by the Universities of Michigan and Alexandria, to examine the royal mummies using X-ray analysis, with particular reference to the condition of their teeth.[21]

In 1975 the French government made an unprecedented request. There was to be a 'Ramesses the Great' exhibition – one of many successful Ramesses exhibitions held all over the Western World – and it was hoped that the pharaoh himself would be allowed to visit Paris. With international attention now focused on his mummy, it became obvious that Ramesses was in dire need of some urgent repair work. Permission was given for Ramesses to fly to Paris, where as a deceased head of state he was greeted by a military guard of honour. Ramesses was immediately installed in a purpose-built 'Laboratoire Ramses II' at the Musée de l'Homme, where from September 1976 to May 1977 he became the focus of a multi-disciplinary team of over a hundred specialists dedicated to the study and preservation of his body. Ramesses was subjected to intensive X-ray analysis. He was measured and observed, his skin, hair and teeth were examined and various samples were taken from his wrappings and his body cavities, although due to a prior agreement with the Egyptian authorities no samples were taken directly from the body itself.

Much of this analysis confirmed what was already known or suspected, but one curious discovery was of fragments of nicotine-bearing leaves recovered from Ramesses' abdominal cavity. Whether this is the result of modern contamination, or whether it reflects the use of an unknown plant related to the tobacco family in the embalming rituals, is not yet clear, but it seems extremely unlikely that this could be read as simple evidence for dynastic tobacco use. Tobacco is a New World plant so far unknown in pharaonic Egypt. Two further surprises were the presence of peppercorns stuffed up the king's nostrils, and the replacement of the heart, inadvertently removed by the embalmers and sewn on the right rather than the left side of the chest.[22]

With all studies over, the damage to Ramesses' skin was repaired as far as possible with natural products such as beeswax, turpentine and petroleum jelly. Ramesses was then rewrapped in his original but now clean bandages and placed in his restored wooden coffin base, which was in turn housed in a specially designed show-case provided with a ventilation system and dust filters. Finally the king and his coffin were sterilized using gamma radiation which would destroy his fungal, bacterial and insect infections. Some eight months after his departure the much restored Ramesses travelled back to Cairo in a sterile plastic tent. Ramesses the Great was reinstalled in Cairo Museum, in the presence of the Egyptian authorities, on 15 May 1977.

Notes

1 For a discussion of Merenptah's Levantine campaign as a genuine historical event consult Hasel, M. G. (1998), *Domination and Resistance: Egyptian military activity in the southern Levant*, Leiden, 178–89.

2 For a full translation of this text consult Lichtheim, M. (1976), *Ancient Egyptian Literature 2: the New Kingdom*, 73–8.

3 For a complete listing of Merenptah's monuments, in order of location, see Sourouzian, H. (1989), *Les Monuments du Roi Merenptah*, Mainz.

4 For a discussion of this palace, with further references, consult O'Connor, D. (1991), 'Mirror of the Cosmos: the palace of Merenptah', in E. Bleiberg and R. Freed (eds) *Fragments of a Shattered Visage: the Proceedings of the International Symposium of Ramesses the Great*, Memphis: 167–98.

5 Smith, G. Elliot (1912), *The Royal Mummies*, Cairo, 65–70.

6 British Museum Papyrus No 10055. For a full translation and discussion consult Cerny, J. (1929), 'Papyrus Salt 124', *Journal of Egyptian Archaeology* 15: 243–58.

7 For details of the reign of Ramesses III consult Grandet, P. (1993), *Ramses III: histoire d'un règne*, Paris.

8 Edgerton, W. F. and Wilson, J. A. (1936), *Historical Records of Ramses III*, Chicago.

9 Quotation after Redford, D. B. (1992), *Egypt, Canaan and Israel in Ancient Times*, Princeton: 249. Redford gives a full account of the rise of the Sea Peoples.

10 This translation after Peden, A. J. (1994), *Egyptian Historical Inscriptions of the Twentieth Dynasty*, Jonsered, 23–36.

11 This version of the story is taken from the Papyrus Harris; Gardiner, A. (1961), *Egypt of the Pharaohs*, Oxford: 287.

12 For a full translation of this text with notes consult Peden, A. J. (1994), *Egyptian Historical Inscriptions of the Twentieth Dynasty*, Jonsered: 195–210.

13 A good popular account of corruption at this time is provided by Vernus, P. (1993), *Affaires et Scandales sous les Ramses; la crise des valeurs dans l'Egypte du nouvel Empire*, Paris.

14 Diodorus Siculus, *Histories* 1.63: 1.

15 For a full translation of this damaged text with commentary see Peden, A. J. (1994), *Egyptian Historical Inscriptions of the Twentieth Dynasty*, Jonsered: 181–

6. The 'recoiling' or movement of the god was the statue's only means of communicating with his devotees.

16 British Museum Papyrus 10053. For a full translation of this text consult Peden, A. J. (1994), *Egyptian Historical Inscriptions of the Twentieth Dynasty*, Jonsered: 265–70. See also Peet, T. E. (1930), *Great Tomb Robberies of the XXth Egyptian Dynasty*, Oxford.

17 See for example Aldred, C. (1979), 'More Light on the Ramesside Tomb Robberies', in Ruffle, J., Gaballa, G. A. and Kitchen, K. (eds), *Glimpses of Ancient Egypt: studies in honour of H. W. Fairman*, Warminster: 92–9.

18 The possibility that Ramesses was buried in the north is suggested by Reeves, N. and Wilkinson, R. (1996), *The Complete Valley of the Kings; tombs and treasures of Egypt's greatest pharaohs*, London: 172.

19 This sequence of events is as outlined in Reeves, N. and Wilkinson, R. (1996), *The Complete Valley of the Kings; tombs and treasures of Egypt's greatest pharaohs*, London: 207.

20 Pierre Loti quoted in Balout, L. and Roubet, C. (eds) (1985), *La Momie de Ramses II: contribution scientifique à l'égyptologie*, Paris: 23.

21 Harris, J. E. and Weeks, K. R. (1973), *X-Raying the Pharaohs*, London; a more detailed report is given in Harris, J. E. and Wente, E. F. (1980), *An X-ray Atlas of the Royal Mummies*, Chicago. It is difficult to accept the statement (1973: 44) that Ramesses 'was about seventy when he died' given that he is known to have ruled for sixty-seven years, and that he had already fathered several children by the time he came to the throne! See the review of the later volume by Kitchen, K. A. (1985), *Journal of Near Eastern Studies* 44:3: 235–7 where Kitchen calculates that, if these X-ray ages were to be accepted at face value, Ramesses would have been minus sixteen years of age at his accession!

22 For a full report on the French conservation project consult Balout, L. and Roubet, C. (eds) (1985), *La Momie de Ramses II: contribution scientifique à l'égyptologie*, Paris.

Further Reading

There is a vast amount of published literature dealing with the life and times of Ramesses II. This bibliography lists the more accessible books, suitable for the general reader, with preference given to books in English. Many of these books provide additional bibliographies. More specialized references have been given in the notes which accompany each chapter.

Adams, W. Y. (1984), *Corridor to Africa*, Princeton.

Baines, J. and Malek, J. (1980), *Atlas of Ancient Egypt*, Oxford.

Breasted, J. H. (1903), *The Battle of Kadesh: a study in the earliest known military strategy*, Chicago.

Corzo, M. A. (ed) (1987), *Wall Paintings of the Tomb of Nefertari: scientific studies for their conservation*, Cairo.

Corzo, M. A. and Afshar, M. (eds) (1993), *Art and Eternity; the Nefertari wall paintings conservation project 1986–92*, Getty Conservation Institute.

Desroches Noblecourt, C. (1963), *Tutankhamen: life and death of a pharaoh*, London.

Desroches Noblecourt, C. (1985), *The Great Pharaoh Ramses II and his Time: an exhibition of antiquities from the Egyptian Museum, Cairo*, translated by E. Mialon, Montreal.

Freed, R. E. (1987), *Ramesses the Great: his life and world (an exhibition in the city of Memphis)*, Memphis.

Gardiner, A. H. (1960), *The Kadesh Inscriptions of Ramesses II*, Oxford.

Gardiner, A. H. (1961), *Egypt of the Pharaohs*, Oxford.

Grimal, N. (1992), *A History of Egypt*, translated by I. Shaw, Oxford.

Gurney, O. R. (1952), *The Hittites*, London.

Habachi, L. (1969), *Features of the Deification of Ramesses II*, Gluckstadt.

Hayes, W. C. (1959), *The Scepter of Egypt 2: The Hyksos period and the New Kingdom*, New York.

Ikram, S. and Dodson, A. (1998), *The Mummy in Ancient Egypt*, London.

James, T. G. H. (1984), *Pharaoh's People: scenes from life in imperial Egypt*, Oxford.

Kees, H. (1961), *Ancient Egypt: a cultural topography*, London.

Kemp, B. J. (1989), *Ancient Egypt: anatomy of a civilization*, London.

Kitchen, K. A. (1982), *Pharaoh Triumphant: the life and times of Ramesses II*, Warminster.

Lichtheim, M. (1976), *Ancient Egyptian Literature 2: the New Kingdom*, Los Angeles.

Menu, B. (1999), *Ramesses the Great: warrior and builder*, translated by Harry N. Abrams Inc., London.

Murname, W. J. (1985), *The Road to Kadesh*, Chicago.

Partridge, R. B. (1994), *Faces of the Pharaohs: royal mummies and coffins from ancient Thebes*, London.

Peet, T. E. (1930), *Great Tomb Robberies of the XXth Egyptian Dynasty*, Oxford.

Redford, D. B. (1992), *Egypt, Canaan and Israel in Ancient Times*, Princeton.

Reeves, C. N. (1990), *Valley of the Kings: the decline of a royal necropolis*, London and New York.

Reeves, C. N. and Wilkinson, R. H. (1996), *The Complete Valley of the Kings: tombs and treasures of Egypt's greatest pharaohs*, London.

Robins, G. (1993), *Women in Ancient Egypt*, London.

Romer, J. (1981), *Valley of the Kings: exploring the tombs of the pharaohs*, New York.

Snape, S. R. (1996), *Egyptian Temples*, Princes Risborough.

Tigger, B. G. (1976), *Nubia Under the Pharaohs*, London.

Tubb, J. N. (1998), *Canaanites*, London.

Tyldesley, J. A. (1994), *Daughters of Isis: women of ancient Egypt*, London.

Waterson, B. (1991), *Women in Ancient Egypt*, Stroud.

Weeks, K. R. (1998), *The Lost Tomb: the greatest discovery at the Valley of the Kings since Tutankhamen*, London.

Index

(Figures in italic refer to a picture caption on that page)